The Siren Call of Hungry Ghosts

By the same author

Game Wardens
Cotopaxi Visions: Travels in Ecuador
Life Between Life
The Case for Reincarnation
Predictions
Toronto
Skin Dive

The Siren Call of Hungry Ghosts

A Riveting Investigation into Channeling and Spirit Guides

by JOE FISHER

PARAVIEW PRESS

NEW YORK

The Siren Call of Hungry Ghosts
Copyright © 2001 by Joe Fisher
All rights reserved, No part of this book may be used or reproduced in any manner whatsoever without prior written permission except in the case of brief quotations embodied in critical articles or reviews. For more information contact Paraview Press, 1674 Broadway, Suite 4B, New York, NY 10019, or visit our website at www.paraviewpress.com.

Cover image courtesy of NASA/JPL/Caltech
Back cover photograph: Sherry O'Neil

Book design by Smythype

ISBN: 978-1-944529-50-5

Library of Congress Catalog Card Number: 00-108792

PRINTED IN THE UNITED STATES OF AMERICA

This book is dedicated to my dear mother, Monica, who has always insisted that demons do *exist.*

Contents

Foreword by Colin Wilson / 9

Preface / 14

PART ONE: **Mysterious Voices**

CHAPTER 1 **An Excitable Young Lady From Greece / 18**

CHAPTER 2 **Stern Warnings / 26**

CHAPTER 3 **First Contact / 33**

CHAPTER 4 **Guides Will Assist You / 45**

CHAPTER 5 **A Cast of Characters / 57**

CHAPTER 6 **'I Can See in Your Mind' / 69**

PART TWO: **The Channeling Saga**

CHAPTER 7 **A Sense of Presence—The Long Tradition / 82**

CHAPTER 8 **Guides, Channels and the New Age / 99**

PART THREE: **Sleuthing Far From Home**

CHAPTER 9 **Ernest the Elusive / 112**

CHAPTER 10 **An Exercise in Reincarnation / 129**

CHAPTER 11 **The Changing of the Guard / 145**

CHAPTER 12 A Surfeit of Spooks / 153

CHAPTER 13 Can We Trust You, Dr. Pinkerton? / 167

CHAPTER 14 Dressing for Yesterday / 184

CHAPTER 15 Misadventure / 200

PART FOUR: Reappraisal

CHAPTER 16 Back to the Fold / 224

CHAPTER 17 One Man's Nightmare / 242

CHAPTER 18 Tales of the Serpent / 257

CHAPTER 19 The Siren Call of Hungry Ghosts / 267

CHAPTER 20 The Challenge of Consciousness / 289

CHAPTER 21 Epilogue / 297

Acknowledgments / 308

Select Bibliography / 309

Foreword

Before I was halfway through this book, I realized that *The Siren Call of Hungry Ghosts* is one of those permanent classics of the paranormal, like Tyrrell's *Apparitions* and Myers' *Human Personality and Its Survival of Bodily Death*. And before I had finished it, I became aware that it is also one of the most disturbing books about ghosts ever written.

To understand just why *The Siren Call of Hungry Ghosts* is so important, it is necessary to speak briefly about the history of psychical research.

Until around the middle of the nineteenth century, the whole subject of ghosts was regarded as highly dubious. Most educated people accepted unconditionally that ghosts were superstitious nonsense which had been unmasked by the great scientific revolution of Galileo and Newton. England had two famous hauntings in the 17th and 18th centuries: the "Phantom Drummer of Tedworth"—a poltergeist that made loud drumming noises and threw objects around—and the "Cock Lane Ghost," which restricted itself to knocks. Both were denounced as frauds—although first-hand accounts now make it obvious that both were genuine—and the unfortunate tenants of the house in Cock Lane were even sentenced to prison. The Age of Reason was quite determined that ghosts did not exist.

All that began to change halfway through the nineteenth century—or, to be quite precise, on March 31, 1848, in the house of a farmer named Fox, at Hydesville, New York. The Foxes had been kept awake for several nights by loud rapping noises, which they assumed to be the shutters banging in the wind. But as James Fox went around shaking the shutters, to make sure they were tight, his daughters observed that banging noises seemed to reply like an echo. So, when the noises began again in the middle of the night, 12-year-old Kate said cheekily: "Mr. Splitfoot (i.e. Mr. Devil), do as I do." And as she snapped her fingers, the rapping sounds imitated her.

Mrs. Fox then asked the unseen knocker whether, if it was a spirit, it would make two raps; two thunderous bangs were heard in reply.

The Foxes called in the neighbors as witnesses, and one of them, bolder than the others, managed to get the "spirit" to answer questions in a code of raps. It explained that it was a peddler who had been murdered by the previous tenant, and buried in the cellar. But digging in the cellar failed to reveal the body. It was not until more than half a century later, in 1902, that a wall in the basement collapsed, revealing another wall. Digging between the two walls unearthed a skeleton and a peddler's tin box.

During the summer of 1849, the rappings in the Fox household soon turned into typical poltergeist phenomena—objects thrown through the air, and people touched, and pinched, by invisible hands. When the two daughters were sent to other homes, the manifestations followed them. Back at home, Mrs. Fox was hit on the head by a hairbrush. Mr. Fox's hair turned white.

The "spirits" eventually dictated a message ordering those who believed in them to start a Church of Spiritualism. "You must proclaim this truth to the world." On November 14, 1849, the first Spiritualist service took place in Rochester, New York, and the new religion spread all over America. A regular feature of these meetings was a "medium" who went into a trance and contacted "the other world." Phantom hands sometimes played musical instruments, and, on occasion, the "dead" even materialized so they could be seen and touched.

Inevitably, the scientists were enraged at what seemed like an outbreak of medieval superstition, as absurd as the witchcraft craze. Yet many scientists who were persuaded to investigate ended up convinced that the phenomena were genuine. In 1882, a Society for Psychical Research was formed in London by eminent intellectuals, scientists, writers, and politicians; its aim was to try to discover, once and for all, whether all this talk about life after death was nonsense—and, if not, then what it was. They were convinced that they would solve the problem before the end of the century—after all, this was the age when science was making tremendous discoveries in the realms of stars and atoms. But the proof they sought eluded them. Clearly, all the phenomena were not fakery. Yet they simply refused to yield up their secrets. There was always just enough evidence to confirm the belief of the believers, yet never enough to convince the skeptics.

As a young man, G.K. Chesterton and a group of friends began to experiment with a "planchette," a pencil on wheels that can produce "automatic writing." Asked the name of a distant relative, the board spelled "Manning." They informed the spirit that this was not true. "Married twice," it replied promptly. To whom? "Cardinal Manning," said the spirit. Chesterton remarked that he had no doubt that some mysterious and unknown force was involved. But there was one major drawback: it told lies.

This has remained one of the major problems of investigators ever since. The evidence that something strange is going on is overwhelming. But it never quite makes sense.

At this point I should say: "Now read on." But perhaps this would be too abrupt. Let me simply say that while Joe Fisher's experience was just as baffling as that of so many other investigators, it makes a far better story than most (so good that I have retold it in three of my own books), as well as raising some worrying questions.

Joe Fisher is a British-born author and journalist—he now lives in Canada—who, in 1984, wrote an excellent book called *The Case For Reincarnation,* which is certainly among the best accounts of the subject ever written. The Dalai Lama himself recognized the seriousness of the work when he agreed to write the preface. I had read the book long before an editor asked me if I would like to review the originally-titled *Hungry Ghosts,* so I lost no time in accepting.

The book was not only as good as I expected; it was so stunning and compulsive that I read it straight through in three hours. When Mr. Fisher and his mother came to visit me a few years later at my home in Cornwall, I found myself looking at this charming and good-looking man with a kind of incredulity, hardly able to believe that he had been through such extraordinary experiences. But our long conversation left me in no doubt that his air of youthful candor masks the mind of a brilliant investigative journalist.

Let me sketch out the theme of the book in a few sentences. Briefly, Mr. Fisher attended a séance in Toronto when he heard that he would be able to see "spirit communication" in action. He got rather more than he bargained for when he learned that his own "spirit guide" was a young

Greek girl who had been his lover in a previous incarnation. The details she gave were precise and deeply convincing. So were those given by spirits that claimed to be an ex-Royal Air Force pilot named Ernest Scott and an amusing Cockney veteran of World War One named Harry Maddox. I must admit that, under the circumstances, I would have been just as convinced. But I might not have shown Mr. Fisher's persistence in tracking down the evidence.

His disillusionment began when he returned to England and decided to verify Ernest Scott's war stories. The airfield under discussion proved to be genuine, so was an enormous amount of geographical and historical information given by Scott. Yet records seemed to indicate that Scott never existed. When Mr. Fisher tried to track down the farm near Harrogate, Yorkshire, where another spirit named Russell claimed to have lived in the 19th. century, Russell proved to be just as elusive. So did the charming Cockney, Harry Maddox.

It would be a pity to spoil this marvelous and compelling story by giving any more of it away. Let me just say that, from the point of view of psychical research, the questions it raises are highly disconcerting. Never have the pitfalls of the subject been shown so clearly. When scientists set out to investigate some mystery—let us say, the great explosion over the Tunguska region of Siberia in 1908—they can at least go and look at the place where it happened, and draw their inferences from the signs which are still so obvious. This was the method Mr. Fisher pursued in his *The Case For Reincarnation*. But when it turns out that half the information has been falsified—not by fake mediums, but apparently by the "spirits" themselves—even the most dogged investigator has to admit that he doesn't know quite where to turn.

The solution that Joe Fisher offers in this book—that many "spirits" are little more than con-men who enjoy telling lies for the sake of it—seems to me highly plausible. But I have to admit that I have caused some consternation when I have spoken about *The Siren Call of Hungry Ghosts* at meetings of the Society for Psychical Research and the College of Psychic Studies. Clearly, Mr. Fisher's views throw an enormous spanner in the works, and raise a whole set of new questions for those believers who accept that mediums are a simple and direct link with the world of the dead.

Yet, in another sense, the author provides as much ammunition for the believers as for the skeptics. The spirits were apparently fakes in the sense that they were not who they claimed to be. Yet it seems equally obvious that they *were* spirits—or, perhaps, some mysterious practical joker hidden in the unconscious mind of the medium herself, which poses just as many questions.

Whatever the solution to this strange problem, there can be no doubt that Joe Fisher has performed a major service for psychical research by presenting the conundrum in such clear and unambiguous terms. He has carved for himself a place in its history—a place as important as that of Daniel Dunglas Home or Conan Doyle or Oliver Lodge. Moreover, he has done it with a book that—unlike some of the great classics of the paranormal—holds the reader from the first page to the last.

Colin Wilson
Cornwall, England

Preface

Sleepwalkers are responsible for the consequences of their actions.

When the opportunity arose to meet my spiritual guide I was hardly a novice in metaphysical matters. I had interviewed many leading practitioners of occult science and had written copiously about prophecy and reincarnation. Moreover, I had worked for years as an investigative reporter and was practiced at distinguishing truth from falsehood. Yet on being exposed to channeling in general and my guide in particular, I must confess to a certain insensibility - an entranced fascination - that left me unprepared for the odyssey which unfolds in the course of this book. In a way, I was sleepwalking as much as any medium who willingly surrenders to a state of unconsciousness.

At the time I first witnessed a channeling session on 20 July 1984, I had much to learn about mediumship, having read only some teachings of Seth, the late Jane Roberts' well-publicized spirit guide, and a sketchy history of mediumistic practice. Hearing the mysterious voices for the first time, I can well remember responding with innocent enthusiasm. Like many other spiritual aspirants who accept non-physical existence, I longed for personal contact with a disembodied source of love, wisdom and intelligence. In reaching across the void that separates earthly reality from the ethereal realms, I yearned to explore vicariously the veiled majesty of the next dimension.

Little did I know that I had embarked on a voyage that would turn my perceptions inside out and bring me to the brink of emotional collapse. Ambling in where angels fear to tread, I was well and truly embroiled in mediumistic phenomena before the realization dawned that my rugged experience as an investigator was about as useful as a swimsuit on the moon.

But there could be no turning back. As the widespread fascination with channeling attained a feverish intensity across North America, I felt compelled to pursue my acquaintanceship with the spirits. Wanting, above all, to know who they were and what they were up to, I pressed on into a psychological minefield.

This, then, is a true story; a cautionary tale of adventure and subjection in the New Age milieu.

Joe Fisher
Adolphus Reach
25 April 1989

The pseudonyms of Aviva Neumann and Louise Oleson are used to protect the identities of mediums who operate on a strictly private basis. Similarly, the names of members of Aviva's group have also been changed, as have the real names of the Graham family in Chapter Ten. All other channelers in the book are identified by their real names. All channeled dialogue is quoted verbatim from tapes and transcripts in my possession.

This book originally appeared in Canada and the U.K. under the title *Hungry Ghosts*. The book you now hold in your hands is the first U.S. edition. It includes a new foreword by Colin Wilson, as well as an Epilogue that updates events since my book was first published a decade ago.

J. F.
29 August 2000

"But 'tis strange:
And oftentimes, to win us to our harm,
The instruments of darkness tell us truths,
Win us with honest trifles, to betray us
In deepest consequence."
>William Shakespeare
>*Macbeth:* Act I, Scene 3

"Beloved, believe not every spirit, but test the spirits ... because many false prophets are gone out into the world."
>1 John 4: 1-3

PART ONE
Mysterious Voices

CHAPTER 1

An Excitable Young Lady From Greece

Aviva Neumann stubbed out her cigarette, removed her spectacles and slung a pillow onto the arm of the sofa in her Toronto townhouse. Then she stretched out, wiggling her arms, shoulders and legs in search of the most comfortable position.

Roger Belancour—tall, balding and withdrawn—sat on a chair facing me, his clasped hands resting on the back of the sofa. In a kindly, avuncular fashion, he waited for Aviva's scrawny frame to shrug off the last tics and twitches.

The delay left me restless. It seemed we had been talking for hours about the voices, the mysterious voices, and I was impatient to hear them for myself. I leaned forward to scrutinize Aviva's face. All was still. Her slippered feet pointed daintily towards the ceiling. Her brow glistened in the oppressive humidity of the July evening. She looked delicate, vulnerable, and completely at peace. In repose, her sharp features had softened perceptibly.

As I studied Aviva's impassivity, Roger began to address her supine form in a somber monotone that fell on my ears like a benediction:

"Your key phrase is to go down to your most suggestible level of relaxation and when you hear that phrase from me you will be at your most suggestible level of relaxation and be able to go deeper from there."

Still she lay there, motionless.

"Your key phrase…." Roger repeated the induction. Then he started again. And again.

The suspense was intolerable. To distract myself, I examined the painting on the far wall. It was an extraordinary piece, at odds with the domesticity of tubular furniture and blue drapes which framed sliding glass doors leading on to a narrow backyard. The painting showed six gaunt and scantily-clad people languishing in a dark cave. Their wretchedly thin arms stretched beseechingly towards a crack of light in the distance. I remained absorbed by this depiction of torment until a change in Roger's phrasing and intonation swiftly returned my gaze to Aviva's face.

"Are we at a level where we may talk with the guides?"

For the first time, her lips parted.

"If...you...wish," she answered drowsily.

Roger glanced at me and smiled modestly as if to suggest that a dialogue would soon begin. He leaned over to a tape recorder which stood on a table behind the sofa and pressed the "record" button. Then, turning back to Aviva, he asked to speak to Russell. They had told me about Russell.

"Russell," Roger asked politely, "could you give us some information about our visitor's guide?"

I stared unblinkingly at Aviva and waited. My stomach leapt as if to straddle the long pause between question and response. When her lips parted once more, her voice was barely recognizable. Gone was the high-pitched jocularity with the pronounced Australian lilt. Her enunciation was now unequivocally masculine; the English accent was unmistakable. This was an entirely different Aviva, strangely assertive and uncompromising. This was a voice which claimed to belong to Aviva's guide, a discarnate individual who had lived as a sheep farmer in Yorkshire during the last century. Speaking with all the conviction of a separate being, "he" was about to divulge the identity of the non-physical personage who was directly responsible for my welfare. My guide!

"The guide is a female."

"Her name?" asked Roger.

"Filipa—in her past life. This is what she is known and goes by."

"And would she be willing to give her charge some information pertaining to herself as to her past life and what nationality she was?"

"She says she has been with him many lifetimes; and he with her. They have alternated roles. Her last lifetime was in what is known now as Greece from the years 1718 to 1771 on the Greek calendar which is five days different from your own."

I was flabbergasted. Aviva's eyes remained closed and her body was immobile, save for the face muscles and larynx. Some part of me wanted to reach out and shake her limp arm and demand: "What are you saying?" But a saner, more settled corner of my psyche knew that Aviva was no longer consciously in our company. Who, then, was this austere character called Russell? Had I *really* lived in eighteenth-century Greece with a woman called Filipa whom I had known, perhaps even loved, over many lifetimes? It was all so instantaneous and overwhelming. But there was no time to be speechless because Russell had already moved on to other things and was demanding that I answer him.

"Have you no curiosity," he inquired, "as to whether you may be a soul or an entity?"

I was expecting this. Roger had explained beforehand that the "guides" who speak through Aviva had insisted that there were two types of human beings on the planet: souls and entities. Souls were said to be created from desire while entities were born of knowledge. Apparently, the two types differed fundamentally.

"Yes, I do," I replied apprehensively. "Will you please tell me which I am?"

"I would ask," Russell responded, "which do *you* think you are?"

Mildly intimidated, I was not about to be drawn into making a choice. Aviva, whom I had met only a week earlier, had invited me to "observe" the guides because she thought I might be able to help her understand the state of garrulous unconsciousness in which she was now enveloped. An observer I wanted to remain. Besides, I knew very little about the concept of souls and entities and had difficulty with the idea that the human race was divided into two streams. I told Russell as much.

"Yes, I know," he intoned sympathetically. "It has been rather poorly explained to you. You are, in fact, an entity... You have reasonable power as an entity. You have, in part, begun some forward development, although not on a conscious level. Most of your forward development has been on what you would term a subconscious level. You have never been a soul. You were always an entity created from knowledge, from the pool of knowledge which has been spoken of many times in many sessions."

My befuddlement knew no bounds. Yet I was ready to believe. My father was a retired Baptist minister and my mother, a staunch Christian whose psychic ability left her fretful lest God be displeased by her involuntary visions, had recently become a Jehovah's Witness. Fundamentalism, naturally, had dominated my childhood. But I had followed a spiritual path of my own and had come to accept reincarnation as integral to the life process, a requirement of human evolution.

Initially, I had been merely intrigued by the proposition that we return to Earth to inhabit different bodies. In time, I concurred with reincarnation theory, which states that both sexes, a variety of races, and ever-changing roles and relationships are often experienced over a succession of lifetimes in order to learn the lessons of life. The more I studied ancient beliefs and the work of modern reincarnation investigators and past-life therapists, the more enthusiastically I responded to a statement of Voltaire's which still strikes me as eminently sane: "It is no more surprising to be born twice than it is to be born once."

Later, I became fascinated by the innumerable references in scripture, mythology, metaphysical literature and, most recently, medical research testifying to unseen presences with whom contact could be made. Russell's invisible yet almost tangible presence confirmed in practice what I acknowledged in theory—that we *are* attended by disembodied intelligences who inhabit a non-material universe. As for the soul entity question, who could say whether Russell was right or wrong? But I was glad, even relieved, to be hailed as an entity, if only because I would rather have been created from knowledge than desire.

The ramifications of this encounter were staggering. While there was much more exploring to do, it seemed that I had stumbled upon a treasure-trove of metaphysical insight, a resource which could yield untold information about life beyond the grave.

Having read about spirit guides such as Seth, I had been perplexed by the trance state in which mediums were said to relay the teachings of these unearthly beings. Now I was witnessing this strangely enticing phenomenon and was having difficulty remaining emotionally detached. No matter how impressive Aviva's self-surrender might be, I told myself the evidence of my eyes and ears must be distrusted. Clearly, the struggle was to keep my head, to remain objective...and hope that this promising *El Dorado* would not turn out to be fool's gold.

Roger broke into my ruminations to ask whether I had any questions for my guide. Although he felt that Filipa would be unable to speak directly through Aviva on this occasion, he assured me that she would soon be able to talk with her own voice. Russell volunteered to act as intermediary in the interim, explaining that guides first had to "learn the energies" if they wished to communicate through a human "vehicle."

"Filipa says," offered Russell, "that she would be most delighted if personal contact were to be made with her. She says your knowledge and your self-discipline and your style of thought processes make you what she calls a good candidate for communication on a direct level. Then you could receive direction from her."

"How should I make this direct contact?"

"She suggests that if you put aside the same particular moment each day on the earthbound plane to establish thought control patterns upon herself, this would be a good start. For one who has contact with a guide has a more open resource for control of his or her own destiny. This would also offer new companionship and she says that there is much instability of companionship in your life."

These words were instantly unnerving, as I had long experienced some difficulty in sustaining romantic relationships. I had barely learned of my guide's existence and now she was identifying this source of personal concern. (Was this apparent weakness, I wondered, already undermining the life I shared with Rachel, my live-in girlfriend?) Silently, I speculated whether Filipa had intimate knowledge of my dealings with others. Though I believed I had some very good friends, perhaps some of my friendships were more flawed than I realized. Whatever Filipa's words were meant to suggest, her immediate recognition of my vulnerability was unsettling, to put it mildly.

"She feels," added Russell, "that she can become the old sock of comfort."

Warming to this remark, I requested some information on the last relationship we had shared on Earth.

"She says this was, for her, during the immediate past life in Greece. You were a male and she was a female. You were to be her suitor. However, you both transgressed in the eyes of the community. You were sent from the village and did not return. She says she did not wish for this to happen. However, the village is more powerful than the one."

The village is more powerful than the one. The phrase was sonorous, poetic, and conjured images of Greece. Ten years earlier, I had composed most of my first novel on the Greek isle of Siphnos. I loved Greece, its culture and its people, and I could readily imagine that I had once incarnated in that richly atmospheric land. Sitting on the floor of Aviva's living room, I found myself breathing the air of a bygone era, roaming parched valleys and ancient crypts. I imagined Filipa's dark eyes and long black tresses.

So magnificently seductive was the moment that I wanted to merge with the reverie. But the skeptic inside screamed in protest, demanding that Filipa's credibility be established before the dreamer was granted any further indulgence.

Could Filipa tell me, I asked, when I arrived in Canada and from whence I came?

"She says your concept of time is quite different from her own and that she has not had to work with earthbound time since her departure from the earthbound plane. It is difficult especially when there has been virtually no contact of a spontaneous nature between herself and her charge. She does not understand what you mean by the term 'coming to Canada.' She says you were born on the earthbound plane and have not left the earthbound plane in this lifetime. What do you mean by 'Canada'?"

I was charmed by Filipa's lack of geographical knowledge. After all, if she hadn't lived on Earth for over two hundred years, her ignorance of Canada was quite understandable.

"She asks," Russell inquired, "was this a known place when she was last on the earthbound plane?"

"No," I conceded. "That's an interesting point because Canada was only formed as a nation in 1867."

"She departed the earthbound plane many years prior to that. She says that in tiny places like Theros, where you and she lived, it was difficult to learn of the outside world. Information could be gleaned only from those who passed through the village, usually from the Black Sea en route to larger centers."

"Theros? This is where we lived together for a while?"

"Theros."

"Is this an island? Or the name of a community?"

"This is a village. It is, she says, only five days' walk from the Black Sea."

Of course, I reasoned, peasants living in the eighteenth century would have measured all journeys in walking time. Once more, I was tempted to follow the images that sprang to mind. But the skeptic within was impatient with such impetuously romantic forays into the old world. First, I needed to ascertain whether Russell and Filipa truly were who they claimed to be. Without knowing quite how to go about it, I pushed Russell for such an assurance. His reply was warm and considerate.

"I feel that if you wish earthbound verification of the guides this course of questioning you have chosen with Filipa is your correct course. However, at this stage, I'm afraid the poor girl is a little flustered. She's an excitable young lady and she's deeply intrigued but I do not think she has fully understood what you were asking of her tonight...I have a feeling—and I will explain to her—that she is being asked to deliver physical proof of her relationship to you...She says that she is still not over what you might call juvenile fascination."

She's not the only one, I thought, as my imagination cavorted in the dust of a remote Greek village. Such was my enchantment that I barely heard Roger invoke the practiced refrain that brought Aviva back from the trance state. I was visualizing secret liaisons with a raven-haired beauty. I was re-living our betrayal and, finally, my despair as a group of wrinkled elders in black smocks ordered my banishment. *The village is more powerful than the one.*

I wanted to believe. But my years as a journalist had bred such caution that the dispassionate observer continued to agitate me. I knew that I must not allow emotional vulnerability and spiritual aspiration to influence my judgement. Non-attachment was regarded as a pearl of great price by the spiritual masters. Non-attachment was the state of mind I strove to achieve.

I was still wrestling internally when Aviva's eyes flickered open and Roger helped her struggle groggily into an upright position. Clearly disoriented, she reached awkwardly for her spectacles and sank back against the sofa, eyes closed, for several minutes. When Aviva opened her eyes once more she sighed and stretched her arms and I told her that she looked as though someone had just woken her up in the middle of a deep sleep.

"That's very much what it feels like," she said languidly. There was no trace of Russell's English accent, nor of his supreme self-assurance. It seemed all that remained from her sojourn in another state of consciousness was a dry and rasping throat. When Roger brought her a tall glass of water she gulped down its contents.

"You get very thirsty," she went on. "Coming back isn't much fun. It's as if I'm being dragged very swiftly up a mineshaft. Or, as you say, it's like hearing an alarm go off when I'm dead to the world. And I am dead to the world, believe me. I'm not conscious of anything I say once Roger puts me out. And I don't remember a thing afterwards."

A few minutes of quiet recovery ensued before Aviva spoke once more.

"Well," she said, "did you meet your guide?"

Roger and I smiled knowingly.

"Well?" Her eyes were wide with inquiry.

"Apparently," I said, "my guide is a Greek woman who was last on Earth in the eighteenth century."

"Greek!" Aviva exclaimed, lighting up a cigarette. "Whatever *next?* It's getting like the United Nations around here, Roger."

CHAPTER 2

Stern Warnings

That hot Friday night in July, I stepped out of Aviva's townhouse feeling like an apostle who had witnessed his first miracle. Never mind the heat, I was shivering with excitement. Walking through the housing estate that wound around itself like a redbrick serpent eating its own tail, I passed people sprawled on their front steps, sucking languorously on beer bottles. *If they only knew....* If they only knew that a sheep farmer from the reign of Queen Victoria had been sounding forth just a short walk from where they were slumped, panting and perspiring. Intoxicated with eternity, I felt like grabbing them by their undershirts and shouting: "Can't you see this sad old world is but one side of the coin we call life?"

Sensibly, I saved my exhortations for Rachel. Given her fondness for Tibetan Buddhism, she was bound to be fascinated with Russell and all he had to say. And so she was. But instead of responding enthusiastically to my description of Filipa, Rachel gave me one of her glum looks which always spelled trouble.

Heeding the implicit warning, I withdrew to my study to mull over the extraordinary events of the evening. I kept coming back to Filipa, kept hoping that I could believe what Russell had said. If indeed we had been lovers in Greece, I wondered what other relationships we had shared across the centuries. I also wondered about the insight she possessed concerning my life and behavior.

The next morning, I started a regimen that I would follow, more or less religiously, for the next three years. Before breakfast, I climbed the stairs to the swivel chair in my study, hoisted my feet onto the oak desk, closed my eyes, and willed Filipa to communicate with me. My efforts were rewarded with fifteen minutes of blankness interrupted by scraps of memory and teeming thoughts about the oncoming working day. In short, nothing happened. But the prospect of enjoying mind-to-mind contact with my guide left me restless with anticipation. Every morning I tried again. Every morning I yearned for a breakthrough.

I did not doubt that such communication was possible. In conducting research for *The Case for Reincarnation*, I had run across references to guides and to a non-physical plane of existence between lives. The ancient Tibetans had named this timeless, spaceless realm the *bardo,* literally, *bar,* "in between"; *do,* "island." Other cultures, from the Hebrews of old to the Okinawans of the South Pacific, also identified and described a dimension that received and nurtured the soul between earthly existences. To my way of thinking, this was heaven: the ocean of life from whence we came and to which we returned.

Metaphysical and scriptural literature abounds with guides, guardian angels, guardian spirits, invisible helpers and other like-minded beings who exhibit benevolent concern for particular individuals on Earth. Throughout recorded history, many people have been sensitive to an accompanying presence in their daily lives. In recent times, those who have reported near-death or out-of-body experiences have often cited an encounter with a guide. Then there are the plethora of mediums who down through the ages have established direct communication with human intelligences on "the other side." A 1982 survey conducted by George Gallup Jr. stated that twenty-four per cent of Americans believe it is possible to make contact with the dead.

Intrigued as I was by the many testimonials of transdimensional communication, a personal encounter with a spiritual being had previously eluded me. I had narrowly survived a motorcycle accident in which my crash helmet was sliced in two and had almost drowned when the boat in which I was sailing capsized in shark-infested waters off the Bahamas. But I had yet to undergo a near-death or out-of-body experience. Moreover, I had never sensed with any certainty an accompanying invisible presence in my life. Even an attempt to explore my reincarnation history had faltered when preliminary tests revealed I was a poor candidate for hypnotic regression. So my natural enthusiasm was tempered by this absence of direct involvement when Aviva Neumann invited me to her home on that muggy July evening to make contact with a group of entities claiming to reside in the next world.

The invitation arrived unexpectedly, soon after I had been interviewed about the evidence for reincarnation on the Toronto radio station CFRB. My Canadian publisher forwarded a listener's letter from Aviva telling how she had involuntarily become a mouthpiece for supposedly discarnate entities calling themselves guides. These entities, she pointed out, also spoke volubly about reincarnation. In fact they claimed to be living in a disembodied state *between* lives.

The tone of Aviva's letter assured me that she wasn't a New Age groupie with metaphysical stars in her eyes. Believing in nothing beyond the physical sciences, she worked as a laboratory technologist and had always scoffed at psychic phenomena. Indeed, she felt vaguely troubled about being a channel for other beings. She was writing to me, she said, because she was looking for a rational explanation for this irrational turn of events. "I am a normal person with normal interests," she declared, "and I don't want to be regarded as a candidate for a psychiatric ward."

Aviva concluded her letter with a formal invitation. "When you are next in Canada," she wrote, "perhaps you would like to attend a session at my house and experience this phenomenon for yourself." Little did she know that, although I speak with an English accent, I lived just a couple of miles from her Parkdale home, a revelation that prompted a gasp of surprise when I telephoned to accept her offer.

In the course of my first visit I was told that Aviva was suffering from chronic myelocytic leukemia, a life-threatening disease. When Roger Belancourt, a neighbor, friend and part-time hypnotist, had learned of her condition two years earlier, he immediately offered to hypnotize Aviva in order to administer corrective medical suggestions to her subconscious mind. Knowing nothing about hypnosis, Aviva felt that she should at least give it a try. So, in company with Roger and her doctor, she prepared nine carefully-worded commands that would be administered while she was in trance. The commands ranged from "Your bone marrow will start immediately to manufacture the extra red blood cells needed by your body" to "The over-production of myelocytic leukocytes will now cease."

Fortunately, Aviva proved herself from the start to be an excellent hypnotic subject. Simple tests to establish her eligibility were passed without difficulty and she was soon being ushered repeatedly into trance. Once the hypnotic state could be attained at will, she and Roger met twice a week so that Roger could recite each medical suggestion six times to his slumbering subject.

Within a few months, it was evident that the suggestions—"hexes," Aviva called them—were helping to keep the leukemia in check. They couldn't prevent Aviva from suffering at intervals from fatigue and sudden attacks of excruciating pain. Nor could they inhibit the tendency of her already slight build to become slighter still. But the persistent commands to her subconscious mind were seemingly capable of eliminating hours of pain and nausea, reducing inflammation of the joints and staving off severe deterioration. Satisfied that the primary objective was being achieved, Roger began to conduct some hypnotic experiments as a postscript to the long-winded chore of recitation. Although Aviva took scant interest in these experiments, she willingly submitted to them. They provided her with a means of rewarding Roger for his care and diligence.

Carefully and with a certain sobriety, like a schoolmaster explaining the laws of physics, Roger told me how the development of his hypnotic technique had led, eventually, to communication with "the guides." Aviva, meanwhile, sat on the sofa smoking one cigarette after another and grinning every so often as if to say: "Don't ask *me* what any of this is about!"

Aviva denied all responsibility for the mysterious voices.

"I just wanted hypnotic medical suggestions to help my mind fight the leukemia," she said. "That was all! But one thing led to another and now these *entities* are speaking through me. I don't know who or what they are. And I don't really care. But, from what Roger has told me, it seems that they are aware of what's going on inside my body and are doing their best to take care of me. Yet I've never believed in the so-called psychic world. I've never had a psychic reading that's come true. I think astrology is absolute crap, and I've got no time for anything that's supposed to be paranormal. Look at my library...."

I turned around to the bookcase behind me, and saw it was crammed with volumes on the works of Karl Marx and Vladimir Ilyich Lenin.

"I think that shows you where I stand," said Aviva. "And it's not in some airy-fairy world between incarnations!"

Aviva may not have believed in the *bardo* but, culturally and clinically, the evidence for its existence was clear. In fact, Aviva's skepticism only left me more inclined to accept the astounding phenomenon in which she was the central participant. She seemed oblivious of the implications that her "sleeps," as she called them, held for humanity. Scientists the world over were spending billions of dollars in a fruitless search for extraterrestrials. Yet here, in an ordinary suburban living room where visitors were not even charged admission, a cynical, forty-two-year-old mother of three was giving voice to disembodied humans who, having passed through death's door, were testifying eloquently to the fact that we do not really die. And that we are never truly alone.

The more I thought about the guides, the more I felt drawn to the idea of writing a book about discarnate beings. I envisaged myself gathering untold knowledge about life in the next dimension by interviewing a wide selection of spiritual guardians speaking through the entranced forms of a host of mediums. I could start with Russell. He would know the best way to proceed.

* * *

I hunched over Aviva's corpse-like figure. Roger sat in his customary position, his hands clasped over the back of the sofa. Aviva's consciousness had been lulled into obliteration and Russell was very much in command, uttering each syllable with confidence in his cleanly-picked English. His self-assurance made me nervous.

"Do you feel," I inquired, "that it would be a good idea for me to write a book about guides?"

"At the moment, no," Russell replied abruptly. "You have not enough knowledge."

"What I mean is, to start researching a book."

"If you research that book and thoroughly research it and take nothing for granted. And if, when you are satisfied with your research, you research your research…yes, perhaps for you, with the nature of the work you have been involved in, this would be a good thing. But I would say that you are perhaps entering dangerous ground…So long as you continue to ask questions, so long as you continue your own forward development, so long as you do not impede the forward development of guides, yes, this might be very good for you. But…."

I knew from the tenor of Russell's voice that a warning was imminent.

"…I would caution you that nothing is to be taken at face value. If it is easily believed on faith or taken on what you may term face value, then perhaps it is a little…*valueless*."

"Do you feel that I should go to various people who claim to be in contact with their guides to establish what the role of a guide is?"

"Perhaps the first thing you must establish is whether a guide is, in fact, a guide or a playful spirit and not a guide at all."

Naturally, I wanted to know how to differentiate one from the other.

"You will find where there are playful spirits, or indeed what you may term fakes, you will find more souls, more belief, more acceptance without questioning. If you do not recognize one from the other with alacrity, you may find yourself in a soul-entrapment type of situation....You are a very intelligent man. You have chosen well. However, I must caution you...Even the most intelligent among us have, and will be again, caught in soul entrapments."

I asked Russell for some advice on how to avoid this miserable-sounding fate. He replied by cautioning me even more sternly than before to conduct my inquiry armed with a highly-critical attitude and a barrage of perceptive questions.

"You must proceed into this field of work—if you intend to proceed with it—with a deliberate amount of skepticism, a large amount of knowledge and a vast amount of accurate questions that will indeed single out reality from that which is basic belief, mysticism, falsehood. Do not accept at face value. Question! All the time, question! And if questions are not answered satisfactorily, question and question again."

Russell paused. When he next spoke, his voice was softer, more sympathetic.

"You may ruffle and will ruffle a few feathers with this work. However, Filipa says that you have ruffled many before and you will again. You have altered perceptions before with the nature of your work. The pen has a powerful message."

"Have you any idea," I asked, "how long it would take me to do a thorough job on a book concerning guides?"

"I would say, fifteen to twenty lifetimes . . ."

These words left me stunned. Thankfully, Russell had more to say on the matter.

"However, I understand that you would wish to complete this within one lifetime and I understand that you would wish to complete this within a framework that would allow you to pursue other options once you have completed it . . . This might be a very large undertaking. However, it is not an impossible one. If you wish to research guide material, you must do what you consider to be a professional and thorough job. For, you see, when you yourself pass from the earthbound plane and you yourself become a guide, you will take this knowledge with you, and you will be able to see the areas where, perhaps, you made errors...."

Russell was saying, in his distinctly austere manner, that he thought my idea was a good one, And I gathered, too, that he and Filipa were prepared to do all they could to help me. Sensing a heart of gold beneath the bombast, I liked Russell instinctively. But it was Filipa, my own guide, with whom I really wanted to chat. All I could do was wait. Russell, by his own admission, had spent an entire year preparing to talk through Aviva's voice box, measuring his exertions in earthly time. On the other hand, Roger's guide—a Dutch woman named Hanni—had spoken out within a few weeks. I hoped earnestly that Filipa would be able to emulate Hanni's vocal dexterity.

When Aviva was roused from her trance, she rubbed her eyes, reached for her spectacles, drained two tumblers of water and agreed, reluctantly, to listen to a tape recording of the session. When she heard Russell use the word "alacrity," she couldn't restrain herself.

"*Alacrity?*" Aviva mimicked, rather poorly, her guide's English accent. "*Alacrity?* I never use that word. What the hell does it mean?"

CHAPTER 3

First Contact

When we met in July, 1984, Roger Belancourt was fifty-two years old and a veteran explorer of occult alternatives to religious orthodoxy. While working in jobs that ranged from tool-and-die making to the sale of automotive chemicals, he had devoted much of his life to a self-styled spiritual inquiry. This inquiry had wound to and from psychic readers, mind-development classes, the Spiritualist Church and a variety of groups dedicated to self-realization and enlightenment. As a sideline, he had practiced hypnotism for more than seventeen years and had worked with doctors, dentists, psychiatrists and psychologists to help people rid themselves of such problems as depression, obesity and cigarette addiction.

In the early 1970s, Roger became convinced he was attended by a non-physical human presence. This awareness began, somewhat shakily, when he tried automatic writing and scrawled a message which read simply: "My name is Jai-Lin. I am your guide. I was a Tibetan lama and am with you constantly." Believing his own mind had invented the words, Roger promptly relinquished automatic writing. But a few weeks later, when attending an aura-balancing session, he found reason to wonder whether he had made the right decision. The practitioner told him, "Do you know that you have a large Oriental man dressed in monk's clothing who is with you?"

After a brief flirtation with belief, skepticism returned once more. But not for long. Newly enrolled in a mind-development course, Roger was meditating with others in a classroom setting when, to his surprise, he felt someone shake him roughly by the left shoulder. "Naturally, it broke my concentration," he said. "I looked around but no-one was there. When the class finished, the person in charge came over to me and asked whether I knew what had happened. He said that he had seen a huge hand belonging to a large Oriental man in a long robe reach out for my shoulder and shake me. From that point on, I accepted that I had a guide and that the guide was a monk or lama of some kind."

Long before contact was made with the guides, Roger found in probing Aviva's state of unconsciousness that he could monitor the efficacy of the hypnotic suggestions by eliciting slow, dreamy, monosyllabic answers on the state of her health. He also found that Aviva's subconscious mind would deliver—in the third person—information apparently pertaining to her experience in previous lives. She related details of her last life as a Czechoslovakian teenager called Stanislav who, when German forces occupied Czechoslovakia in World War II, was taken from school and put to work in labor camps. Stanislav's fate at the war's close was to be executed and thrown into a pit with twenty others.

The same expressionless voice that had narrated Stanislav's history described a life as a peasant woman named Svetlana who lived through the Russian Revolution; recounted a brief existence as a Punjabi infant who, in 1802, died of malnutrition before his first birthday; and told of an incarnation as Sybil Handley, an English seamstress, who was born in London in 1741. Sybil bore thirteen children and died of tuberculosis in 1796.

In time, Roger was able to retrieve direct past-life memories from his subject. As Stanislav, Aviva produced, on request, verifiable words and phrases in Czech. Such hypnotic feats, more common today than ever, have a long and involved history.

Hypnosis was practiced in ancient Egypt and ancient Greece and was rediscovered in the late eighteenth century by the Austrian physician Franz Anton Mesmer who gave his name to the art of mesmerism, also known as animal magnetism. Mesmer, who did not attempt to carry his patients back beyond birth, induced the trance state by conducting transverse and longitudinal passes with his hands. A similar technique was used by a Frenchman, Colonel Albert de Rochas, who towards the end of the last century became the first modern practitioner of past-life regression. In his radical experiments, Rochas tried in vain to achieve that which many therapists of today claim on a routine basis: the retrieval from entranced subjects of precise past-life information which can be supported by historical fact.

For all the research conducted into the trance state, there is no consensus of clinical opinion as to the nature of hypnosis. This little-understood zone of unconsciousness may be entered by a seemingly limitless number of doorways or inductions and the depth of trance can vary tremendously from subject to subject. In deep trance, surgery may be conducted on an oblivious subject without the aid of anaesthetic, thereby confirming the reality of this altered state.

Roger won his own confirmation by observing, week after week, Aviva's progressive slide into slumber and by listening to her faraway responses to his questions. Keen to do away with the protracted patter which ushered Aviva into the hypnotic state, he successfully accelerated the process by substituting a key word—"relax." Although this one-word wonder rushed her into unconsciousness, it was fraught with menace. Twice Roger used the word by accident and found that he had to act quickly to rouse his swooning subject. One of the two blunders took place during a telephone conversation when, momentarily perplexed at his friend's sudden silence, Roger was obliged to shout corrective instructions into the receiver! On regaining consciousness, Aviva reacted angrily at being plunged randomly into trance. Had she been smoking, she argued, a disastrous fire might have ensued and, in protest, she called a halt to the sessions.

The sessions resumed a couple of weeks later when Roger suggested changing the key word to a key phrase. This development not only acted as a safeguard against unwanted hypnotic paralysis but also served to stretch the horizons of the trance state still further. By repeating the key phrase, Roger found that he could reach a deeper part of Aviva that was even more knowledgeable and creatively alive than the subconscious mind. He listened in awe as Aviva intoned in trance:

> When you give the key phrase over and over and over, it alters the state of consciousness, allowing the conscious to leave....The alter-consciousness that you have induced here is the same person that you have always dealt with. It is simply that the conscious mind has departed for a time, which frees up the information from other sources.

It appeared that Roger had plugged into the switchboard for another level of awareness. Initially puzzled by this development, he soon discovered that there were a huge number of alter-consciousnesses, each with its own voice. At will, he could converse with a separate alter-consciousness for every organ of the body and aspect of the self, ranging from the lungs to the liver, from her health to her humor. All he had to do was select the part of Aviva, physical or abstract, with which he wished to speak in the same way that one might call up a file from a computer. Often, if Roger was unsure of what department to ask for, the connection was made through an interrogative two-step. After the initial inquiry was made, Aviva would respond with: "To whom do you wish to speak?" and Roger would rejoin: "To whomever can answer the question."

The answers were objective and explicit. And they considerably enhanced the process of monitoring Aviva's health. For example, after the medical suggestion was given to promote the red blood cell count, the alterconsciousness for the blood would inform Roger that the count had been increased substantially—a statement confirmed by laboratory reports when Aviva next visited the hospital.

The scope of the alter-awareness was vast indeed. It could read the mind as well as the body and would give fascinating discourses on an immense range of topics involving this world and the next. It could also talk at length about itself. As the entranced Aviva stated methodically:

> ....alternate awareness is not only aware of the physical Earth plane but aware of other planes...It is not subject to the time and space valuations that you have on the earthbound plane. It is subject only to the time and evaluation centers within the mind itself. Those forever go on; they do not cease. Once the body has gone the mind does not stop...Only the conscious mind is dimmed and shut down until it can be renewed in a new entity.

The switchboard of the alter-consciousness quickly established itself as an infinitely abundant source of knowledge. Both Roger and Helen Fields, a new friend of Aviva who adopted responsibility for transcribing the tapes made at each session, grew to crave opportunities to converse with "the other Aviva," who placed current human existence into extraordinary perspective. In trance, Aviva declaimed authoritatively about "the real world" of the non-physical planes, the nature of earthbound existence, reincarnation, the structure of the mind and the functions of ego and personality, to name but a very few topics.

The goal of reincarnation, Roger and Helen were told, was "forward development," a phrase which was to be reiterated countless times over the next few years. On requesting a definition of forward development, they were told: "Forward development is understanding of oneself."

Perhaps the most riveting material concerned the distinctions between souls and entities. Roger and Helen were assured that they were entities and, as such, were distinguishable from the larger stream of humanity made up of souls. New souls and entities, it was said, were unknowingly brought into being by incarnate entities' thoughts and behavior. That is, entities and entities only were able to generate unconsciously the non-physical essence—a necessary preliminary to incarnation—of future human beings. Entities were created from knowledge. Souls were born of desire.

I must admit that I found the idea of two streams of humanity divisive and difficult to grasp. Metaphysical teaching, however, has always promulgated the esoteric fact that thought is energy. Apparently, any thought one might have discharges energy into the cosmic flux, the nature of one's thoughts determining the type of energy disseminated. The soul-entity concept consolidated and developed such awareness of thought forms. It also fostered among the "entities" gathered in Aviva's living room a common sense of supremacy over the masses of souls in society.

Nevertheless, Roger and Helen were initially bemused by the insistence of the after-consciousness that they were able to procreate without any conscious awareness. I never overcame my aversion to this strange method of giving birth, if only because it was unusually disquieting to learn that one was creating a soul. This meant, of course, that desire of some kind—ranging from wanting to help others, to cravings for sex or alcohol—had become sufficiently entrenched to form, in embryo, an often unwanted "mind-child," a discarnate presence that yearned for an earthly body. While the creation of souls was a relatively common occurrence, only very rarely was anyone said to be in the process of creating an entity. Desire was clearly far more prevalent than knowledge.

First the alter-conscious and, later, the guides told how souls and entities thought and behaved differently because they were cut from separate cloth; their mind structures were entirely different. This distinction was liable to lead to conflict and had been instrumental in starting wars as well as in provoking discontent and disharmony in marriages and partnerships. At death, souls were said to occupy a non-physical plane of existence removed from the world of discarnate entities. If they wished, however, souls were able to transform themselves into entities over transitional periods of several lifetimes dedicated to forward development.

Entities tended to be loners and individualists whereas souls—who were more single-minded, but less influential than entities—preferred to assemble in groups such as church congregations and sports crowds. Although entities appeared to be the superior species, it was said that neither entities nor souls could claim superiority. They were simply different, just as men and women were different from one another.

While Aviva had no conscious memory of where she had been or what she was doing while in trance, her alter-consciousness insisted that she thoroughly enjoyed the respite from physical existence. Indeed, Aviva would much rather be allowed to remain out of her body....

> ...when she comes back from the unconscious into the conscious, sometimes it is very difficult for her to reorient. She finds that in what you might call the astral realm, the alternate awareness realm, it is far more comforting as she is so extremely and intensely aware and stimulated all the time. She almost resents coming back into the conscious body.

No matter how ardently the other Aviva enthused about the wonders of unconsciousness, the waking Aviva fought hard to discredit everything she said while in trance. The laboratory technologist whose hero was Lenin and whose attitudes and ideological principles were solidly grounded in the material world swore Roger and Helen to secrecy about the sessions because she feared being classified as mentally disturbed. As she grudgingly listened to tapes of the sessions, she complained that the information could not be verified, properly understood or used in the here and now. Moreover, she maintained the material contradicted her conscious knowledge. Aviva's griping became so virulent that Roger decided to consult his entranced subject about her antagonism. This is how she responded:

> Whether she at this time believes the information is not relevant. What is relevant is that she questions and starts to seek and therefore opens more the door to knowledge....Do not underestimate the power of questioning. There is no contradictory information. What she finds contradictory merely contradicts her own beliefs. In acknowledging an understanding of the material, she must also acknowledge, therefore, that her beliefs are in jeopardy.

The waking Aviva was not about to be persuaded by such sophistry. Weary of postulation, she wanted to know whether her altered state could produce something of practical benefit, such as the coveted digits that would bring home a lottery jackpot! Dutifully, Roger broached the topic at the earliest opportunity. Much to Aviva's subsequent irritation, the exchange went like this:

"Are you able to go into the future and look at a newspaper?"

"Yes."

"Would you be able to retrieve winning lottery numbers for us?"

"If it is part of your plan to have that amount of money, you could influence the numbers yourselves. Monetary gain is nothing that can be lasting."

Although he had conveyed Aviva's wishes, Roger felt that metaphysical knowledge was not to be used for material gain. Even so, he would have rushed off to buy a lottery ticket had Aviva's alter-consciousness produced an all-important number. But winning the lottery wasn't uppermost in Roger's mind.

Urged on by the alter-consciousness to pursue his forward development, he had received answers to many of his questions. Yet there was one outstanding matter that had yet to be broached. Roger had never spoken to Aviva about Jai-Lin. Now it occurred to him to ask whether his hypnotized subject would confirm the existence of spirit guides in general, and Jai-Lin in particular. Initially, he raised the question with the alter-consciousness for health while checking on Aviva's physical condition. But this awareness, narrowly myopic in its knowledge, knew nothing of guides.

Some months later, Roger tried again. On the night in question, Aviva had been grappling with an excruciating bout of pain. Lying back in agony, eyes closed, she started to recite the alphabet backwards to herself as an aid to concentration. Helen looked on helplessly while Roger leaned over Aviva's prone form, steadily and soothingly repeating the key phrase. Her retreat into unconsciousness was impeded by the acute and lengthy discomfort, which she likened to "a black void full of spasms like lightning bolts." Eventually, however, her pain was surmounted, the letters of the alphabet retreated into insignificance, and she lapsed into trance.

Once the medical suggestions had been administered, Roger instructed Aviva to descend to the threshold of the alter-conscious state. Then he posed his all-important question:

"I understand that my spirit guide is Jai-Lin. Is it possible for me to contact him in this manner?"

"To whom do you wish to speak?" Aviva responded sluggishly.

"To whomever can answer the question."

Roger and Helen waited patiently. They were used to waiting patiently at the altar of the alter-conscious. But this pause seemed to last forever. When the reply finally came, Roger and Helen found themselves staring at each other, stunned and incredulous.

"Yes…It is possible to contact the guides."

The guides' distinctive voices, however, did not materialize overnight. For several months, the alter-consciousness acted as intermediary, relaying messages from the next world. Aviva's guide was identified as Russell Parnick, who, in his previous life, had lived as an illiterate sheep farmer in the Yorkshire Dales more than one hundred years earlier. He also claimed to have been Aviva's wife during a fourteenth-century existence. Helen was said to be guided by an entity called Mi-Lao, who had last incarnated as a peasant woman in the walled city of Chutsu in China's Hunan Province during the seventeenth century. And then there was Jai-Lin. Although Roger never heard Jai-Lin speak directly, the shadowy Oriental monk was demonstrably as close to him as the clothes that he wore and as readily available as the trance state.

Whenever Roger ushered Aviva into an altered state of awareness all he had to do was ask for the alter-consciousness responsible for guide contact and the responding voice, devoid of all expression, offered Jai-Lin's answers to any questions. These answers were always prefaced with "Jai-Lin says," the "J" being uttered harshly and separately, rendering the name audibly alien to Roger's customary pronunciation.

Jai-Lin was said to have personified wisdom during his one earthly incarnation. That made sense to Roger, not only because of the earlier intimations that he was attended by an Oriental monk, but also because Jai-Lin's discourses were those of a sage; their heady content often sailed over the heads of his listeners, leaving them bemused and uncomprehending.

Speaking via the alter-consciousness, Jai-Lin, Russell and Mi-Lao demonstrated a knowledge of their charges that was both comforting and unnerving. Their counsel ranged from the universal to the intensely personal. A lecture on "functional development within the second level of the mind" might be succeeded by a warning to Roger to curb his negative thinking.

> Jai-Lin says that your thoughts are, at this time, as you know, in a very negative cycle, You must always think positive thoughts. Do not allow your thoughts to become scattered. You have much to learn in self-discipline. This is one of the things you must be taught. This is one of the things he is trying to teach you. By consciously trying to contact Jai-Lin, you will learn discipline of self-thought…He says…if you cannot control your own thoughts, how can you be aware of others?

Jai-Lin presented Roger with an exercise, telling him to observe an object closely for fifteen minutes each day in order to "clarify the mind and begin to teach it concentrative thought." Jai-Lin went further still. He offered to nudge Roger physically whenever negativity was foremost in his mind. Exactly how this was to be accomplished was not discussed and Roger did not consider that a developing tendency to rub his forehead could be attributed to his guide. But he was later informed that an intermittent tingling beneath his scalp was indeed Jai-Lin's signal. "He was hoping that it would come to you without his having to tell you," Aviva intoned. "However, now that you are in the know, you will be able to do something about it."

Roger must have been either unable or unwilling to take the necessary corrective action because Jai-Lin did not stay for very much longer. One day the alter-consciousness explained in its characteristically emotionless way that the Tibetan guide had moved on to meet fresh challenges elsewhere. Roger's besetting negativity was cited as the prime reason for his departure. Forward development, Roger was told, is of first priority to guides as it is to their earthly charges and Jai-Lin's progress would have been impeded had he maintained his guardianship. Not that Roger was left stranded. Incarnate individuals, it was explained, are never without a guide.

Nevertheless, the guide named Sebotwan who filled Jai Lin's unearthly shoes was a far from heartwarming prospect. Considerably less advanced than his predecessor, Sebotwan took little interest in Roger. Where Jai-tin had been vibrant, wise and solicitous of Roger's welfare, Sebotwan exuded lassitude and indifference. For several months, the hypnotist tolerated Sebotwan's apathetic attentions. Then, in March, 1984, coinciding with the resolution of certain issues in his life and the adoption of a more positive frame of mind, he learned that his efforts had been rewarded by another change of guide. Her name was Hanni.

Hanni mastered the art of manipulating Aviva's vocal cords within a few weeks, speaking so softly and tenderly that she could barely be heard. In explaining her obvious affection and concern for Roger, Hanni disclosed that he had been her son during her previous life in the Netherlands. Tragically, he had drowned as a boy while attempting to swing across a canal on a rope and she had blamed herself for his death. Nevertheless, Hanni did not allow the trauma to stifle her sense of humor, as this exchange illustrates:

> Roger: How was your day today?
> Hanni: In which time reference—mine or yours?
> Roger: In yours.
> Hanni: It has been an exceptional two hundred years.

Hanni, however, wasn't the first guide to make herself heard directly. That feat belonged to Russell, whose forceful voice had shattered the membrane of the altered state in February, 1983. Suddenly, as if under pressure, Aviva's speech changed in the course of a few words from a dull monotone to the matter-of-fact stridency that was to characterize the sheep farmer's diction. There he was, loud and clear, answering a question as to how his "charge," as he routinely called Aviva, might overcome stress and fatigue in her life.

For the remainder of 1983, Russell sometimes spoke directly but often relied on the alter-consciousness to relay his knowledge and advice. As he explained later, it was a question of "learning the energies" while simultaneously coping with the unrelenting demands of his many other earthbound charges. By the beginning of 1984, however, Russell was adept at speaking through Aviva's voice box and was readily available for consultation.

In his practical and autocratic way, Russell took firm control of the sessions and, although keen to expound on metaphysical knowledge for the sake of promoting forward development, he placed Aviva's physical welfare above all other considerations. His terse observations were invaluable in helping Roger to chart the fitful course of Aviva's leukemia. It was evident that Russell knew his charge thoroughly, as this warning of her worsening condition indicated on 20 February, 1984:

> Her health is deteriorating. She has become aware of what she calls palpitations, pains other than the pains that she feels within her bones. This will frighten her....She rationalizes that she cannot afford to slow down. Either she slows down or she will depart from the earthbound existence. The white blood cells at present are substantially up to a critical level. She is supposed to be resting, which she is not doing. And even you can see that she is hyperactive, as usual. This, we must curb.

Aviva wanted the best from both worlds. Eventually she had decided to draw on both conventional and non-conventional resources in her fight against leukemia. Even as she visited Toronto's Princess Margaret Hospital for blood tests, drug maintenance, and the occasional chemotherapy session, she was relying on Roger's medical suggestions and, to a lesser degree, Russell's advice. Although she grudgingly acknowledged the presence of her guide, Aviva found it difficult to follow the recommendations of someone she wasn't supposed to believe in. Russell was plainly frustrated with this attitude and he complained frequently to Roger that Aviva wouldn't listen to him. Aviva responded in her wakeful state by calling Russell "a jerk," saying she would relish the opportunity of being able to tell him so directly.

To an outsider, the alliance was as humorous as it was bizarre: a brusque discarnate and his rebellious ward locked in a dependent and yet mutually resentful relationship. Gradually, however, Russell was winning her over. The very fact that she was leaving questions with Roger to ask of her guide vouched for that. To inquire of Russell was to affirm his existence. But to inquire of Russell and call him a "spirit" was to invite his wrath.

"We're not spirits!" he fumed on more than one occasion. "We're people just like you. It's just that we don't have bodies any more."

CHAPTER 4

Guides Will Assist You

Regular weekly attendance at the Friday night séances left me increasingly convinced that the guides were indeed who they claimed to be. My incipient conviction was attended by progressive enthrallment. Just as each morning I hoped to achieve mind-to-mind communication with Filipa, each Friday evening I set out for "session," as our gatherings were known, eager with expectation. Tramping through the city streets, I wondered whether the voice of my guide—the woman I had loved and lost more than two hundred years ago—would pierce the somnolence of the trance state. But, for ten tremulous weeks, Aviva's alter-consciousness kept me waiting. Grateful though I was for the relayed messages, I could hardly wait for Filipa to break through.

"Have you been aware of my attempts to contact you?" I inquired nervously of Filipa as the summer of 1984 edged into autumn.

"She says," responded the alter-consciousness, "that when you make attempts to contact, you must not allow other thoughts to flow across your mind. When this happens, contact is very difficult. She says concentration for this sort of thing is something learned, not something that one is naturally gifted with. She must learn also and she asks that you understand that."

Knowing that Filipa was also struggling to communicate gave me the incentive to keep on trying. Not all was well at home, however. Rachel was offended by the avidity with which I would discuss the guides and I learned to mention Filipa as little as possible in her presence. Perhaps she questioned my loyalty, sensing my attraction to this unearthly lover of old. Anyway, Rachel no more than tolerated my striving for communion with the next world and, over a period of several months, her pained forbearance turned imperceptibly into withdrawal.

Not that I deserved any better. The guides' gripping expositions of life beyond the body left me increasingly preoccupied with the non-material universe and less and less willing and able to respond to Rachel on a basic human level. Aside from renouncing my otherworldly aspirations—an unthinkable course of action—there seemed little I could do to prevent our feelings for one another from drifting into cold storage.

Filipa's remarkable understanding and empathy cushioned my progressive alienation from Rachel, my friends, and the world about me. In any case, I told myself, personal happiness in the current existence was a small sacrifice to make for one's immortal welfare. Besides, I was as happy as I could reasonably expect to be. If life was sometimes distressing, it was because Rachel and I were always arguing. We loved one another, but we had little in common and were loath to compromise with each other's views and preferences.

I did, however, manage to persuade Rachel to accompany me to Aviva's house one Friday night and looked on enviously as her guide was not only identified but started to speak with his own distinctive voice! The session was only a few minutes old when the dull monotone of the alter-consciousness turned in mid-sentence to a thick Scottish brogue. So unexpectedly rich was the accent that we wondered, momentarily, whether our ears could be deceiving us.

The guide gave his name as William and told us he had last lived in Edinburgh from 1642 to 1665. In an earlier Scottish life in the thirteenth century, Rachel had been his son who had died as "a wee young child" at the hands of the English garrison. While William and Rachel had strong karmic ties as a result of sharing more than twenty lifetimes, William had also guided Rachel during her last life in Italy earlier this century. In the years leading up to World War II, she had honed her skills as a blacksmith to become a master of weaponry in the service of the Nazis.

William had a way of communicating which made Rachel's forehead throb. He always called her "Lass" and, at times, made her uncomfortable by teasing with serious intent about her tendency to drink too much. Rachel grew to love William but she preferred, nevertheless, to stay at home rather than attend the sessions. For all their signs and wonders, the guides gave her the creeps.

Rachel couldn't really explain why she was repulsed by the sessions. But she did mention that she felt a certain intangible negativity in the air, and maintained that Russell interpreted material from his timeless, spaceless, genderless dimension in a patriarchal, linear way. To my mind Rachel was merely jealous of Filipa's obvious affection for myself as well as our effortless intimacy. Yet I had difficulty accepting this reaction of hers. Surely an attractive, intelligent woman of the twentieth century could not justifiably envy a peasant girl from the eighteenth century who no longer occupied a physical body and who, moreover, was working on behalf of my spiritual welfare.

Technically, at least, I was clinging to my stance as the objective observer determined to test the claims of Filipa and the other guides. Yet I grew to crave the emotional attunement invariably experienced in Filipa's company. No explanations were necessary; there were no battles of will. In a way, talking to Filipa was like talking to myself.

Although Rachel's affections ran deep, she neither accepted my personality nor my outlook on life. She protested that Filipa catered unfairly to my idealistic impulses and grumbled that my guide should be more considerate of her emotions. But I refused to listen to these complaints. So far as I was concerned, Filipa loved me unreservedly as I was. And that meant a lot.

I was determined that Rachel's ambivalence would not deter my spiritual quest. Filipa was that quest. In getting to know my guide, I was honing my immortal destiny while preparing for the time when we would be together once more in the between-life state.

Filipa was still speaking via the alter-consciousness, but I was left in no doubt that I was conversing with an individual as unique and multi-faceted as anyone occupying a physical body. Where Russell appeared to conceal his true feelings for Aviva beneath a verbal mask of imperious efficiency and Hanni was unfailingly maternal towards Roger, Filipa gave the impression that, could she only have materialized, she would snuggle romantically beside me. Her messages may have been delivered in public and in the third person, but they hinted at tenderness, seduction, shared confidences.

Filipa wistfully recalled our days spent together in the little Greek village of Theros, somewhere near the Turkish border. As Andreas Cherniak, a militiaman born of a Greek mother and Slavic father, I had led a small group of guerillas against the Turks. As Filipa Gavrilos, she had toiled in the fields outside Theros. Frequently she would ask, "Don't you remember?"

> Filipa says you were very tall for a man in a Greek village. You were five...Russell is telling her...five feet ten inches. She is not familiar with these measurements. You were swift. You were very good in shape—very dark of skin with dark eyes and dark hair. You had rather large feet and hands. You were usually quite proper. You were very much in love, but this was not seemly in Theros. You were judged by the priest and sent from the village, for they did not wish you corrupting the girls of the village. She herself—somewhat smaller, she says, and a little more round—had black hair and much fairer skin than yours.

I did not remember, but my reverie of Grecian images was revived once more. I had lived in Greece, after all, and it was easy for me to travel there in my mind, a Greece shorn of modern accoutrements, a landscape unspoiled by the motor car. I did not recognize Filipa by her description and her words failed to summon unconscious memories to my awareness. But I was moved and fascinated by this love story from the past and wondered whether my fondness for small, dark-haired women had grown out of this tragic romance. Rachel, too, was small and brunette. Then I wondered about myself. I asked Filipa what connection there was between the Greek soldier and the person of today.

> She says that from that time you have learned about discretion. However, between you then and now the mind is essentially the same. The brain is obviously quite different . . .You are far more at peace with yourself. There is not such bravado, not such careless disregarding of authority. You have learned to be subtle. You have learned also ways that do not antagonize those about you....She says the quality which makes your mind active is the same quality. It is a little more agitated and a little easier to speak with. You tended to be much in the line of a bull-headed, take-charge person. Now you will act thoughtfully. This did not happen before and this led to many of your problems.

It all made sense. I had learned to be subtle and not antagonize others.

My mind was active and prone to agitation. If this much were true, could not the past life itself also have validity? Filipa said that I would feel affinity with this life in Greece if only I could hear the folk music of the Thrace region that I used to sing so heartily and raucously.

> She says you sang so many different songs and often mixed many together. Especially at the plaza, where you would sit with your friends and drink much. There were times, especially in the springtime, when you would most love to sit and sing. And when you would sing of your homeland tears would always come into your eyes.

In one of Toronto's largest record stores, I found a recording of traditional Greek music played on traditional instruments. Although the tunes were pleasing to the ear, no long-lost memories were evoked and I was hardly stirred to the depths of my being. I wondered about that as I tried unsuccessfully to explain to Filipa's eighteenth-century understanding what a stereo system and a record actually were. Disappointed in my failure to respond emotionally to at least one of those Greek folk songs, I was consoled by a memory that had surfaced only a few days earlier. As a boy, the name Philippa had held a strange fascination for me. Finally, I understood why.

Other guides had struggled to break through the impassivity of the alter-conscious like baby chicks pecking through a confining eggshell. But on 12 October 1984, when Filipa managed to speak out for the first time, there was no transitional phase of any kind. Suddenly, to my intense delight, she was responding in her own voice, her Greek inflection leading charm to broken English. Her delivery was subdued, pensive and poignantly tender, although she was later given to occasional outbursts of volatility. Sometimes her speech was clearly enunciated and easy to understand. But at other times I had difficulty comprehending her strange juxtapositions and faulty word endings. Strangely, Filipa refused to admit that her diction fluctuated in this way and, because she struggled so gallantly with the language, I did not have the heart to insist otherwise.

Whatever the quality of her speech, Filipa always spoke to me like a lover for whom the fire still smoldered. She said that in order to communicate she tapped my knowledge of English while also making the best of a primitive version of the language spoken during an earlier incarnation of hers in Scotland. Mi-Lao, on the other hand, had never been exposed to the English language and said she was using her charge Helen Fields' linguistic knowledge exclusively, sounding very Chinese as she did so. The guides explained that just as they could read our minds, so they were able to assimilate our grasp of the language. Russell had spoken a broad Yorkshire dialect in his last life, a dialect he occasionally savored, much to our mystified amusement. But there wasn't a trace of dialect in his normal speaking voice because, he said, clarity was essential for the task at hand. Accordingly, he had dipped into his knowledge of English in previous lives, reinforcing this capability by helping himself to Aviva's idiomatic inventory.

My confidence in Filipa grew as we came to know and understand one another. In a succession of conversations, my curiosity about our reincarnation history was satisfied by a wealth of detailed information spanning millennia. I learned that I had lived 2,046 lives—many ending in stillbirth and infancy—since coming into being 21,000 years ago. Filipa told how we had spent seventeen incarnations together, both of us changing sex and race repeatedly in the course of our expeditions into earthly reality. We had first met as members of opposing warring tribes, an initial antipathy that was transformed in the course of several incarnations into a bond of love. Twice, we had perished together in the region now known as the Philippines; long, long ago in a volcanic eruption and, more recently, as brothers when our fishing boat capsized in rough seas.

Our ever-strengthening karmic ties led eventually to the passionate relationship in Greece where we "broke all the rules," behavior which apparently dictated that we share more earthly experiences. "We will be earthbound again together," said Filipa, "and this time I hope we do it right." Since the life in Greece, I had incarnated three times, most recently as a black male in Mozambique who was murdered by a sibling at the age of thirty-seven.

Filipa, on the other hand, had remained in the *bardo* since her death in Greece at the age of fifty-three. Unlike myself, she preferred to pursue her personal development in the between-life state.

You enjoy the physical experience. You enjoy the challenge. You are one who seeks great challenges and you do so in your earthbound existence each time. You defy authority. You've done it many, many times. You have defied convention many, many times. And you are not one who seeks and pursues knowledge lightly. When you do pursue, you have a burning yen to really pursue it and learn all you can. This is good...[The earthbound experience] is one of the more restricted areas of learning. It is an area of learning that takes great fortitude, and I would almost say courage....We must all build up that courage. We must all learn the specific lessons that only the earthbound plane can give us...I am unencumbered by the physical and the material...I feel I progress faster here. Here, knowledge and learning are not restricted by silly beliefs and attitudes that are pushed and fed into an entity on the earthbound plane.

But so many times, I told Filipa, I had read and heard that spiritual progress could be achieved only by meeting the challenges of earthly existence. She responded, somewhat testily:

That is certainly not so! And you use that awful word again. Spirits! There are no spirits. We are all people. People are people. It is your own growth as an entity which is the most important thing you should be seeking. There is nothing spiritual or ethereal about it. We all come from the same place and we will all arrive at the same place. We are all people. We are not spirits.

"You know what I mean," I replied. "Personal growth."
"That's a far better term," said Filipa.
Apparently, the mutual attraction and affection between Filipa and myself kept us in touch with one another as we cycled in and out of incarnation. In fulfillment of a pact made several lives earlier, she had leapt at the chance to become my primary guide when the opportunity arose in my thirty-fifth year. In any case, she said, we had already worked with one

another as apprentice guides. Our present situation was just another way of being together out of choice. In a few words, Filipa summarized our past and present involvement:

> I had much love for you on the earthbound plane. We were both having much love for each other. Now you are on the earthbound and have no knowledge of that love, but I still have the knowledge of it. I still have all my memories and you will, too, when you also come here, be able to have those memories with me.

Filipa and I seemed to think alike, feel alike and see the world from a near-identical perspective. Knowing that she understood my motives, my behavior and my reactions better than I did myself both confirmed my belief in Filipa and left me feeling intensely vulnerable. I learned to accept this vulnerability and grew to trust that she would not exploit my defenselessness. No matter what I said or how I said it, my words were always interpreted just as I had intended them to be. And she proved time and time again that she knew my inner nature and my tendency to lapse, occasionally, into self-loathing. Often she would counsel me as to how I could be more loving:

> When you open yourself to the love of learning, you will open yourself to love what you are as an earthbound human in this life. And when you open yourself to what you are and can love what you are, you will have capabilities of much love for other people. Ask yourself: What do I like about myself? Do I love the talent that I have brought with me? Do I love the way I look? Do I love what I believe in and what I am striving towards? If you can like yourself, it is a beginning. If you can love yourself and open to that love, you will find that you will open to others around you.

Much more than a subject of research and a wellspring of information on discarnate life, Filipa rapidly became an adviser, a best friend. And my ideal lover. Sometimes I fantasized about our sex life in eighteenth-century

Greece and imagined with relish the passion that would erupt if only we could be together again, sharing hungry bodies as well as hungry minds. The notion was by no means extraordinary. The casebooks of past-life therapists are replete with examples of couples who have shared loving relationships over many lifetimes.

In contrast, Rachel and I were growing apart and our sexual relations had deteriorated accordingly. We were feuding much more than we should, mainly because we thought differently about so many things. Our difficulties were only compounded when we learned from William one Friday evening that we had shared only three incarnations together—as distant relatives, as teacher and pupil in a seminary, and as business acquaintances. Three shared lifetimes of minor emotional attachment were decidedly secondary to my seventeen highly-charged lives with Filipa.

"You do not have very strong karmic ties," said William, stating the obvious. That was the last thing we needed, or wanted, to hear.

For all her ethereality, Filipa was gradually taking Rachel's place. At first, though, I had serious doubts about her intelligence and her ability to understand and answer my questions. Her initial responses were almost juvenile, prompting me to remark to Roger and Aviva that I had attracted a "disco queen" for a guide. It was as if she were overwhelmed by the experience of making contact and to hide her fluster she pretended to know more than she actually knew. She was "winging it," one might say, claiming to be an old hand at trans-dimensional communication when she was but a novice.

Strangely immature behavior, I thought, for a guide. But then, as Russell often reminded us, the guides were only human and we had no right to expect them to behave like gods. Typically, Filipa confronted me with my own misgivings:

> I know that I am learning from you. I am not as accomplished as you. And I know that I am not, perhaps, as smart as you would like me to be. But I am trying and I think that maybe we can work together.

Such unabashed self-deprecation roused my sympathy as well as my affections. When I responded by saying that I was impressed with her progress, she explained that she was shy and ill-at-ease during our early dialogues.

> I now have some experience with this and I am knowing you better and becoming friends with you. It is difficult to walk in where there are strangers and participate in conversations which have obviously been going on long before.... It is a most uncomfortable situation. So it does take a little time. But I am enjoying those with whom I am here and I have encountered much in the way of forward development.

I was becoming disconsolate about my failure to achieve mind-to-mind contact with Filipa. More than three months had passed and still, with the zeal of a religious celibate, I trained my mind each morning to hurdle space and time in one concentrated blast of mind energy. All in vain. The daily endeavor had resulted in nothing but a turmoil of teeming thoughts or, at best, an empty screen for the mind's eye. Filipa did her best to coach me in the task of dissolving the non-material veil. Just relax, she would tell me, insisting that success would be achieved through receptivity and openness rather than effort and exertion.

"Don't try so hard," she counseled on more than one occasion. "Sometimes when you try very hardly it is impeding for it brings too much brain—not mind—and this makes for very difficult."

Russell described guide contact as a joining of mind energies. These energies were perceived and translated by the respective guide and charge. He likened the communication to a farming procedure practiced in his native Yorkshire:

> When we needed water in far fields we would dig trenches all the way along and let the water empty into them to form a channel. Imagine that the astral realm is the body of water and the charge is the field. The idea is to create a form of trench to carry the water or, in this case, the flow of energies.

Hanni, in advising Roger on the best way to make contact with herself, instructed him in her self-effacing and gentle fashion: "Tug on my skirt as you did when you were a little boy." She recalled that in the Dutch incarnation they shared Roger would sit on the floor and tug at her skirt and when her apron fell down he would giggle and squeal and run away with it. And Hanni would chase him and they would giggle and squeal together. "The warm little boy who had no chance to grow to adulthood has now grown to adulthood," said Hanni. "You should just relax and let the warm personality that was so much a part of you become you again. Practice. Be warm and friendly and uninhibited and communicate in an open fashion when you feel totally at ease...and it will happen."

Late in November, 1984, my daily meditation began to yield results. For the umpteenth time, I went upstairs to my study before breakfast, hoisted my legs on to the oak desk, closed my eyes and breathed deeply. I had learned to harbor no expectations; I had learned not to try. That morning, particularly, I surrendered utterly to the experience of sitting there, ushering my thoughts effortlessly in Filipa's direction. And that's when it happened. An image swam into view, an image of a dusty pathway winding past two large boulders and leading in the distance to a stand of tall, spindly trees. Birds scattered from the topmost branches.

Having no understanding of what this image represented, I could hardly wait for the next session and the opportunity to consult Filipa. When Aviva sank into trance, I listened impatiently to a typically stentorian address from Russell before my turn came and I was able to tell Filipa exactly what I had seen. Her response was feverish in its intensity.

"That's our spot!" she exclaimed. "That's our place. Did you see the underbrush and the cots where we used to sit?"

"It's very arid," I said. "Dusty."

"Yes—and prickly bushes," said Filipa. "It's one of my most favorite spots. If you can describe our place of years ago, I would think that would be a progression [in making contact]. It was not a pretty place, but it was ours. It was all we had. For you see, where we lived, the small villages, everybody knew everybody else and what they were doing and when they were doing it and who they were doing it with. There were others doing it too. We weren't the only ones. But we got caught. You see, that was the difference."

Hugely encouraged in the pursuance of my morning meditation, I recalled the itchiness that Jai-Lin had provoked in Roger's forehead and

I asked Filipa whether she, too, could provide a physical indication of her presence. I suggested that she induce itchiness in the soles of my feet.

"Do you walk barefoot often?" she inquired.

"No, not very often. You're saying it's going to be awkward....?"

"Well, you'd have to keep removing your sandals each time so that you could scratch."

"What about the back of my neck?"

After a ludicrous exchange as to whether "prickles" or "tickles" should be generated there, it was agreed that Filipa would endeavor to attract my attention by cultivating a prickly sensation under my collar. For the next few days, I waited in vain for my neck to bristle with sensation. And as much as Filipa insisted that she tried to make me scratch, I did not feel a thing and the scheme was abandoned.

Yet in my daily attempts to communicate with the next world I was beginning to develop a sense of what contact actually meant. When I was "there," a loud buzzing would reverberate in my ears, a sound that could be likened to an internal droning of cicadas. When the buzzing began, I felt tuned in to Filipa's presence and I would continue to be aware of her closeness for as long as the sensation lasted. This communication usually took place beneath a huge sign nailed to the wall of my study proclaiming, in bright red letters, GUIDES WILL ASSIST YOU. The sign was left over from Pope John Paul II's visit to Toronto in September, 1984 where it had advised the Roman Catholic faithful of the availability of marshals at an open-air mass. Perceiving its alternate meaning, a friend had collected the sign from a scrapheap and presented it with a smile at my door one afternoon.

The buzzing in my ears was always accompanied by a strange sense of contentment and reconciliation and a suspension of worldly anxiety. Occasionally, when I was feeling particularly relaxed and at peace with myself, mind-to-mind conversations would erupt in my head. But once the meditation had ceased and the buzzing had retreated, doubt often filled the void. Part of me poured scorn on the notion that communication was possible with beings in another dimension even as the rest of me insisted that I must trust and accept what I was experiencing.

But is it experience, retorted my inner interlocutor...or merely self-delusion?

CHAPTER 5

A Cast of Characters

Mindful of Jesus Christ's injunction not to cast pearls before swine, I was careful to avoid mentioning the guides within range of unsympathetic ears. Even so, I made errors of judgement. Evangelizing about my friends in the next dimension cost me at least a couple of earthly pals who apparently decided that undue exposure to the occult had ravaged my senses beyond repair. As one friend of mine told another, "We've lost Joe."

I was intrigued to learn that the guides were faced with the same dilemma. "We are looked upon," confided Russell, "as perhaps a little strange in the eyes of many in our world who share the knowledge of our contact. Some believe us to be inadequate intellectually because they feel that realm-to-realm discussion is something that cannot occur. Sometimes we are looked upon as crackpots, to use one of your terms."

Roger told him that while some of our associates would also see us as crackpots, Christians would consider we were talking to the world of the dead. Necromancy, it was called.

"But what is the world of the dead?" Russell demanded. "Departing the earthbound plane is only a departing from physical experience. It is not anything else than that. What else could it be construed as?"

"They tend to believe," Roger explained, "that the dead go to their graves and will remain there until such time as Jesus Christ returns. Then they will be raised up and judged according to their deeds and either taken to heaven to be with Him or to hell to be with Satan."

Even though such belief was current in Victorian society, Russell was shocked by this disclosure.

"How incredible!" he exclaimed. "Most incredible! It is quite unfortunate when people base their lives on a myth. However, they will learn. Between their earthbound experiences, they will learn. It does not necessarily make them any smarter next time."

Fortunately, there were people of my acquaintance who would neither scoff at my involvement with the guides nor contend that communication with discarnates was impossible. And, thankfully, they weren't about to protest that we were consorting with the Devil's minions. Indeed, I knew they would be just as astounded and as intrigued as myself if they could only witness Aviva in action. Towards the end of 1984, I invited some of these individuals to attend the Friday night sessions. In turn, they brought still more visitors and, by springtime 1985, Aviva's entranced and supine form was regularly attracting from ten to thirty people for each session. No fee was ever levied for the "performance." Aviva simply liked meeting new people. Their goodwill and conviviality was payment aplenty so far as she was concerned.

The budding group represented a wide cross-section of society. There were several journalists, a nurse, a storekeeper, a waitress, an entrepreneur, an inventor, a probation officer, a veterinary worker, a soldier, an aeronautics company manager, a couple of students, a social worker, a chiropractor, a management consultant and a poet who was also a practicing psychic. As the number of embodied individuals grew, the cast of discarnate characters expanded to accommodate them.

The presence of a guide was announced for any newcomer who was declared by Russell and his colleagues to be an entity. We watched in awe as the initial announcement of a guide's name gradually developed—usually in the space of several sessions—into a distinct voice with its own reincarnation history. It was intriguing to observe how people were paired with the type of discarnate individual that, consciously or unconsciously, they appeared either to want or need. There were mother figures, father figures, quarrelsome eccentrics, big brothers and sisters, simple pals, gentle counselors, prattling comics.... And, in my case, a dream lover.

No guide was ever available for anyone who was classified as a soul. The guides of souls, it was said, occupied a separate plane, a plane inaccessible to entities. So it was that many people were politely turned away, though some souls became so fascinated with the proceedings that, regardless, they continued to attend.

I wrestled with the soul/entity concept for a long time, if only because there was no precedent for such an idea in the history of human thought. And while I eventually acceded to the guides' greater wisdom and knowledge, there were times when I questioned my deference. For example, I wondered why Bernard Vesey, a professional editor, was identified as a soul even though I knew him to be an individualist of considerable perception, a keen seeker after truth and a student of metaphysics. Effectively excluded from the "club" of entities on his first visit to Aviva's living room, Bernard did not return. I was troubled by this, but the matter was out of my hands and I accepted the guides' judgement.

As for Bernard, he was not only deterred by his designation; he was disturbed by its implications. It was pointless to try to coax him back into the fold. There was no personal guardian with whom he could converse.

The parade of guides was endlessly fascinating. Embracing a wide variety of cultures, eras, lifestyles and personalities, they spoke in separate accents and, if requested, languages.

Aside from Filipa, Russell, Mi-Lao, Hanni and William, the burgeoning cast of characters included Ernest, who had fought in World War II as a bomber pilot with the Royal Air Force; Sonji, a wealthy landowner from Kathmandu, Nepal, who died of natural causes at the age of sixty-six; Tuktu, who lived in Ceylon in his most recent incarnation yet whose name hailed from a life in Korea; Kinnggalaa, an African huntsman from the fifteenth century who lived "on the Mother River near the Mother Lake"; Franco, an Argentinian tailor who died in political upheaval in 1903; David, a farm boy from South Carolina who loved fishing...

We watched spellbound as Aviva cruised from tribal African bass to prim upper-class English to rippling Anglo-Indian to Carolina drawl to broad Scottish and back again. If she was acting, she was not only brilliant, she was inhumanly so!

Even the most skeptical of observers had to concede that Aviva—who was incapable of successfully imitating a foreign accent in her waking state—could never consciously produce the stream of accents that flowed so effortlessly from her lips. Immobile save for the muscles in her face and larynx, she gave riveting performances week after week. There were awe-inspiring soliloquies, tales of sadness and nostalgia, snippets of humor, moments of heart-stopping perceptiveness and extraordinary medical analyses. Advice was dispensed in abundance to the distressed, the sick, the metaphysically maladjusted...to anyone, souls included, who made an inquiry.

Russell and his colleagues, however, preferred questions related to forward development. Invariably they urged us to strive for mind-to-mind contact with themselves and gave tips on how this could be achieved. They offered specific advice on how to shield oneself from negativity, gave tutorials on subjects such as "love," "guilt" and "creativity," and vented their opinions on everything from abortion to vegetarianism. A pithy wisdom was commonly expressed, as in these extracts from Russell's discourses:

> In his earthbound form, man does not wish to know about his true origins. He prefers the security of a deity.
>
> You cannot have freedom without discipline. But you can always, once you have mastered discipline, arrange freedom.
>
> Action is learning; pondering is regression.

The more sessions I attended, the more I attempted to learn about the guides' world and our inter-dependent relationship. The guides represented an open resource of knowledge and information about anything, anything at all, concerning the mysteries of existence here and hereafter. In a sense, it was like talking to agents of the Creator. All one had to do was ask.

Step by step, the guides told us about the realm in which they lived. It sounded marvelous. Space and time did not exist, love and mind-to-mind communication reigned supreme and the utter lack of physicality was seen as joyous deliverance from the trammels of earthly confinement. The all-encompassing, overwhelming love that embraces everyone at the point of death was often remarked upon. Said Russell:

> When you enter this plane...you will feel the love that your guide is bringing to you. This is much the same as grasping a rope and following it through a storm to go back safely from your outer shed to your house. You feel it and you can follow it....Here the feelings of love are far stronger, the ties with others and the feelings that go with those ties are far deeper than you can experience on the earthbound plane.

The guides' descriptions of the between-life state closely approximated ancient scriptural accounts as well as the testimony of deep-trance subjects and the statements of those who had undergone near-death experiences. But the guides' portrayal went farther, deeper, in relating details of roles and motivations beyond the grave.

Each guide was responsible for a number of charges—possibly as many as one hundred or more, depending on ability and experience. These charges were people living on Earth with whom they were karmically bonded as a result of having shared intense experience in previous incarnations. We who were incarnate today could, in turn, become guides ourselves after death or "transition." Conversely, the guides—our co-explorers aboard the seemingly endless shuttle of rebirth—were expected to return to the earthbound plane in the cause of their own personal evolution. The guides were assisted by "apprentices" who were also linked to the embodied personality through shared past-life experience.

The very lack of physical encumbrance in the *bardo* granted deeper understanding and clearer perception, allowing for an overview of the human condition that was inconceivable to those of us struggling with the limitations of terrestrial life. Shorn of material cares and considerations, the guides were free to cultivate an attribute said to be indispensable for guiding: unconditional love. Indeed, it seemed our allies in the next dimension were able to avail themselves of love and knowledge as easily as we received the blessing of sunshine. Although they retained human traits and foibles, the guides *knew* so much more than their incarnate counterparts, most of whom were stumbling around on Earth unaware of their origins and their history of past lives and equally ignorant of any life after death. The guides possessed this knowledge on their charges' behalf and they knew, also, the blueprint or "karmic script" of goals and lessons that those in their care had drawn up before birth for the life to come. Russell outlined the guides' mandate:

> Our aim as guides is to see that the individual does not drift too far from his path, although we cannot prevent this. Most charges do not understand energies. They understand only their own motivations and feelings, for they do not have the other levels of awareness of themselves open. And that is

primarily where we do most of out guiding—in the level of self-awareness, giving impetus to the opening of channels in the mind and the brain.

I could scarcely believe how privileged we were. While the rest of humanity floundered in a fog of oblivion, we were in direct communication with disembodied beings who had the maps of our lives laid out before them! With their help, the road to the Godhead could surely be negotiated much more swiftly and assuredly than would otherwise be possible. But if our good fortune was incalculable, I cautioned myself, our responsibility was correspondingly all the greater. As if to acknowledge our enlarged sense of obligation, Russell commented:

> The prime responsibility of each human being is to advance his own development, but not at the cost of others. It is to learn. It is to love. Primarily, to learn to love.... The essence of you on the Earthbound plane is to learn the lessons of love and acceptance.... Each time you learn one of these lessons, you are taking one more step towards the aim and goal of the human existence. Each time you learn to accept limitations and aggressions in others and in yourself, you are learning. The most basic learning is to love and accept yourself and those with whom you are in association.

Both guides and charges were said to have originated from "the great pool of knowledge." By means of successive incarnations and subsequent progression through non-physical planes, we were making our way back to that pure state of being where individuality would be freely and willingly surrendered. The information relayed by the guides, while "interpreted" for earthly understanding, was retrieved from this vast knowledge pool. "It is as a well," noted Russell, "where you can take what you need and it will always be replenished."

While writing *Life Between Life* with psychiatrist Dr. Joel Whitton, I often consulted Filipa, Russell and the other guides on the nature of discarnate existence. As well as corroborating the testimony of Dr. Whitton's patients who tasted the between-life state while under hypnosis, the guides went further still. They explained the role of the guide at the death of an individual, spoke rapturously about "our natural home"—Filipa's epithet for the *bardo*—and discussed the "assessment board" of higher beings which helps an individual to evaluate his most recent existence and to choose the next incarnation. Their insights were so valuable that Russell and Filipa were accredited in the book's acknowledgements as "eloquent ambassadors of between-life consciousness."

Guides were not necessarily wiser or more evolved than their charges. In the group setting, we were inclined to defer to them as senior partners because they occupied higher ground; theirs was the expanded vision of the between-life state. Yet guides and charges were often together because they had reached a similar stage in their personal evolution. Russell explained:

> ...Our paths are similar. We are working upon much the same things at the same time....If you start to outstrip your guide, you will find that you have a guide who is more at the level to which you have progressed. Conversely, if you begin to decline, slip backwards—as Roger well knows—you are left with a guide who is at the same level of development as yourself.

As earthbound entities, we were individualized by thousands of different energy types which blended to represent a unique person, just as the ingredients of a cake combined to produce a distinct flavor. These energies provided the guides with valuable information. Displaying somewhat erratic diction, Filipa said:

> Your energies are our eyes, your energies are our ears, your energies are our shapes and form and substance. Picturing of you is not as you would see, with two eyes. What we seeing is you, insiding and outsiding. We knowing of beauty or coarseness or defaultness—all these and more are known.

By reading our energies, the guides knew the precise state of our emotions. Thus informed, they could take appropriate action, including physical intervention. "When we have to intervene physically," said Russell, "we do so through the mind, but we can also come in control for a brief moment of the body.... We are able...to divert movements and increase attention span." We were told that a guide might infiltrate a driver's mind, initiating sudden attentiveness before a dangerous situation revealed itself on the road ahead. As David explained in his pronounced Southern accent:

> Physically, we are not going to put down a hand and drag you away. I mean, that's not something that we can do. We don't have a physical body but, physically, we can make energies do very powerful things.... It's more like an energy that we would throw around you or knock you down with.

And he gave an example:

> I've got at least two charges that I've got to be very close to when they're sleeping because they tend to forget to breathe sometimes. We can tend to have a little input there, raise their awareness levels so that they wake up just a little.

On a routine basis, however, our discarnate friends chose to attend and influence us in less dramatic ways. Insisting that guides did not "spy" on their charges, Russell explained:

> We must have basic information. And basic information is given to us many times through your sleep stages, many times through your dream stages when we are the influencers of your dreams. We can also gain it through your times of introspection.... At a glance, we can see various aspects that deal with your daily survival.... It is vital information.

Russell stressed on several occasions that only in extreme circumstances would the guides meddle in earthly affairs. Free will was a prime requirement of accomplishment and nothing could be accomplished in terms of personal advancement if guides were to lead their charges hither and thither. In fact, such behavior was counterproductive to the very purpose of incarnate life, which was learning. The best guide was like the best referee: unobtrusive. The best guide was skilled at helping the individual remain true to his or her between-life intentions while stimulating the greatest possible measure of personal growth.

Just as the guides would reach into our minds for linguistic knowledge, so they would tap the same source for past-life information. Reincarnation history was a favorite topic on Friday nights. Group members who wanted to learn about past-life ties with their guides, relatives and friends, as well as the anterior causes of various situations in their present lives, were presented instantaneously with plausible scenarios from the past.

Aside from rare exceptions such as Jai-Lin, who achieved huge advances within one incarnation, cosmic infancy was said to extend for up to seventy or eighty lifetimes. Management consultant Sandford Ellison, the "youngest" member of the group, was said to have led 112 lives. At the other extreme, the most earth-worn entity was poet Tony Zambelis who was told that he had lived 4,208 times and had spent some of his earlier existences on the vanished continents of Lemuria and Atlantis. Tony's guide, Ernest, said that they had shared as many as three hundred relationships in and out of incarnation. Such statistics were mind-boggling and the rest of us were relieved to hear Russell say that the quality of the lives rather than the quantity indicated how far one had traveled along the road to enlightenment.

Although I had never been one to join groups of any kind, it was easy to become addicted to the Friday night sessions. With the guides' help, Helen was becoming remarkably adept at identifying auras as well as differentiating between souls and entities. Tony was able to detect various colors displayed by the guides as they manipulated Aviva's vocal cords. Franco's charge, Erik Muller, a magazine editor, would enter lengthy discussions about the non-material terrain encountered during his frequent out-of-body experiences. And Jane Barkalow, Kinnggalaa's charge, was the envy of all in that she chatted silently and interminably with her African companion about all aspects of her life. Whether she was at home, at work, or driving her car through the city streets, Jane enjoyed apparently effortless communication with her guide.

Having been betrothed during their time in Africa some five hundred years ago, Kinnggalaa and Jane shared a similar relationship to Filipa and myself. They chatted on Friday nights with great affection and familiarity; their rapport was a joy to witness. Hailing from Liverpool, Jane was all warmth and effusiveness and, amusingly, she would address the less than ebullient Kinnggalaa as "Love." He, in turn, would urge that Jane put on more weight, even as she was endeavoring to diet. "I like to have proportions on my females," he said in a deep monotone resonant with wisdom and experience. "Plumpness of more than your proportions was considered quite attractive when we were together."

Outside Aviva's living room, certain members of the group could sense the guides in a variety of ways—from the buzzing in my ears to the throbbing forehead that Rachel felt in William's presence. The most efficacious calling card of all, however, was dealt by David, the farm boy from South Carolina. When his charge, Valerie Edson, failed to notice him in her daily life, David vowed to send her an unmistakable indication of his attentiveness: the reek of rotting fish from his much-loved days in the Deep South.

It was a grand claim, if only because Valerie—who worked at rehabilitating alcoholics—was so unimpressionable, and we all waited expectantly to see whether such an outlandish link would ever be established. Doubts pressed in as several weeks went by without Valerie detecting the slightest fishy whiff. When David swore he was doing his best, Valerie pleaded with him: "Make the smell stronger still."

"You want me to send you the whole dockful?" David drawled.

Soon afterwards, Valerie was awakened at 4 a.m. by an insufferably strong stench. "I woke up wondering who on earth was barbecuing fish at that time of the morning," she said. "The place was filled with the smell of fish that was just turning rotten."

At the next Friday night session, after David had expressed his customary "How are you tonight?" Valerie told him that his efforts had succeeded.

"Oh good!" he said. "Aa've bin tryin' every night."

"I was almost sick!" Valerie protested.

"It was catfish."

In the weeks and months to come, Valerie was often surprised by the stench of fish—sometimes in the house, sometimes at work and sometimes in the street. It was always the same foul odor of rotting fish on the barbecue.

"Aa know you don't like my fish but aa kinda love it," David told his charge. "Aa see an instant change in your energies when you're not likin' fish. Well, *aa* like fishin' and the next time we're together on the earthbound aa reckon we're goin' to do just a lot of fishin'."

In the so-called civilized world of the late twentieth century, most people roll their eyes at any suggestion of guide contact and mind-to-mind communication. Yet in ancient times when the unseen world was considered to be just as habitable as the physical environment, primitive man was in constant communion with invisible beings in the next dimension. Russell lamented the passing of this dialogue, blaming man's isolation on the steady rise of materialism. "The accumulation of things has preoccupied man for the last few hundred years," he said. "And with this preoccupation, people have lost the ability to use their minds. They have relied on the brain instead of the mind."

These days, we were told, guide contact is achieved only by approximately one person in ten thousand—a statistic which confirmed our communal feelings of pride, privilege and gratitude. Not that we needed to be reminded we were special. We already saw ourselves as honored guests at a banquet where the dining never stopped. Or as seekers after truth who had found a secret doorway in a world of walls. Nothing, nothing on this earth could emulate the thrill and reassurance of communicating with one's guide.

The group members were quite different from one another in temperament and association and there was little fraternizing outside the womb of Aviva's living room. But the weekly hour or two of trans-dimensional communication bound us together as one family. No matter how moribund or heavy-laden we might have felt at the beginning of the evening, we were usually energized and uplifted by the time we left. As for Aviva, I drew comfort from knowing that Russell and his colleagues were doing all in their power to restore her to full health.

The sessions drew to a close when Russell signaled that his charge's energies were wearing thin or that the communicating "vehicle" was becoming dehydrated. Reluctantly, we bade fond farewells to our guides for another week and Aviva was hauled up the "mineshaft" from deep trance to waking reality. For her, the evening was only just beginning. Once she had sat up and gulped down a couple of tall tumblers of mineral water, her grogginess would begin to dissipate. Around the living room, in the kitchen and in the hall, people would be animatedly discussing what the guides had said. And, for a while, she would feel like a stranger in her own home because she had no memory, no idea at all, of what the voices had said even though the talking had been hers. All hers.

Gradually, however, the debate would become less trenchant, people would pay more attention to the snacks on the coffee table, and Aviva was able to settle comfortably into what she liked best about Friday nights—socializing.

CHAPTER 6

'I Can See in Your Mind'

The exquisite moment I had longed for swept in briskly and without fanfare one overcast morning in March, 1985.

As I lolled at my desk in meditative repose, I received a distinctly visual impression of a woman walking towards me wearing sandals and a long white wrap. Although her face was partially hidden by the garment, I knew at once I was staring directly at Filipa. Within seconds, my body was racked with the most profound and unrestrained emotion. I wept out of joy and sadness and loss and anguish, yet to this day I don't really know why. Intellectually, I cannot find reasons for my tears. All I can say is that it was one of the most moving experiences of my life.

The following Friday night, Filipa was quick to acknowledge the vision. We had barely exchanged opening greetings when she declared: "We have made success, yes?" Carefully avoiding any mention of my weeping ("I did not think that would be good for all to know," she explained later), she spoke of the communication as "very deep heart" contact stemming from our life together in north-eastern Greece. "Is many times I think his mind is going to shut," she told the group. "But you make it. Not too clear, but you make it. It is nice."

Several months later, I experienced another powerful surge of communicative energy. After working on *Life Between Life* for several hours, I decided to lie down in the middle of the afternoon. Within a few minutes, I was mind-gliding in a state of utter euphoria. A clamorous buzzing in my ears told me that contact had been well and truly established. Next, I remember being overwhelmed by the feeling that Filipa and myself were of like mind. My fatigue forgotten, I got up, made a cup of tea, and spent the next hour and a quarter suffused with an ecstasy as spontaneous and all-consuming as my tears had been. So long as the ecstasy lasted, I chatted silently to Filipa as if she were beside me. Which, of course, she was.

When Filipa next spoke through Aviva's lips, she spontaneously expressed her pleasure at our blissful communication. She intimated that my passive and relaxed state had contributed inordinately to the parting of the veil.

Each morning, we were having more and more fun as I dedicated myself to making contact. In stepping up my meditative exercise, I had taken to visualizing myself hugging Filipa, a development that drew a number of appreciative comments. She seemed to crave the developing closeness at least as much as I did.

"I think sometimes I get more selfish as we get more…because I want more," Filipa confessed one Friday night.

"Do you mean that you want me to spend longer with you in the morning?" I asked. "Or do you want me to contact you on more occasions?"

"I think I just want more hugs."

If Filipa could have assumed a physical body, I'm sure I would have married her. But she was only a voice, a voice that resonated with more love, compassion and perspicacity than I had ever known. Within the space of a few months, she had demonstrated an acute awareness of my feelings and foibles, she knew the people in my life and their effect upon me, and she was even able to relate specific circumstances in which I had found myself, situations unknown to Aviva or anyone who attended what Filipa chose to call our "groupings."

In learning to accept my transparency, I anticipated our chats with a potent mix of longing and apprehension. Waiting for Filipa to speak through Aviva's lips, I felt nervously vulnerable. And why wouldn't I? She was able to discern my every thought and deed—an attribute which made her love even more remarkable. Just as she knew me, I felt intuitively that I knew her too. But such intimacy brought in its wake a certain terror that sometimes curdled my elation. True privacy had been surrendered to Filipa's loving attachment and, though I was grateful for her ministrations, my life was no longer my own.

At the time, I would have denied that the guides were exerting great influence over my attitudes and behavior. Yet every time I contemplated a major decision in my life, I sought Filipa's approval. Would my anticipated course of action contribute to my goal of forward development? Before, such thinking had always been unconscious; I had tried to do that which would not wage war on my conscience. Now my conscience had become personified as Filipa who, for all her love and devotion, was an all-seeing inquisitor. Knowing that she was watching my every move left me self-absorbed, tense, and less inclined to act spontaneously.

Though at first I doubted our mind-to-mind communication, proof that we were genuinely in touch was soon forthcoming. Filipa was able to confirm, via Aviva's voice box, messages that had been delivered in silence, when no one else was around. On one occasion, while cross-country running, a voice or implanted thought form made itself heard as I huffed and puffed up a steep hill. The idea that came to me was: "Imagine that your feet are not touching the ground. Pretend instead that they are pushing off from mid-air just above the surface. Then, both physically and psychologically, the climb will be much easier." I obeyed the advice as it was communicated—mid-way up the gradient—and found that the strain was lessened considerably. When I next spoke to Filipa in a private session at Aviva's house, I asked whether she had been speaking with me while I was out running. "Yes," she replied evenly, "I was telling you to imagining that your feet are placing one above the other in air."

Sometimes, however, I was able to do no more than approximate what had been said during our private dialogues. I am thinking particularly of the time I asked Filipa for my nickname during our time in Greece. I understood her to transmit in reply the word "Gilead." When asked the same question at the next Friday night session, Filipa responded with the word "Gideon," adding…"because you always brought me nice things when we met." My nickname for her, she said, was *Micro Laluda* or "Little Flower." And so we came to know one another by the names of Gideon and *Micro Laluda,* or simply *Laluda.* Whether we were chatting publicly or in private, we always began by exchanging the traditional Greek greeting of *Yassoo.*

Several times, Filipa described situations familiar to myself but known to no-one else attending the sessions. For example, after interviewing an extraordinary psychiatric patient who subsequently appeared in *Life Between Life* under the pseudonym of Jenny Saunders, I was curious to glean Filipa's impressions.

Jenny was unusual in that she was a source of psychokinetic activity—the physical manifestation, psychically induced, of subliminal tension. Unconsciously, Jenny's mind had, among other things, shattered glass tumblers and created bloodstains on the wall of her apartment. Without revealing any clues, I simply asked Filipa whether she had any comment about the person I had encountered three evenings earlier. "Ah," was her reply. "The woman with the strange energies! I didn't like you being around her. I was trying to give you energy and protection."

Filipa invariably contacted me when I was at work, especially when I was seated at the computer, my fingers running over what she called the "buttons" on the keyboard. Sunk in concentration, I would suddenly be aware of the familiar buzzing in my ears. When questioned about this, Filipa replied: "When you are working with your brain, it is much easy to make the contact with you, for you have your mind free from blockings."

Occasionally, however, I was too exhausted or preoccupied with earthly cares and considerations to achieve the relaxation necessary for effective guide contact. At times like these, Filipa longed for a physical body:

> I try when you are this to smooth these feelings for you. Sometimes I wish that I could stand there and wipe your face and hold your hand. But it becomes too personal, it becomes...I have to remain in my position of objectivity, cloudy as it may get.

Filipa offered much in the way of practical advice. There were tips on nutrition—"take fresh figs and goat's milk as you did in Greece; this, for you, is most goodly." She pinpointed a weakness in my lungs (I have latent tuberculosis) and warned several times that undue stress would aggravate this condition. She suggested a cold remedy whereby I was instructed to cover my head in sacking and then bend, breathing deeply, over a pot of boiling balsam. Further, I was urged to take five-minute "brain rests" from my work every hour. Elaborating on the value of such mini-breaks, Filipa harked back to Greece for a suitable analogy:

> When you were working in the fields or when you were with

your militia, you would walk and walk and walk for days. And you would come in and your feet would be big and sore and all red. And if you had made little stops all along the way—and sometimes you did—your feet did not get big and sore and red. And then you did not get a big face, all red and cranky. It would work the same way in these days. You resting the brain little bit, too. Just like you would rest the body a little bit.

Repeatedly, Filipa advised that I protect myself from negative energies by visualizing the shielding influence of my Greek soldier's uniform. And she suggested that I divide my daily life into separate undertakings, allowing no merging of interests or responsibilities. By way of explanation, she presented me with another vignette from our days in Theros:

Now I know that you are going to tell me that you don't remember, but I am going to describe to you a little room that you had in your house when we were together. It was almost square with a wooden door....And all around the walls you had driven wooden stakes and put up planks and made yourself shelves. You were very neat, I suppose, and you made not only shelves. You put little walls along the shelves that made them into little rooms.

And you had in these little rooms all your clothes and your boots and your medals and your hats and your gloves and your coats. You had each little room on the shelves for one thing. And never ever did I see you put your hat in anything but a little room that was meant for that.

Now you should apply that very same technique. You must make a little room for your work, a little room for your contact, a little room for private time and a little room for rest time. You see what I mean? And if you do this, you will find you are quite capable of achieving what you want. Don't try to relate one room to another. You see, when you put on your hat, you didn't try to relate it to your coat. You simply took your coat and put it on and the two came together....

It was good advice. But Filipa did more than act as an agony aunt equipped with an array of stop-gap antidotes. She was working invisibly to help me accomplish what I had planned for myself while inhabiting the *bardo*. I was glad to learn that I was indeed treading the path delineated in my karmic script. My principal goal for this incarnation, Filipa explained, was to disseminate, on a wide scale, knowledge of that which lies beyond earthly reality. Apparently this objective had been karmically inspired by an earlier desert life in Sumeria in which, following a volcanic eruption, I deliberately kept secret the whereabouts of a supply of fresh water. Many perished, I was told, because I withheld this life-giving information from others. Today, although circumstances were very different, my predicament was the same. Once more, the challenge was to spread the news rather than keep it to myself.

Somehow, Filipa had to be either living inside me or hovering perpetually close by, picking up via some otherworldly antennae my organism's every twitch and shudder. How else could she read my thoughts and feelings, sit in on my compositions at the computer keyboard, observe my contacts with others, assess my health and nutrition, listen to the jazz and rock 'n roll that I played on the stereo—"noises," she called it—and even hear the tunes I habitually hummed in my head? "I can see energies," is how she explained her ability to know me inside out. "I can see in your mind. If you make in your mind, I can see."

The guides were doing much to enrich our quality of life, both emotionally and materially. They often displayed the ability to read the state of our physical bodies and prescribe minerals, foods or medicinal herbs to enhance performance and well-being. Russell would occasionally perform psychometry—that is, while turning over in "his" hands a personal item belonging to someone unknown to himself and Aviva, he would give incisive readings as to the individual's character and personality.

Sometimes, group members whose energy levels were depleted through stress or overwork would be instructed to hold the entranced Aviva's hands so that they could receive a steady influx of energy fed through her body from the guiding plane. As far-fetched as this might sound, I can attest to the marvelously restorative effect of these energy boosts. Feeling like an empty jug being filled to the brim, one knew instinctively when the transfer was complete.

On countless occasions, the guides claimed responsibility for beneficial physical intervention in the lives of their charges. Rachel was jolted out of a prolonged state of depression by a coursing wave of energy, running the length of her body. "It was such an extreme sensation and it took place unexpectedly and without apparent reason," she said. "I've never felt anything like it in my entire life." William later admitted that he had effected the change.

When Sandford Ellison persistently refused to allow himself to relax, he found himself immobilized in an armchair for ninety minutes. Try as he might, he was utterly unable to move. Tuktu informed his bewildered charge:

> It is called enforced rest. If you will not do it for yourself then I will do it for you.....It was without question that you needed a rest and you would not take one. And if you do not heed my advice, I shall do it to you again.

Russell implied that he had saved Aviva's life many times, often by directing Roger to administer crucial healing suggestions to stem the tide of her leukemia. But perhaps the most sensational example of his guardianship occurred when Aviva insisted—against Russell's advice—on driving through a heavy snowstorm to collect her six-year-old son from school. The incident occurred early in 1983, shortly after Aviva had emerged from assimilating anti-pain suggestions in trance. Russell had told Roger that she would risk death that afternoon if she followed her usual pattern in driving to her son's school. Perhaps thinking that the characteristically willful Aviva might have seen this extreme warning as a challenge, Russell added: "Don't tell her how grave the situation is…tell her simply that she should make other arrangements."

Typically, Aviva ignored the advice anyway and insisted on driving north through the blizzard to her son's school while Roger stayed behind and agonized over her safety. As Aviva recounted later: "After arriving at the school and collecting my son, I was unable to start the car. The engine was in perfect condition and I hadn't left the lights on, but it just wouldn't start. Although I stopped several cars and asked their drivers to give the engine a boost, the car *still* wouldn't start. One woman I asked to help me couldn't even start her own car. For a long time, I kept turning the ignition key without getting any sign of life. But as soon as the snowstorm abated, the engine started perfectly, as if nothing had happened."

Later, Russell intimated that he had instigated the temporary engine failure so that enough time would pass to keep his charge from encountering a potentially fatal accident on the way home. Said Aviva: "At the time, I pooh-poohed the idea that Russell had somehow interfered with my car. Now I'm not so sure. But we could have frozen to death—the jerk didn't think of that!"

* * *

Nothing could have prepared me for the extraordinary experience of communing with the guides. Had I devoured every occult volume ever written and debated metaphysical concepts nightly unto the grave I doubt very much whether my state of unreadiness could have been ameliorated in any way. Really one was *never* ready to meet the guides, if only because—for all the beneficial aspects of the weekly exchanges—one couldn't help but feel as vulnerable as a person standing on the blind side of a one-way mirror. The disembodied entities could read our minds and bodies but all we had to go by were their voices. They evinced familiarity with our world but we didn't know theirs, at least not consciously.

It was an addictive process: the more counsel I received from the guides, the more I wanted. But there were times when their counsel left me shaking my head in disbelief. It didn't quite make sense that, while stressing the importance of free will, they should intervene—physically and emotionally—in our lives. "We will not impose upon you," Russell had said. Yet, by their own admission, they *had* imposed upon us.

While I hastened to agree with the guides' assertion that orthodox religion was littered with half-truths and mistaken notions about non-physical reality, I was surprised, very surprised, to hear Russell state one evening that Jesus Christ was no more evolved than any member of our group. We were chatting about great religious leaders and their ability to influence the masses when Russell announced:

"The one you call Jesus Christ has, of course, been back to the earth-bound many, many times."

"Has he?" I replied incredulously.

"Heavens, yes."

"Even after living the life of Jesus Christ, one still needs to return to the earthbound plane?"

"He was just a man."

"But he accomplished so much in terms of knowledge and...."

"No, he didn't, He managed to get people to follow him. All he did was speak the truth. He never faltered in his own religion; he never faltered in his own morals. He simply acted as any teacher acts and engendered no more karma than any other teacher."

"But wouldn't you say that he was a particularly evolved human being?" I persisted.

"No," Russell declared. "No more than the rest of you. It was just that he spoke out and people needed something to hang onto for they were desperate times. In desperate times, there's always someone who will speak out and gain a following."

"But few people could speak out as he did, Russell."

"I think you will find that what has been received about his life has been quite distorted. The fantasy has hung on long after the man has gone, and it has been blown bigger and bigger with each generation."

"What about Buddha?" I inquired. "Has he reincarnated, do you know?"

"Buddha has a different aspect, altogether. The one who you call the Buddha has not reincarnated to my knowledge."

"So what sort of status would Jesus Christ have today?"

"I don't believe he's on the earthbound at the moment."

"Does he still have lots to learn?"

"Oh, the same as yourself," Russell said dismissively. "If you were living in desperate times and you spoke out with your books you, too, might be revered. In two, four, five, seven hundred, eighteen hundred years, you too might be painted as some savior when, in fact, you were no more than a man who spoke his mind. You see, a man who is emboldened by fear and injustice is often given statutory leanings by others when he is no more than a mere man. Fables will be written around his life and they will be distorted into what you call scripture. Stories abound that are merely mouthings from one to another and, as you mouth from one to another, the stories grow larger and more colorful until one day they are written down in their large, colorful, magnificent setting...yet all along they were nothing more than simple acts of kindness."

***

With great reluctance, I decided in September, 1985 that Rachel and I must part. Although the break-up was not precipitated by the guides, they were decidedly a factor in our failure to close the gulf that separated us. My guide, after all, was not only a guide, she was a lover who talked to me as such. Rachel's jealousy, I realized at last, was perfectly understandable.

Later, Rachel confessed that she had known our relationship was doomed as soon as I was introduced to Filipa's unconditional love. She knew that she would never be able to compete with such affections and spoke of feeling "heart-sick" when listening to Filipa's amorousness. Rachel insisted that it was relatively easy to conduct a relationship with a discarnate entity but much more taxing to apply oneself to making a partnership work in the face of daily pressures. "Talking to Filipa," she said, "is very different from walking uphill with a bucket of water."

I had always known that, in spite of her fondness for William, Rachel had never attended the Friday night sessions with any enthusiasm. Rather than embracing the guides, she had submitted to them. She consulted William only once or twice after our break-up and then renounced all contact with the group.

I reacted quite differently in the wake of our parting. Now that my interest in Filipa and the guides was unhampered by any conflicting considerations, I steeped myself still further in the apparently infinite supply of knowledge which lay on the far side of the trance state. So rich and so abundant were the insights and observations that there were times when I felt overwhelmed by the veritable geyser of information.

We were being regaled with lengthy expositions about life on the lost continents of Atlantis and Lemuria. We were learning about the inner workings of the mind, which was said to have some 10,000 levels. We were lectured, among other things, on the intricate symbiosis of the guide-charge relationship, the pursuit and discharge of one's karmic workload and the process of choosing one's parents. Everyone, it was explained, had strong karmic connections with at least one of his or her parents-to-be, who were identified and selected from the *bardo* long before the actual birth took place. At times the between-life state sounded incredibly complex. Said Russell:

On the earthbound plane, you are dealing with basic energies. You are dealing with visual energies, sound-wave energies, thought energies, pain—these types of energies. You probably have forty or fifty that you work with. And these you perceive and you understand. When you look at a tree, you know that it is a tree. When you hear a musical instrument, you can identify that instrument....On our plane we are dealing with the perceptual capability of over 400,000 energy types and their sub-variants.

As for the process of reincarnation, we learned that we would be aware of our multiple lifetimes as soon as our bodies expired. "Once in transition," Franco pointed out, "you have the instinctive knowledge of rebirth just as on the earthbound plane you have the instinctive knowledge of earthly death." Tuktu added: "The whole reason for pursuing our many earthbound lives is to well round our identities."

Yet even the guides had their limitations. We were told that to explain the nature of God would take three hundred sessions—a daunting project which was never attempted. And in answer to the question "Who created the first soul?" Russell confessed his ignorance:

> I do not have exposure to that type of knowledge and I'll not gain that, in your terms, for some time yet....I cannot even conceive where I might locate information of that description for you. You see, we think more in terms of the movement, accumulation and the use of accumulated knowledge.

So much data was available, nevertheless, that it scarcely seemed to matter that mankind's farthest origins would remain a mystery. In fact, the scales were being lifted from our eyes at such speed that I wondered aloud whether the barrage of information might precipitate insanity.

"Change and difference can overwhelm," Filipa concurred. "It's like taking a long, five-day walk from the village and seeing first time a big city...all those big buildings...much, much horses...much, much mules. Most different from what your slow life was in the countryside."

She went on to say that I would be able to synthesize the material and present it to the general public in a way that would contribute to a sudden leap in knowledge and awareness on the earthbound plane.

Filipa was articulating the very sense of mission I had nursed for years. She was saying that my search for metaphysical answers to the riddle of earthly existence was that mission. She was saying that I had a job to do, that I must withstand the guides' information barrage and turn it to the advantage of others and that I must help my fellow seekers on the path by discerning true guides from the myriad channeled voices. Naturally, her assistance would be unfailing. She was always there, always ready and willing to help. But I didn't realize quite how assiduous she was in her attentions until one Friday night she mentioned, quite casually, that she was aware of every thought I had about her.

The remark left me weak with ardent appreciation. *Every time I thought of her, she knew.* How attentive, I asked myself, can you get?

PART TWO
The Channeling Saga

CHAPTER 7

A Sense of Presence – The Long Tradition

Humanity has always been attended by invisible beings. Guides, guardian spirits and "helpers" populate tribal lore and scriptural texts, they reappear as guardian angels in the Christian tradition, they form the basis of modern Spiritualism and channeling, and they vie for attention in the spiritism of Africa, Asia, the Middle East, the Caribbean and Latin America. Throughout recorded history, an abundance of writings—ranging from the fervently religious to the studiously anthropological—testify to an oft-encountered sense of presence.

Embracing all races and creeds, the non-physical guardian is generally endowed with a common aim: to protect its ward and to promote personal growth by encouraging adherence to the highest ideals. The names assigned to these spirits are as diverse as the cultures in which they appear: the Romans called them *genii;* the Greeks, *daimones;* the Zoroastrians, *fravashis;* the Mongols, *Dzol-Dzajagatsi;* the natives of New Guinea, *tapum,* to name but a few.

Even before history was recorded, shamans worldwide were invoking guardian spirits for the purposes of healing and protection. The means of invocation have taken many forms, from sleep deprivation and the ingestion of hallucinogens to enforced seclusion and acoustic stimulation, usually involving extended exposure to loud and persistent drumming. Shamanic training among the Australian aborigines aimed at developing the "strong eye," that is, the faculty of seeing spirits. The native peoples of North and South America have always been aware of and dependent upon "spirit helpers" or "grandfathers" to sustain their connection with their spiritual source and to aid them throughout incarnate life. "No experience is as important to Indians in at least half the geographic regions of North

America as the gaining of a spirit-helper in a vision quest," declares Jamake Highwater in *The Primal Mind*. "Without it, a person would surely fail in every major activity of life."

Before 1850, native boys and girls often began their vision quest as early as the fifth year, traveling to a remote spot—a mountaintop or the shore of a lake or the depths of a forest. There, the child or youth remained for several days and nights, taking neither food nor water. Growing weakness would lead to a partial loss of consciousness and, often, to visual and auditory hallucinations. Sometimes, the vision included instructions as to what must be collected for a sacred bundle, which was kept for life as a symbolic embodiment of the power that guides one's life and gives protection and good fortune. "Even today," writes Highwater, "successful visions support people for their entire lives. It is a power upon which they can call for protection and good fortune."

The nomadic hunters and gatherers of the now-extinct Charrua tribe of Uruguay conducted a painful version of the vision quest. After making their way to the top of an isolated hill, they would slash and gouge their flesh with their weapons until, in delirium, each was granted a hallucination of a living being. This being was at once adopted by the native and invoked, in times of peril, as his guardian. The Plains Crow tribesman, in seeking the all-important vision, climbed a remote mountain, stripped, fasted, went without water and, finally, cut off one joint of his left forefinger. The dismembered appendage was then held up to the sun as the native pleaded with his guardian for good fortune.

Those living in the classical societies of antiquity, although less inclined to suffer for the privilege of a personal encounter with their guides, were no less knowledgeable about the special relationship existing between the living and the so-called dead. Socrates, the great Athenian philosopher, spoke in the fifth century B.C.E. of a being whose voice, from time to time, dissuaded him from some undertaking but never directed him as to what he should do. Socrates told his friends that when a man dies his guardian spirit, which has watched over the course of his life, escorts him to the place of judgement from whence he will be guided to the initial stage of the *postmortem* existence. The wise and disciplined soul, he said, will follow the guide. But the soul that is deeply attached to the body and its pleasures will hover around the visible world for a long time. Origen, a father of the early Christian Church, held a similar view. He wrote: "At the hour of death the celestial escort receives the soul the moment it leaves the body." In *Work and Days,* one of the earliest of Greek poems, Hesiod envisaged "deathless beings" who were ... .

> Keepers, unseen, of mortal men
> In airy vesture dight
> Their good and evil deeds they scan
> Stern champions of the right

The Bible, of course, mentions "ministering spirits" (Hebrews 1.14) without spelling out their perpetually watchful responsibilities. But *The Egyptian Book Of The Dead,* which dates back to 1300 B.C.E., succinctly expresses the unremitting vigilance that attends all who walk the earth. In Egyptian times, death was welcomed as a release from the gods' dogged attentiveness. "Behold," quoth the soul in transition to the next world, "I who was kept under guard and watched continually am now released."

The angel—meaning "one who is sent; a messenger"—personifies spiritual guardianship in Christianity, the guardian angel being a particularly potent symbol to Roman Catholics. As recently as 6 August 1986, in a general audience at the Vatican, Pope John Paul II spoke at length about the reality of guardian angels. They were purely spiritual beings, he insisted, which had no body, although they occasionally revealed themselves in physical form "because of their mission for the good of men."

Catholics insist that man's goodness, or lack of it, has no bearing on the quality or degree of angelic attention. "Every single human being on earth, whether Christian or non-Christian, whether in grace or in sin, remains during its entire life under the care of a Guardian Angel," states Jesuit theologian Joseph Husslein in *Our Guardian Angels.* The Bible mentions angels on nearly three hundred occasions, citing their power and solicitousness—from an angel "strengthening" Jesus Christ on the eve of his crucifixion in the Garden of Gethsemane (Luke 22:42) to the angelic intercession which gained Peter's release from prison (Acts 12:5-11).

The Popular Dictionary of Spiritualism equates the guardian angel with the guide figure which has its genesis in pre-Biblical times. According to the dictionary, the guardian angel is, "a guiding spirit, control or guide." The guiding spirit who is charged with a medium's wellbeing—often known as the "doorkeeper"—is said to be especially deserving of this title. Russell, ostensibly Aviva's control or doorkeeper, concurred with this definition. In his words:

> Guides have been a known fact for thousands and thousands of earthbound years. And, as a fact for thousands of years, they have been mis-translated. What people have considered as guardian angels have merely been the guides.

Later, Filipa urged me not to be hoodwinked by the Church's grandiose and winged interpretation of herself and her colleagues, pleading:

> Just be fair in your analysis....Do not make us sound nonhuman. Then people will understand that we are people too, not something that has been made by religion called angels. We do not have wings; we do not make soap bubbles in the air. This is...earthbound unthink.

For centuries, wings have been considered an anatomical imperative in drawings and paintings of angels. Yet in the first known depiction of angels—wall paintings, dating back to 300 C.E., decorating a large catacomb in Rome's Via Latina—there are no wings to be seen. Though absent from the majority of passages in the Bible, angelic wings were adopted by a later breed of Christian artists who wanted to highlight the distinction between earthly and spiritual beings. Chronicling the visits of guides to the dying in his *Deathbed Visions* (1926), Sir William Barrett noted that children would sometimes exclaim with great amazement that an angel without wings was present at the bedside.

Children and Biblical characters are not the only witnesses. In the book *Private Dowding,* Wellesley Tudor Pole carefully described his observations at the bedside of his friend, Major P., during the last hour of his life:

> 3 p.m.: Death seems very close at hand....Directly above the dying man I can see a shadowy form [a counterpart of the

body] that hovers in a horizontal position about two feet above the bed. The form is attached to the physical body...by two transparent elastic cords...and as the physical body grows more lifeless, the form hovering above seems to become vital.

3:15 p.m.: Two figures have now appeared and stand, one on either side of the bed....They seem...to be of some finer form of "matter" than the "double" that is hovering above the bed....

3:55 p.m.: The two figures stoop down over the bed and seem to break off the "cords" at points close to the physical body. Immediately . . . the form or double rises about two feet from its original position but remains horizontal, and at this same moment Major P's heart stops beating . . .

The astral double, which normally resides within the body, tends to become partly dissociated during sleep and even more separated when a person is in trance or shock. The double is said to be tethered by an invisible cord—the "silver cord" mentioned in Ecclesiastes (12:6)—so that it may rejoin the body when normal conditions are resumed. The cord is finally severed at death.

A distinctly visual sense of meeting his guide left an indelible impression upon Mark Eveson, a Toronto psychologist. The encounter would probably not have happened without a nasty accident which left Private Eveson, as he was then, heavily concussed after driving an army truck into a tree just before Easter, 1949, near Dorchester, England. His skull and jaw were fractured in the collision and it wasn't until a week later that he regained consciousness to find himself in a bed at Aldershot Military Hospital. Eveson, who remembered nothing of the accident, describes his awakening:

When I came to, I found that I was able to leave my body and look down at myself from the rafters. I could do this for any length of time.

I was aware of a white figure. At first I thought it must be

Jesus, but then I thought it was very naive of me to think so. The figure was male, dressed in white clothes and positioned on my left side. He was exuding feelings of great warmth and great attraction and I knew him—very definitely, I knew him. There was a welcoming and a beckoning from this figure and I had a strong sense that he was my guide. He was showing me a host of figures beyond, all of which expressed enormous love and compassion. There was a total acceptance of me that I had never before experienced.

Then two orderlies came to my bedside. As I was looking down on them, I heard one say to the other: "This one won't last the night." This made me very angry and, in a deliberate act, I went back into my body. Outside my body, everything had been beautiful. When I returned, existence became normal and painful.

There are many accounts of people who, after "dying" for a matter of moments, return to their bodies eager to tell of having become acquainted with discarnate overseers. Often, these witnesses have been resuscitated on an operating table or at the scene of an accident and, invariably, they speak of having absorbed intense feelings of love and well-being from their involuntary encounters. One woman told Dr. Raymond Moody, whose book *Life After Life* documents case studies of those who have revived after brief spells of clinical death, that she detected the presence of two beings who identified themselves as her "spiritual helpers." Dr. Moody learned of some who believed they had met their "guardian spirits"; others mentioned that they had heard voices telling them to return to their physical bodies because they were not yet dead.

Research in hypnosis points to the attending presence of spiritual beings before birth as well as after death. When the hypnotic subjects of Dr. Joel Whitton are ushered into the between-life state, they often encounter guides who help them acclimatize to the *bardo* and act as consultants and comforters before the next expedition into earthly reality. The late Dr. Helen Wambach, a clinical psychologist from San Francisco who regressed thousands of people into past lives during the 1970s, heard repeatedly about guiding presences when she asked 750 trance subjects to relay their experiences of the birth process. In answer to her primary question "Did you choose to be born?" the majority answered "Yes," saying they did so reluctantly after consulting with advisers. Those who described guides indicated that these figures were not necessarily superior to themselves, but rather colleagues who just happened to be discarnate. Here are some of the responses:

> Yes, I chose to be born. Someone helped me choose, and this person was a complete friend.

> I think I was reluctantly talked into being born. A wise male whom I respected, obeyed and loved helped convince me it would be good for me to be born now. He was a gentle, kind, but firm man.

> I was aware of guides that seemed to be large light-beams, guiding me not to be born now—but I was determined.

Clinical hypnotist Frank Baranowski of Mesa, Arizona, related a rare case in which one of his in-depth research subjects, Sarah E., claimed—when regressed in trance—to be a guide occupying the space between a life in Germany which ended in the 1870s and her current incarnation. In hypnotic sessions conducted in 1974, Sarah spoke of guiding a man named Andres. She told of trying to influence and make contact with him, maintained she was in touch with Andres' deceased relatives, and said of her charge: "He is doing less than he is capable of."

In response to Baranowski's questioning, the hypnotized Sarah was able to describe the Chicago apartment building in which Andres resided; gave an address—near the intersection of Milwaukee Avenue and Damen Avenue—and a time frame: March, 1929. She said Andres was uncomfortable living in an area where so many people spoke Polish, a language he did not understand. In one exchange with the hypnotist, she spoke of trying to influence Andres not to commit suicide by stepping in front of traffic on Armitage Avenue. Sarah E. pointed out, however, that she was not to be Andres' guide throughout his life. "I am to move on," she announced. "I am to be replaced."

Later, Baranowski traveled to Chicago where he located a seven-story apartment building—built in 1922—that appeared to fit Sarah's description. The building was placed in an area that had supported a large Polish population since the turn of the century. Unfortunately, there was no way of establishing whether a man named Andres—the only name given by Sarah—had lived there in 1929.

American consciousness-researchers Dr. John Lilly, Dr. Stanislav Grof and Robert Monroe have all encountered guiding presences in the course of their unusual work. In his book *The Center of the Cyclone,* Dr. Lilly describes meeting two guardians in a succession of close brushes with death as well as in subsequent deliberate attempts—by taking doses of LSD in an isolation tank—to recapture the elevated state of consciousness he had enjoyed involuntarily. Dr. Lilly told of leaving his body while in a state of coma, becoming a "single point of consciousness" and meeting two beings who transmitted guiding and teaching thoughts.

> They tell me it is not yet time for me to leave my body permanently, that I still have an option to go back to it. They give me total and absolute confidence, total certitude in the truth of my being in this state. I know with absolute certainly that they exist.... They say that they are my guardians, that they have been with me before at critical times and that in fact they are with me always, but that I am not usually in a state to perceive them. I am in a state to perceive them when I am close to the death of the body. In this state there is no time…

Later, in a conscious effort to regain the "peaceful, awesome, reverential space" in which the meeting with the guardians had occurred, Dr. Lilly swallowed 300 micrograms of LSD in the controlled environment of an isolation tank and soon found himself occupying the same landscape of exhilaration. Slowly but surely, he noticed the approach of the two guides from a vast distance. And as they drew closer he could sense, at an astonishing rate of speed, their thinking, their knowledge, and their feeling. In the last of the series of LSD experiments, Dr. Lilly says he experienced "a fantastic feeling of smallness" as the guides showed him the entire universe.

The universe expands to its maximum extent, recollapses, and expands three times. During each expansion the guides say, "Man appears here and disappears there." All I can see is a thin slice for man. I ask, "Where does man go when he disappears until he is ready to reappear again?" They say, "That is us."

Encounters and interaction with "guides, teachers, and protectors" have cropped up routinely in the course of many hundreds of experimental LSD sessions conducted by Czechoslovakian-born psychotherapist Dr. Stanislav Grof. As Grof wrote in *Realms of the Human Unconscious: Observations from LSD Research,* the recurrence of this ancient theme "is one of the most valuable and rewarding transpersonal experiences" resulting from the sessions. He continues:

> Sometimes, the spirit guides are a source of light or energy with or without concomitant vibrations of a high frequency; usually, the individual only senses their presence, and receives messages, instructions, and explanations through various extrasensory channels. Typically, the ego identity of the subject is preserved, and he relates to these entities as separate from himself; it is possible, however, to experience various degrees of fusion or even full identification with them.

Robert Monroe, founder and director of the Monroe Institute of Applied Sciences in Faber, Virginia, is arguably the world's leading authority on out-of-body traveling. He has developed what he calls Explorer Communication in which human "explorers"—each one lying on a waterbed in a soundproof, temperature-controlled booth—make contact with friendly entities during monitored out-of-body experiences.

In approximately one-third of hundreds of hours of such communications, discarnate beings take over the explorers' bodies and speak using their vocal cords. The remaining two-thirds comprise contacts in which the explorer relays to a monitor in a control room his or her conversation with the non-physical being. In *Far Journeys,* Monroe tells how these discarnate entities radiate a friendliness that evokes complete trust on the part of the explorers. Moreover, the beings are touchingly solicitous as to the explorers' well-being, exerting themselves to help advance the mental and physical health of those with whom they are "associated." The discarnates are not always guides, although they frequently identify themselves as such. For example, a social-services executive reported:

> ...he told me that he is kind of my overseer. And he is responsible, somewhat responsible, for my growth and development. Apparently he has been through a lot of lives and different lifetimes...and I don't know if they are a part of him or not. I feel very comfortable here, like this is where I belong and I have felt like this before.

These last few examples of contact with discarnates have relied upon manipulation of some kind to achieve another level of consciousness where the intelligences are readily perceived. But there are those who sense a guiding presence in their daily lives without contrivance. Children who converse with a so-called "imaginary playmate" would sometimes fall into this category. So would those of us who, either in dreams or waking reality, are suddenly inspired by an illuminating image or idea.

Then there are the thousands of people in Britain who responded positively to a question—first posed by Oxford University's Sir Alister Hardy Research Centre in 1969—asking whether they have been aware of or influenced by a presence or power different from themselves. Such a response suggests that, worldwide, there are millions of people who feel a distinct sense of otherworldly accompaniment in their everyday lives. Answers to the question, which was made public on the radio, in newspapers and magazines, were divided into ninety-two categories of experience, many of which cover terrain ("voices guiding," "sense of protection," etc.) occupied traditionally by the guides. The results prompted Sir Alister Hardy to write in *The Spiritual Nature of Man,* "The feeling of being guided is very strong in the lives of many people . . . I suspect that there are many who feel that their lives are being guided towards a particular goal and yet shrink from admitting it, entirely for reasons of modesty." Here are three typical responses to the Oxford survey:

> Gradually I became aware of this power and began really to

court it. It has come to me often—once in a dream—as light, warmth, comfort and love past understanding. It has walked with me and sometimes I hear something or someone calling my name.

…there is a definite sense of presence which, though not physical, is strong enough to be felt. I feel able to communicate with it as if to another human being.

One day I asked the rhetorical question, "But who is there to talk to?" To my astonishment, a voice replied: "There's me." This was the beginning of conscious contact with a guide figure.

Extreme situations—particularly of isolation, danger and despair—have generated voluble testimony about guiding, presences, many of the witnesses being soldiers and explorers. It seems that undue hardship and the imminence of death can heighten sensitivity. From the time of the Crusades to the battles of modern warfare, there are countless examples of fighting men being comforted, and even miraculously aided, by unseen presences. American soldier W. H. Ziegler met his guardian soon after landing under heavy fire on the island of Iwo Jima in August, 1945. He and his comrades dug in frantically as the shells rained down. Ziegler describes the events that followed:

> Things kept getting worse out there and I thought it was the end of the line for us all. Then suddenly someone was there in the hole with me, someone had come to protect me. This invisible guardian angel stayed with me all through that long and terrible night. Once when things were quiet for a minute I decided to look out but an unseen force shoved me down just as a bullet whizzed by my head.

Adventurers play variations on the same theme. After Charles Lindbergh had made his historic thirty-four-hour flight across the Atlantic in 1927, he described how the fuselage of his aircraft had been crowded with ghostly human presences:

> The spirits seemed to be able to appear or disappear whenever they chose, passing through the walls of the plane as though no walls existed. I heard familiar voices in the plane advising me, encouraging me, and giving me instructions, as though I'd known all of them before in some past incarnation.

Myrtle Simpson was one of four intrepid skiers who traversed 440 miles in forty days across Greenland in 1965. At one point, deep into the trek, she became aware that "someone else" had joined them. "'He' kept looking over my shoulder," she remarked. Navigator Roger Tufft confessed that he, too, had felt the strange, unseen presence. A similar feeling of being accompanied possessed British climber Frank Smythe—a leading member of the Mount Everest expedition of 1933—as he attempted a difficult solo assault high on the mountain's icy flank. In *Camp Six,* his account of the expedition, he writes:

> This "presence" was strong and friendly. In its company I could not feel lonely, neither could I come to any harm. It was always there to sustain me on my solitary climb up the snow-covered slabs. Now, as I halted and extracted some mint cake from my pocket, it was so near and so strong that instinctively I divided the mint into two halves and turned round with one half in my hand to offer it to my "companion."

Hauntings and apparitions, though infrequently linked to guiding, have astounded and bedeviled people the world over since the beginning of time. The sightings of luminous beings are innumerable—from the appearance of the deceased at the bedsides of surviving relatives to visions of restless spirits patrolling the territory they once occupied. Paracelsus, the sixteenth-century Swiss doctor, scientist and philosopher, wrote that in life and in death each person has a body of light or "subtle flesh" that is able to walk where it pleases, passing effortlessly through walls and any other material obstacles. In the *postmortem* state, it appears that such light bodies are often drawn to certain people and places by lingering emotional attraction.

The ghostly encounters of English psychic Matthew Manning illustrate how bonds of attachment can survive death. Between 1971 and 1974, Manning "met" Robert Webbe, who had owned Manning's house during the eighteenth century and still believed the home to be his own. Principally through automatic writing, Manning gleaned information which established Webbe's identity and learned that his visitor was puzzled by his presence and resented sharing his property. Webbe also expressed confusion at the changes that had taken place and was perplexed by the appearance of modern appliances. Manning writes in *The Strangers:*

> I hold the view that a part of the consciousness of Robert Webbe survived his physical death, and continued to exist—I do not say "live" because I cannot regard it as a life—in my house. I could only conclude that he must be trapped in some kind of postmortal nightmare, unable to leave the house on which he had spent so much money and of which he was so proud. Sometimes he remembered that he was no longer physically alive, and at other times he was still trapped in the time at which he died.... The more I thought about it, the more convinced I became that Webbe's "spirit" was like some kind of incandescent light. A bulb will only light up when connected to a source of electricity, like a battery; I was the battery for Robert Webbe.

There is a proliferation of dramatic accounts by those who have felt an almost tangible sense of presence at life or death junctures in their lives. A driver might hear a loud inner voice shout "Stop!" seconds before an out-of-control vehicle appears around a corner. Or a soldier in the trenches might be overwhelmed with an incomprehensible sense of peace even as he is caught in a machine gun barrage which fells many of his comrades. In her autobiographical *Spirit River to Angel's Roost,* Canadian writer Patricia Joudry gives a moving description of what it feels like to sense a guiding, supportive presence at a time of personal confusion and distress. She recalls crying out "God Help Me!" in utter desperation. And then....

...in a hush, in a great silence, without sound or movement, there was a Presence beside me. It was not a nebulous sort of force in the air, it was a being, a specific someone. It occupied space at my level and was geographically located at my right side. I couldn't see it with my eyes, yet with some new organ of perception I knew it was there just as surely as I was there myself, and maybe more so.

I turned to it and asked out loud: "Who are you?"

It stayed mum. But I felt its whole attention focused on me. There was a pervading sense of peace around me, an awareness of love... I knew I had an ally.

I walked around all day in a state of wonder, filled with an inner quiet, a peacefulness and sense of security such as I hadn't experienced in all my life. Every step I took, the Presence took too. It was like a shadow, but lighting me instead of reflecting me in darkness.

I talked to it all the time in my mind. I said, "I don't know who you are but I believe in you, I know you're here. I trust you. You're here to help me. Help me to let you help me. Keep me tuned in."

That's what it was, a matter of tuning in. I wondered about all sorts of things, such as had the Presence been with me always, and I only managed to tune in today? Or had it come to me now as a result of my desperate prayer? Who was it? What? How could I have this certainty about something—someone—entirely invisible to the eye?

My mind flew in all directions like a bird let out of a cage, a bird that hadn't even known it was caged but had believed its little space was the universe. I went around looking as though I were alone but accompanied by a companion closer to me than any human being had ever been. I didn't know if it was male or female. It was still there at night when I had my bath, and I felt a little embarrassed. I asked if it would step outside, but I don't think it did.

Many famous people have claimed to share communication with entities in the next dimension. Joan of Arc conversed with a disembodied voice which inspired her to great deeds in France. Robert Louis Stevenson credited the whole of his published fiction to "the single-handed product of some unseen collaborator." Daily experience convinced the poet W. B. Yeats that "there are spiritual intelligences which can warn us and advise us." Napoleon Bonaparte believed that he had a guiding spirit which appeared to him either as a shining sphere or a dwarf clothed in red who came to warn him. And Henry Miller commented that he was "in the hands of unseen powers" while writing his powerful novel *Tropic of Cancer*. Someone, he said, "is dictating to me constantly—and with no regard for my health."

Carl Jung, the great Swiss psychoanalyst, regularly encountered a guardian spirit named Philemon, a "force that was not myself" who "seemed quite real, as if he were a living personality." Sir Arthur Conan Doyle, the creator of Sherlock Holmes, was told independently by seven mediumistic individuals that he was accompanied by an elderly, bearded man with tufted eyebrows—the marked characteristics of deceased naturalist Alfred Russel Wallace, who was actually named by several of those who were able to perceive him. In his later years, Conan Doyle asserted that he was consciously aware of Wallace's presence, intervention and assistance. As if in anticipation of his activity after death, Wallace had written that earthly evolution "must be directed and aided from outside by superior and invisible intelligences..."

Like Wallace, the writer Malcolm Lowry had a strong, if more intimate, sense of being watched and guided. In *October Ferry to Gabriola*, Lowry was clearly struggling with his feelings concerning this unseen presence:

> Could it be that...some guardian spirit causes our attention to be drawn...to certain combinations, whether of events or persons or things...which we recognize as speaking to us in a secret language, to remind us that we are not altogether unwatched, and so encourage us to our highest endeavor...?...But if beneficent, if not diabolic, then what is it, if it is not God, or of God, this eye that hears, this voice that thinks,

this heart that speaks, this embodied hallucination that foresees, with more than crystal clarity and divine speech. Like light, but quicker than light, this spirit must be, and able to be in a thousand places at once in a thousand disguises, most of them, as befits our intelligence, absurd, this spirit that terrifies without terror, but that endeavors above all to communicate, to say no more than perhaps, "Hold on, I am here!"

Whereas Lowry wrestled with the significance of perceived discarnate attentions, author Richard Bach is much more accepting of what he considers to be a perfectly natural state of affairs. He puts these words in the mouth of the narrator of his book *Illusions:*

I'm guided, yes. Isn't everyone? I've always felt something kind of watching over me....

A prolonged study by California psychologist Dr. Wilson Van Dusen has indicated that hallucinating mental patients could well be making contact, in some cases, with guides or guardian spirits. In studying hundreds of patients—including schizophrenics, alcoholics, the brain-damaged and the senile—Dr. Van Dusen consistently found that they felt they were able to communicate with other beings who, according to their behavior, could generally be divided into a higher and lower order.

The higher order, which accounted for only one fifth of the hallucinations, was supportive and inclined to think universally, with greater richness and complexity of thought than the patient's own. But the lower order harangued and tormented the host, threatening pain or death, suggesting lewd or foolish acts, or finding and working interminably upon a weak point of conscience. The higher order usually communicated directly with the patients' inner feelings whereas the lower order chattered endlessly in voices resembling normal speech.

"The higher order," noted Dr. Van Dusen, who relied upon the patients' co-operation in order to speak at length with the hallucinations, "tends to enlarge a patient's values, something like a very wise and considerate instructor [might do]." Moreover, he spoke of them as helpful guides who were far more abstract, symbolic and creative than their lower order counterparts. What amazed Dr. Van Dusen about his findings was their remarkable similarity to descriptions of the world of spirits made by eighteenth-century clairvoyant Emanuel Swedenborg, who would have classified the higher order as attending angels and the lower order as evil spirits.

Although history is replete with recognition of discarnate guardians, it wasn't until the flowering of modern Spiritualism in the second half of the last century that self-proclaimed spirit guides made themselves known in the western world through the increasingly popular practice of trance mediumship. The large-scale revival of the ancient art brought the next dimension—and knowledge of personal spiritual stewardship—magically within reach of any inquiring individual. The marvel of Spiritualism was that it materialized the ethereal in opening up a transmission system between the living and the dead. The strength of Spiritualism lay in its appeal to the practical side of human nature. Here was a religion in which our discarnate allies would, obligingly if fleetingly, step back across the threshold of death in palpable affirmation of their care and concern.

CHAPTER 8

Guides, Channels and the New Age

The birth of modern Spiritualism can be traced to the year 1848, when the youthful sisters Maggie and Katie Fox made contact with a source of poltergeist disturbances by "rapping" in answer to mysterious knocking on the walls of their home in Hydesville, New York. Rapping—in which messages were spelled out in exchange with supposedly discarnate communicators—quickly became a craze which spread all the way to the salons of Europe and created a need for more direct communication with the other side. In answer to this call, mediumship grew and multiplied on both sides of the Atlantic.

The séance room became almost an institution in late Victorian society; a place where the dead were invited to show just how alive they really were. As the stars of the show—the mediums—were swallowed up in trance, their voices and sometimes their bodies were expropriated by non-material intelligences. On occasion, entirely unconscious of their behavior, they would walk about the room making gestures as they spoke to those around them. The intruding entity or "control" would often introduce himself or herself as the guide or teacher of the medium. Usually, the entity would claim to have links with the medium spanning many incarnations, would speak authoritatively about discarnate life and would impress the medium's "sitters" with clairvoyant abilities—a draw which ensured the trance sessions were well-attended. Frequently, the "control" or "doorkeeper" would step aside to allow other voices to express distinct individualities with varying degrees of eloquence.

North American Indian and Chinese guides were particularly common; so were guides who bore the prefix of "doctor." Their teachings, though often at variance, were generally positive and uplifting, stressing the unity of a vast spiritual universe and the individual's right to creative self-determination in successive lifetimes. Silver Birch, a world-renowned guide who first commandeered the voice box of an atheistically-inclined young man named Maurice Barbanell when he was asleep in 1924, had this to say about otherworldly supervision: "Everyone has a guide, a guardian, a helper, who is attracted and desires to serve . . . Because of the constant vigilance which is exercised, you receive the protection of those who love you in our world."

Leading Spiritualist Sir Arthur Conan Doyle maintained that this world and the next were separated by no more than a "difference of vibration," a difference he likened to an electric fan moving from its stationary position to a blur which cannot be apprehended by the eye. Mediumship's accomplishment was to bring that which defied perception within range of the senses. The Reverend William Stainton Moses, an outstanding medium who, through automatic writing, contacted entities known by such names as "Imperator" and "Rector," referred to these beings as intelligent operators at the end of the line. He wrote in *Spirit Identity* (1879):

> Spirits are very *human;* as a rule, they are men and women with the frailties, and passions, and peculiarities, and characteristics of their Earth life. They are just what they made themselves, and so they remain till they make themselves something else.... To commune with them is to be raised above the cares of Earth and to see with keener insight "the one thing needful"....

The most impressive mediums were usually women, notably America's Leonora Piper and Eileen Garrett and England's Gladys Osborne Leonard. Their abilities outlasted the denigration of skeptics as well as the poking and prodding of psychical researchers who were looking for proof that mediums were truly unconscious in the trance state. The entranced Mrs. Piper unflinchingly endured untold indignities in the name of research, having salt placed in her mouth, a feather poked up her nostrils, a small incision made in her left wrist and a needle thrust into her hand.

Mrs. Leonard went so far as to communicate a *postmortem* message about guides from an entity claiming to be Sir Oliver Lodge, one of the world's most renowned psychical researchers. "I have met them," the message said in part, "and I have recognized them as old-time friends, friends from a very long time ago, and I appreciate, I deeply appreciate, their faithfulness and their patience with me." Perhaps this was a conscience-stricken reference to the many times Sir Oliver had challenged the very phenomena in which he was now participating; it was he, after all, who had plunged the needle into poor Mrs. Piper's hand!

Mediumship has its roots in shamanism, the cataleptic utterances of the Biblical prophets and the oracles of Greece. In the first century C.E., Philo Judaeus explained what happened when an inspired prophet became unconscious:

> ...thought vanishes away and leaves the fortress of the soul; but the divine spirit has entered there and taken up its abode; and this later makes all the organs resound so that the man gives clear expression to what the spirit gives him to say.

In the century that followed, Aristides wrote about the mediumistic priestesses of Dodona. He could have been cataloguing Aviva's experience 1800 years later in telling how they

> ...do not know, before being seized by the spirits, what they are going to say, any more than after having recovered their natural senses they remember what they have said, so that everyone knows what they say except themselves.

In the third century the historian Tertullian remarked that the world was "still crowded with oracles." In time, such practices incurred the wrath of the newly-established Christian orthodoxy, which chose to act with increasing harshness on the commandment in Deuteronomy 18 (10-11): "Let there not be found among you any one...that seeketh the truth from the dead." Christian writers, while recognizing the oracles' clairvoyant and healing abilities, decreed that evil spirits were at work rather than divine inspiration. Although the revered Biblical prophets of old were often participating in a similar process, the Church ruled after the fact that the prophets were possessed by God; they alone were conduits of sacred revelation.

Contemporary communicators, on the other hand, were seen as degenerate practitioners of necromancy and witchcraft, heretical crimes which, in the Middle Ages, were punishable by death. Some unwitting mediums, however, were so confounded at having the "gift" thrust upon them that they supposed God himself must be the benefactor. John Lacy, an eighteenth-century Englishman, was such a person. In a tract published in London in 1708 under the title *A Relation of the Dealings of God to his Unworthy Servant*....Lacy tells of having succumbed for a full year to "agitations" stemming from "an agent separate and distinct from me." Saying that he was just one of two or three hundred people in London to be so affected, he explained:

> Under this influence the respiration of my breath hath, for sundry days, beat various tunes of the drum, sometimes six hours in a day, without my voluntary operation, or thinking of it—nay sometimes without being able to stifle it. Under this influence I have experienced, sometimes a voice so strong and clear, sometimes so harmonious, as my natural one never did nor could furnish…I am at times under the agency of another distinct being, in which times the tongue also is at the direction of that foreign agent, and no more under mine than the motion of other parts of my body.

Had John Lacy lived in North America during the late twentieth century he would have been hailed as a channeler. Channeling—the latest and, for many, the most electrifying indicator that we are not alone—reproduces Lacy's experience thousands-fold. Such "agency" has long been demonstrated in tribal spiritism where possessing deities, ancestors, guardians or random spirits testify impressively to a sense of presence. No more than the renaissance of mediumship under another name, channeling is simply White Man's spiritism.

The rise of channeling's mass appeal in 1985 and 1986 indicated that Spiritualism had been rediscovered for an entirely new audience. But there were differences from the Victorian stereotype. Rather than contacting spirits, channelers were contacted *by* them. Also, the channeled intelligences tended to be more wide-ranging and exotic than their predecessors while being philosophically more in harmony with one another.

Independently delivered teachings stressed the unity of a vast, multi-dimensional cosmos which was frequently described as *All That Is*. God was immanent, rather than transcendent. No longer remote and unreachable, God was integral to everything in the universe. Humanity, therefore, was also divine—we *are* God. Each of us was in communion with this transpersonal force which granted endless opportunities to reincarnate. And while destiny was ours to choose, we were invited to check our critical faculties at the channeler's door before surrendering to the loving omnipotence of The One. So far as the communicating voices were concerned, the rational mind was decidedly secondary to the promptings of the heart.

American writer Jane Roberts, who channeled a widely-respected guide called Seth between 1963 and her death in 1984, pioneered the continent's near-obsession with discarnate authority. Starting in the early 1970s, a succession of Seth books—dictated by the entity who referred to himself as an "energy essence personality no longer focused in physical reality"—sold millions of copies and prepared the way for massive acceptance of the phenomenon. Seth's most influential message, oft repeated, was that we create our own reality by our beliefs and desires.

Jane Roberts was rudely appropriated as a channeler one September day in 1963 in her apartment in Elmira, New York. It was, she recalled, "as if someone had slipped me an LSD cube on the sly." She spoke of being overwhelmed by "a fantastic avalanche of radical, new ideas" which "burst into my head with tremendous force, as if my skull were some sort of receiving station, turned up to unbearable volume. It was as if the physical world were really tissue-paper thin, hiding infinite dimensions of reality, and I was suddenly flung through the tissue paper with a huge ripping sound."

If Seth, a highly intellectual entity, was a prime catalyst of the emerging New Age, Ramtha soon became its most dramatically vociferous spokesman. Speaking through the entranced body of a slender, attractive blonde called J. Z. Knight, Ramtha called himself *The Enlightened One* and said his wisdom had been garnered in 35,000 years of existence.

Commanding and ambulant, Ramtha harangued his followers for high fees in seminar halls and proclaimed his universal message to talk show hosts on national television. Among his many declarations was the edict that there is no such thing as sin and therefore no reason for guilt. Devotees commonly testified they were "hooked" the very first time they saw J.Z./Ramtha or heard his message, attributing their addiction to the depth of his wisdom and the power of his love.

Ramtha first appeared to J. Z. Knight in the aftermath of a silly joke. She was teasing her husband by putting a paper pyramid on her head. When the pyramid fell down over her face, they both started laughing helplessly. Then . . .

> I lifted the pyramid up from over my eyes and looked toward the other end of the kitchen. Through my tears I saw what looked like a handful of gold and silver glitter sprinkled in a ray of sunshine. A very large entity was standing there...he looked at me with a beautiful smile and said, "I am Ramtha, the Enlightened One. I have come to help you over the ditch."

J. Z. Knight, a former cable television executive from Yelm, Washington, later defined channeling as "the catalyst that sparks our inward understanding and allows us to reach our unlimited potential." She spoke of channeled teachers as being inspired by the spirit of God. And she predicted that channeling—by fostering the search for the Godself that lives within each of us—will dramatically affect the future of mankind. "It is this 'within' process," J. Z. Knight declared, "that will put to rest the pages of history filled with war, hatred, inhumanity, bitterness and enslavement of the human mind."

Actress Shirley MacLaine, a fervent New Age convert who maintained she "knew" Ramtha had been her sibling in a previous life on Atlantis, turned the spotlight on channeling with her bestselling books *Out On a Limb* and *Dancing In The Light*. Consciousness-raising, she proclaimed, could be accelerated if we hearkened to the advice of our friends in the supersensible realms. By 1987, tens of thousands of channelers were in business across the continent, giving voice to disembodied intelligences with names such as Hilarion, Emmanuel, Mafu, The Master

Adalfo and Angel Dispatcher.

And then there was Lazaris, a disembodied personality calling himself "the consummate friend" who claimed never to have incarnated in the flesh. Channeled by Jach Pursel, a bearded former insurance adjuster, Lazaris rapidly amassed a huge following on the West Coast. His stilted English, gentle voice and slight lisp drew, among other high-profile personalities, actress Sharon Gless, who publicly attributed her success to Lazaris when accepting an Emmy for her role in *Cagney and Lacey*. In 1987, Pursel was charging $275 for a weekend seminar with the consummate friend. Six hundred participants ensured a weekend's channeling raised $165,000.

A reporter once asked Pursel about the incongruity of a "spiritual" entity like Lazaris attracting so much material wealth. Pursel replied: "I find it strange that spiritual entities need fancy business cards, that they need press secretaries....yeah, I do. And I don't like it that that's happened." But he also observed: "You don't have to have a miserable life to be spiritual. You don't have to sacrifice everything for your spirituality. You can have everything—*and* be spiritual!"

As the channeling voices multiplied, their teachings outsold all other titles in the New Age bookstores and there was a growing selection of books, tapes and videos giving advice on how to communicate with guides. Magazines such as *Spirit Speaks* and *Metapsychology: The Journal of Discarnate Intelligence* were striving to meet the increasing demand for messages from the next world. For those encountering difficulty in making personal contact, retired IBM scientist Marcel Vogel—who had earlier demonstrated through infrared photography that quartz crystals store and release energy—invented a device called Omega Five. Shaped like a suitcase with twelve dials, the device measures the energy field of a crystal held in the hand and, by so doing, is said to be able to detect and tune in to non-physical presences in the immediate vicinity. In the Autumn 1986 issue of *Metapsychology,* editor Tam Mossman enthused that "communication with discarnates is becoming more and more common—just as a number of entities predicted it would!"

Indeed, channeling was everywhere—even in the kitchen! In 1988, Christina Whited, a thirty-eight-year-old mother of three from New York City, claimed to be entertaining an unusual visitor: James Beard, the dean of American gastronomy, who had died of a heart attack three years earlier at the age of eighty-one. Beard was said to be dictating recipes for such diet-conscious nibbles as tofu pudding pie, rye sesame sticks and carob cookies—a far cry from the Lucullan feasts for which he was renowned. Whited told *People* magazine that Beard, who called her "My Dear," dressed casually in khaki pants and Oxford shirts, always wore a white apron and looked about half the age he was when he died. She said her children were not surprised when they saw their mother talking to Beard because "they have invisible playmates too."

The great allure of channeling lies in its ability to offer solutions to the abiding human need for greater meaning in life. It caters to gnawing spiritual hunger, attracting refugees from the traditional religions as well as those sated with materialism's bottomless banquet. Whereas the orthodox religions merely relate the influence of supernatural beings, channeling puts the truth-seeker directly in touch with the next dimension. It's all thrills and immediacy; the source of instant psychotherapy for the insecure, a wellspring of information for the relentlessly curious and an endless fount of fascination for the 67 per cent of Americans who, according to a 1982 Gallup Poll, believe in life after death. In *Channeling: The Intuitive Connection,* William H. Kautz and Melanie Branon predicted the spiraling phenomenon would soon be embraced by the establishment:

> The numbers of skilled channelers will multiply as intuitive counseling becomes a more accepted and respected profession. Their work will achieve greater public credibility and acceptance, first on the individual level and then on the institutional level.

Some communicating entities claimed to be "off-planet" beings who had never incarnated in the flesh. Others maintained they were ascended masters who had outgrown the need for rebirth. Many claimed to be Jesus, one of whom dictated in Biblical terminology a three-volume work entitled *A Course in Miracles.* A channeler called Ceanne DeRohan even had the audacity to maintain she was receiving messages "directly from God in the first person." But the majority of communicators insisted—much like Russell, Filipa and friends—that they were ordinary humans who, while still involved in the process of reincarnation, had graduated as guides or teachers in the next world. Whatever identity was claimed, the messages were overwhelmingly positive and crammed with exhortations to love, help and serve. "They're so cuddly and friendly," Harvard theology professor Harvey Cox said of the voices at large. "They seem to be yuppified versions of the demons and spirits of another time."

Many adherents swore by the quality and accuracy of the channeled communications; others decried the information as vague and stereotypical. And while attempts at explanation placed the source of the pronouncements everywhere from genuine discarnate beings to the unexplored labyrinths of the unconscious, no-one could say with any certainty what was represented by this computer age revival of the ancient conundrum. Psychology professor Jon Klimo, whose book *Channeling: Investigations On Receiving Information From Paranormal Sources* failed to penetrate the haze, summed up the confusion and perplexity when he wrote: "This is a mystery of awesome proportions."

When our group was in its embryonic stage, channeling had yet to establish itself as a major force in North America. But as time went by, we became increasingly aware of the sensationalism it spawned in newspapers and magazines as well as on radio and television. So far as we were concerned, channeling was a fad of dubious integrity. True, Aviva could be said to be no more and no less than a channeler herself. But we had observed Aviva week after week until all conceivable doubts about her trance state had been banished. And, unlike the vast majority of deep-trance practitioners, Aviva neither asked for hard cash nor invited media coverage. There was a certain purity and innocence about her way of operating. We weren't so sure about all the others. We were openly cynical about the fortunes being made from Malibu to Manhattan in the name of spiritual consciousness.

The struggle for greater meaning and awareness implicit in the burgeoning New Age movement was not the issue. We were all in favor of living more consciously, of crusading against the prevailing ideology which denies the existence of anything that cannot be touched or seen. Too often, however, the term "New Age" seemed to be synonymous with blatant commercialism, narcissism and spiritual pride, while the movement appeared to function as a metaphysical bolt hole for all who wanted to escape from reality. To their credit, our guides stressed the importance of confronting, rather than sublimating, the challenges of daily existence.

It had not been easy to acknowledge the existence of our own guides, no matter how persuasive the evidence might have been. Knowing the practice of occultism could be fraudulent and deceptive, I wondered how many of the innumerable "guides" really were who they said they were, never mind the slew of extraterrestrials and ascended masters. I wondered about self-delusion, material ambition and duplicity on the part of the channelers. As for their clients, I speculated on the gullibility so often displayed by those who crave answers to life's riddles.

The various entities, it seemed, often told inquiring clients that they had many guides working on their behalf; it was said that specialist guides were in place for health, career, romance, creativity and so forth. This state of affairs contradicted the teachings of our guides who maintained that each of us had but one personal guide who was assisted by a retinue of apprentices. Russell felt that many channelers who believed they were making contact with personal guardians were actually only bringing forward their own alter-consciousnesses or past-life personalities.

We, at least, were speaking with beings who displayed refreshing common sense and down-to-earth sanity. I was also encouraged by our guides' obvious humanity and unfailing humor, their urgings that we differentiate—by tough interrogation—true guides from mischievous spirits, their reluctance to make predictions, their admission that they made mistakes, their touching innocence about contemporary global events, their utter lack of knowledge concerning modern technology, and their ignorance of earthly time and inability to tell night from day in our world.

"What year is it now?" various guides inquired on different occasions. Russell, aware that our sessions were held after supper, would usually announce himself with a hearty "Good evening!"—a greeting that remained the same when Aviva was ushered into less frequent morning or afternoon trances.

Were our guides telling the truth, the whole truth and nothing but the truth? Were they legitimate heirs to the longstanding tradition of a sense of presence? These questions, I knew, had to be answered, and answered objectively in my study of our allies in the next dimension. Mind-to-mind contact, paranormally-acquired information and uncanny intervention were all very impressive to individual witnesses within our group setting. But they were as empirically inadmissible as the guides' assertions about discarnate life, if only because they could not be validated.

However, our guides' insistence that they had spent previous existences on Earth opened up a much more promising avenue of exploration. Mercifully, this insistence carried within itself the seeds of the ultimate test. For if the guides had lived before in relatively recent times, surely traces of their lives must still exist. And if I could recover these traces—in records, deeds, registers—I would have incontrovertible evidence that the mysterious voices had, indeed, once inhabited human bodies. Most exhilarating of all, this evidence would confirm the knowledge of our hearts: the knowledge that love and concern rain down on us routinely from the next dimension.

PART THREE
Sleuthing Far From Home

CHAPTER 9

Ernest the Elusive

The more I loved Filipa, the more I hungered for tangible proof of her existence. That proof, I knew, lay in establishing beyond all doubt whether at least one member of our group of guides had lived and breathed on Earth. Evidence, yes, I might find evidence. But *proof?* Even if I could match the guides' claims with records of earthly identity, how would I know that the guides actually *were* the individuals whose names were in the registers? For inspiration, I looked to the astounding partnership between English spiritual healer George Chapman and William Lang, a deceased ophthalmic surgeon.

For the first twenty-five years of his life, Chapman, a former firefighter who now lives near Aberystwyth, Wales, had no indication that he would become a healer. Then, in 1945, the premature death of his infant daughter, Vivian, appeared to awaken his latent powers. Chapman soon found that going into trance was easy, like dropping off to sleep, and at regular weekly sessions held among friends he gave voice to various entities with such names as Ram-a-din-i and Chang Woo. It wasn't long before the kindly Dr. Lang began to make himself heard, revealing that he was to use Chapman's mediumship to heal the sick. Speaking with an upper-class accent, Dr. Lang would walk around the room gesturing compassionately at those around him. Yet the entranced Chapman was unaware of anything that took place when he surrendered control of his mind and body.

At first, Dr. Lang spoke sparingly about his earthly existence as a medical practitioner. But in time he revealed that his full name was William Lang and that he had worked for many years at the renowned Middlesex Hospital in London. Inquiries made of the British Medical Association by Leslie Miles, a friend of George Chapman, showed that William Lang had been a distinguished surgeon and ophthalmologist.

Born on 28 December 1852 in Exeter, Devon, he had practiced at Middlesex Hospital from 1880 to his retirement in 1914 and had died—while Chapman was a teenager in Liverpool—on 13 July 1937.

Dr. Lang's healing partnership with George Chapman evolved rapidly. With consummate ease and skill, he would control Chapman's body for hours at a time in order to "operate" invisibly on the etheric or shadow bodies of those who entrusted themselves to his care. Healing was accomplished as treatment of the etheric counterpart of the afflicted organ produced a corresponding effect on the physical body. Since the 1940s, Chapman—who has collected many of Lang's possessions and even sleeps in the doctor's bed!—has traveled the world so that his discarnate partner can proceed with his mission to alleviate suffering. Hundreds of successful operations—many of them watched in awe by orthodox medics—have been conducted on ailments ranging from gallstones to cancerous tumors. Just as impressively, surviving relatives and patients of Dr. Lang were able to communicate with the spirit surgeon during trance sessions and confirm that he is the man they had known so well.

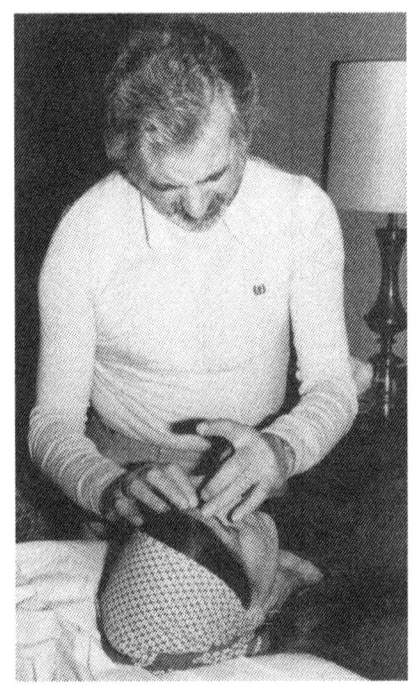

The entranced George Chapman performs an operation with the invisible assistance of Dr. Lang. (photo courtesy of George Chapman)

Dr. Lang's daughter, Marie Lyndon Lang, was naturally skeptical when she heard in 1947 that her father had returned to inhabit, at intervals, the body of George Chapman. But after hearing his voice, observing his mannerisms and asking personal questions concerning events which only she and her father knew about, she made this declaration: "The person who speaks through George Chapman and claims to be

William Lang is, without a doubt, my father." For thirty-one years, until her death at the age of ninety-four in May, 1977, Marie Lyndon spoke regularly with her deceased father. At her request, however, both her intimate connection to the increasingly popular Dr. Lang and her consultations with him were kept secret until her passing.

Vowing "I am going to put this quack to confusion," Dr. Lang's granddaughter, Mrs. Susan Fairtlough, reacted with angry derision when she heard that a healer was "pretending" to be her grandfather. But after meeting George Chapman and Dr. Lang, Mrs. Fairtlough had this to say: "To my great horror, or rather stupefaction, the man who was in this room was indisputably my grandfather. It was not him physically, but it was his voice, his behavior. It was unquestionable. He spoke to me and evoked precise events of my childhood. And I was so impressed that all I could say was, 'Yes, grandpapa, no, grandpapa.'"

There was recognition, too, from Mrs. Katherine Pickering who, as a child, had been a patient of Dr. Lang's, and from Dr. Kildare Lawrence Singer, who had received instruction from Lang at the Middlesex Hospital. The spirit surgeon greeted him with the words "Hello, my dear boy, I *am* happy to see you again."

Testimonials to Dr. Lang's brilliance have been furnished by a host of living doctors, few of whom wished to be named for fear of professional censure. After meeting Dr. Lang for the first time in December, 1969, Dr. Robert Laidlaw of New York told how he discussed in a professional manner certain ophthalmologic conditions and techniques, and added "I fully believed then, and I believe now, that I was conversing with the surviving spirit of a doctor who had died some thirty years ago."

While by no means underestimating the importance of the healing accomplished by his spiritual partnership, Chapman feels the main intent of the surgeon's return is to convince people of the reality of life after death. And he considers the authenticity of Dr. Lang's claim to having lived before as fundamental to this cause. In his book *Surgeon from Another World,* Chapman stresses the importance of verifying sources of channeled communication:

> Too many alleged spirit guides do not stand up to critical examination. I believe it is essential for those who develop

trance mediumship to ensure that their spirit controls are examined thoroughly to prove their identities. The spirit communicator should speak as near as possible to the way he spoke on earth, using the same phrases and mannerisms and manifesting other personal characteristics. He should be able to give dates, names and details of his earthly experiences that can be verified, and be able to discuss intimate matters with relatives and colleagues still on earth. All too often, a "spirit control's" claimed earthly existence is outside the memory of those living, while others deliberately cloak their identities in a shroud of mystery...

Of the more than twenty guides who had communicated through Aviva's voice box, only four claimed to have lived on Earth as recently as the twentieth century. There was Franco the tailor, an accomplished guide with 111 charges and more than forty apprentices, who perished during political upheaval in Buenos Aires in 1903. There was Sonji, a wealthy landowner from Kathmandu who died of natural causes in 1920 at the age of sixty-six. There was David, the farm boy from Anderson, South Carolina, who remembered the first airplanes and professed a fondness for buttercups but preferred to talk in his lazy, Southern drawl about "fishin'," especially "fishin' for catfish." And then there was Ernest, a self-confessed "proper Englishman" who had fought in World War II as a bomber pilot with the Royal Air Force.

As guide to poet Tony Zambelis, Ernest displayed the intimate knowledge of his charge that we had come to expect. Advice was dispensed concerning Tony's domestic and professional life and there was elaborate discussion of his past lives, especially those lives in which he and Ernest had known one another. But there was no reference to Ernest's flying career until, after two months of messages relayed by Russell, Aviva's body twitched and shuddered and a rather pompous English accent issued from her lips. Evidently, Ernest was pleased to be speaking with his own voice.

> I think perhaps I've mastered the trick. It takes quite a lot of energies. And I will learn it better. Ah, my, this is a little tougher than I thought. Certainly not like aviation, is it?

The room was hushed by the new vocal presence. Surprised to see Aviva's frame move in trance, Tony told Ernest what he had witnessed and asked whether his inexperience was to blame.

"Well," Ernest replied, "I did something that was not on the books, you might say. I made a descent down the shaft and right through Russell's charge...."

The "descent down the shaft" was a reference to the central chamber of Aviva's mind, which the guides had mentioned many times. This central chamber connected with the "fourth level of mind"—the specific area used for making contact. The comment about aviation naturally inspired further questioning. And when Ernest proudly informed us that he had been a pilot in the RAF, I decided that this life—recent enough to be confirmed or denied through war records and the memories of Air Force veterans—would be my evidence: the lodestone on which I would build my confidence. For the project to succeed, I knew that I must obtain a wide selection of facts—the more detailed and idiosyncratic the better—which could be checked against documents and personal testimony. Other members of the group were equally keen that Ernest be put to the test. So it was that he was invited to divulge the contents of his memory, paying particular attention to names, dates and events that could be corroborated. According to Russell, my request was by no means unreasonable. "We have no impediment to memory here," he stated flatly.

Each guide was unique in character and temperament; each voice expressed singular emotions. With Ernest, the overriding sentiment was sadness; there was something inconsolable about his delivery, even as he strove to maintain a "stiff upper lip." Early on, he confided that Ernest had not been his name in the most recent life. He had adopted "Ernest," he said, because it had been his name in a particularly beloved incarnation fifteen lifetimes ago. Had we been more perceptive we would have understood from the beginning that this statement implied a general dissatisfaction with his existence during the last war. The reason for his despondency became apparent, however, as time passed and he revealed more of himself and his feelings. These feelings notwithstanding, Ernest fully understood my desire to learn details of his life and then to seek corroboration. With a certain eagerness in his melancholic, well-educated voice, he agreed to provide me with all the information he could muster.

In his last life, said Ernest, he was Flying Officer William Alfred Scott of 99 Squadron, Group Three, Bomber Command. He described himself as five feet eleven inches in height with dark hair and dark brown eyes. His comment, "I used to try to trim my weight at eleven stone [154 pounds]" suggested that he was inclined to be overweight. He was born in Brighton, raised in Bristol (the names of streets and schools were provided) and for three years had attended Bristol University where he studied mathematics and engineering. He even named one of his professors, Jonathan Langley—"quite a colorful chap"—who taught mathematics.

Ernest joined the RAF in 1937 at the age of twenty and, as a member of 99 Squadron, was based at RAF Mildenhall, Suffolk from early in 1939, moving to Newmarket Heath in September that year just before the outbreak of war. Some eighteen months later, he was transferred with the rest of the squadron to RAF Waterbeach, an air base that was "cut into the Fens" (the name given to that low-lying area of East Anglia) in "Cambs," a typically English abbreviation for Cambridgeshire. It was from Waterbeach, he said, that most of his bombing missions were conducted. He spoke with great affection and enthusiasm about the aircraft he flew, the "Wimpey" or Vickers Wellington Bomber.

> Do you know what a Wimpey is? Well, a Wimpey had 1,000 horsepower Pegasus motors—wonderful! She was of geodetic design. She was the pride of our air command, as far as I was concerned anyway. Perhaps others would see the Lancaster [bomber] as being the finest, but I would disagree....

Ernest told how his squadron went "nickling" or leaflet-dropping over Nazi Germany. He talked about participating in anti-shipping strikes, said that his colleagues had chased the German battleship, the *Tirpitz,* and he spoke of conducting bombing missions over Norway and Germany, specifically Cologne and the Ruhr valley. He recalled, somewhat wistfully, the strong sense of camaraderie prevailing among the men of Bomber Command.

> You see, when you're flying, when you're under stress and under the circumstances that we were...ah...familiarity

becomes very thick and it comes very quickly. You grow very much in a situation like that.... You know, crews changed, crews were not together for very long.... We lost a lot of friends. You must also remember that that was a time when you made friends quickly and did not grieve at their loss because there were many losses....

In response to my interrogation, Ernest delivered more and more detailed information. He said that 99 Squadron was known as the Madras Presidency Squadron—"it was all terribly suitable and all that"—with its badge featuring a leaping puma and the Latin motto *Sisque Tene* or *Sisque Tenax*. The motto—which actually reads *Quisque Tenax,* meaning "Each Tenacious"—was, said Ernest, commonly referred to as "Sisky Tenants" by the bomber crews. He went on to name his commanding officer—Wing Commander Linnell—as well as Air Vice-Marshals Cochrane and Harrison who were successively in charge of Group Three. And he described a number of noteworthy wartime incidents.

Ernest, one of the many guides channelled by Aviva, claimed that when he was alive during World War II, his squadron had to sleep in the grandstand at Newmarket Racecourse. This photo confirms that the squadron did in fact stay there. Pictured are Jim "Ginger" Ware (center) and fellow members of 99 Squadron. (photo courtesy of Jim Ware)

In February, 1941, while he was based at Newmarket Heath, a bombing occurred on the Norwich Road which "took out" the White Hart Hotel ("one of the favorite establishments of our class") and the post office, killing a number of civilians. The attack, said Ernest, was the work of a German bomber, a Dornier DO 17, "an amazing little creature that had the gall to fly." He mentioned that when he and his colleagues first moved to Newmarket Heath "it was quite uncomfortable for a while" because they slept in the grandstands of the Rowley Mile Racecourse owing to an utter lack of accommodation in the area.

Ernest told of two spectacular crashes that took place while he was stationed at Waterbeach. In one, a Wellington bomber "took a little while longer getting off the runway than it should have and they piled her up with a nice big 4,000-pound bomb underneath her. The little lady didn't go off and the crew did manage to get out but, my goodness, it did make quite a show." Some six weeks later, another Wimpey—piloted by Harry Sergeant, codename Q for Queenie—crashed into the orchard at the end of the runway after failing to take off. "Everything went up," said Ernest, noting that, although some crew members escaped, others were trapped in the blaze which was "seen over at Lakenheath" (a village to the north-east, some seventeen miles distant).

Some "Wimpeys" were said to have been equipped with forty-eight-foot hoops fastened under the wings of the aircraft. "They were against Hitler's newest tactical weapon," he told me. "Well, you can find that one out...it'll make things a little interesting for you." Ernest told how Wellingtons from 99 Squadron were based briefly in Salon, France in order to conduct bombing raids on Italy. And he indicated that the squadron moved to Ambala, India in 1942, although he had been transferred to 147 Squadron by then. He went on to provide the names of relatives: a nephew, William Scott of Bristol, who was "twenty years younger than me," an uncle, Wilfred Scott of Lyme Regis, and an aunt on his mother's side, Lilly Williams of Brighton; and friends, too, among them Flying Officer Willie Douglas—"he and I were very thick before he was killed"—and Derek Watford, a "rather touchy" flight lieutenant of whom he said: "When he was drinking, he was a good man."

When I asked Ernest whether he was given a nickname by his friends and colleagues, he replied somewhat hesitantly "Well, you often had nick-

In confirmation of Ernest's testimony, a Welllington bomber is shown equipped with a hoop of insulated aluminum for clearing home waters of enemy mines. (photo courtesy of the Imperial War Museum, London)

names. I don't think that most of them would be *right*.... I see you have mixed company here." Loud laughter greeted this remark and only when it had subsided, Ernest added: "Well, 'Scotty,' I suppose. We were all called Scotty, weren't we? That is the...*cleanest*."

During his few years as a bomber pilot, Ernest said that he was convinced he was acting impeccably in fighting what he felt was humanity's last war against "the little clown," Adolf Hitler. But he told how his return to the between-life state changed this self-assessment, bringing the realization that he had incurred karmic debt with all the victims of his bombing raids—debts that he was now obliged to repay. "Now that I'm here," he said ruefully, "I can think only of all the deaths in which I played a part." This, then, was the reason for Ernest's overweening sadness and remorse. He was carrying the burden of having been a mass-murderer in a worthy cause.

Ironically, Ernest said that he did not die in the air but in a bombing raid on Coventry in 1944. He was twenty-seven years of age. Just why he was in Coventry remained a mystery because Ernest refused to talk candidly on this subject. On one occasion he suggested—discarnate tongue placed firmly in cheek—he was "on business." On another occasion, when I suggested that he might have been "visiting somebody," he replied: "That's a nice way of putting it, yes." Whatever his reason for being in Coventry, he said that he was not killed instantly, although he was "long gone" by the time his body was finally discovered under a collapsed building on a street called Sandrich placed approximately 1¾ miles north-east of Coventry Cathedral.

Ernest had delivered the information spontaneously, without pause and at times with considerable emotion. He impressed us all as being eminently human and entirely plausible. His speech was a catalogue of specific detail that could be either verified or refuted. Everyone in the group was excited when my preliminary research in Toronto libraries swiftly confirmed the locations of East Anglian bomber bases at Mildenhall, Newmarket Heath and Waterbeach as well as the existence of 99 Squadron and its use of Wellington bombers in wartime. I learned, too, that, just as Ernest had said, 99 Squadron was called the Madras Presidency Squadron and bore the leaping puma on its badge and that the Vickers Wellington bomber was known as a Wimpey, the name being derived from, J. Wellington Wimpey, a character in the Popeye cartoons who had an insatiable appetite for hamburgers. Appropriately, an article on Wellingtons in the *Air Enthusiast* had commented four years earlier: "There cannot be many instruments of destruction which have gained for themselves a pet name indicative of regard, even warmth."

There was still a wealth of detailed information to check out—information that was practically impossible to find in Canada—and this I decided to pursue in England. It must be noted that Aviva, who was born and raised in Australia, had yet to be conceived at the time Ernest claimed to have died. Furthermore, she had not the slightest interest in the activities of Bomber Command during World War II and in her entire life has spent only four months—back in 1967—in England. In the course of that visit, she did not travel to the various places named in Ernest's account. Listening to tape recordings of my conversations with Ernest, Aviva declared: "He's talking about things of which I have no knowledge whatsoever."

Before the Ernest sessions took place, I had already intended to go to England to visit my parents and had mentioned my travel plans to Filipa.

She couldn't seem to understand that I was able to jet across the Atlantic Ocean in the space of a few hours. My unsuccessful efforts to explain the logistics of aeronautical transportation were met with, "What happens to the mule?" Sensing the impossibility of describing an airplane, I asked her to consult Ernest for a satisfactory explanation, but even Ernest was not fully conversant with jet propulsion. He remarked that when he was last on Earth "the mechanics were on the drawing boards but I did not really think that much would come of it." To an eighteenth-century peasant girl, the notion of wide-bodied jet aircraft flying around the world must have sounded quite outrageous.

That was the way it was with the guides: any technological innovation beyond the time frame in which they had last lived was an object of wonder and incomprehension. In most cases, the concept of motorized travel was understood with difficulty and Russell habitually translated our twentieth-century hardware into terms that he could readily understand. Any writing instrument was "a quill," television and photography was "a magic lantern" and the telephone—which occasionally rang during trance sessions—was branded "that invasive instrument." The Toronto subway system proved to be another stumbling block for Filipa's outmoded perceptions of scientific progress. "How fascinating!" she exclaimed when I mentioned that trains traveled rapidly underground. "But how do you breathe? Surely the body must get flattened!"

Armed with notes and tape recordings of the "Ernest" sessions, I set off for England on Friday, 1 February 1986. I left a deposition of transcribed material with a lawyer in Toronto to establish that the information had been gathered in Canada prior to departure. Boarding the plane, I took a few moments to contact Filipa and pass on word of our imminent flight so that she could experience with me the sensation of being airborne. At her request, I had tuned in to her several times before stepping into subway trains. Vicariously, she had enjoyed the thrill of high speed travel.

I settled back in my seat, became aware of the familiar buzzing sound in my ears and felt at peace with my extraordinary mission. I was convinced that I would find Ernest, or rather, William Alfred Scott, somewhere in the vaults of the Public Record Office at Kew, near London, and hoped that I would be able to track down one of his surviving relatives who would regale me with fascinating memorabilia of the long-lost flying officer. I would find Ernest and, in so doing, I would confirm my love for Filipa.

If I had any doubts at all they revolved around Ernest's tendency to lapse, very occasionally, into American pronunciation. For Norwich, he had said *Naw-witch,* rather than *Nor-itch;* lieutenant had been pronounced *lootenant* rather than *leftenant* and he had sometimes referred to 99 Squadron as "the ninety-ninth." But these discrepancies seemed hardly worth worrying about.

Little did I know as I sped across the Atlantic that Ernest was making an important announcement to those gathered in Aviva's living room. He was telling the group of his intention to reincarnate within a matter of months. It was said that a fetus had been located in southern England, a bodily "vehicle" placed in ideal circumstances to provide Ernest with the opportunity of repaying many of the karmic debts he had incurred. Tony, quite naturally, wanted to know whether Ernest was training a particular individual to succeed him as his guide. To which Ernest replied:

> I have had others here who have been observing and learning for several of your earthbound years now. Don't worry, they are all people with whom you've had quite strong ties and are all quite learned and capable, if I should indeed make the choice. Now you must think it rather strange that, with just a few months of earthbound time to go, the choice might not be made. Indeed, the choice can even change at the last minute, which is why you get things like miscarriages and infants suddenly dying. It is simply that, well, you know.... "Maybe I did rush into this and did not think it through quite properly and perhaps this is not going to be right for me." And so the entity departs and leaves aggrieved parents behind which is unfortunate but perhaps it is also their learning experience; learning to cope with grief, learning to cope with each other in difficult times. Negative can always produce positive....
>
> If I do decide to make myself available to this vehicle, then I will be leaving forty-three other charges as well and they must all be taken care of. It is not just yourself. At each and every available opportunity, others are given responsibili-

ties for a part of your day-to-day existence....

Preparing to be born, said Ernest,

...is a bit like flight school actually, where you go through the motions until you know the motions so well that you do not make a mistake when you are given the actual vehicle to work with.

After landing at Gatwick Airport and spending a few days with my mother at her guest house in Worthing, Sussex, I traveled to the Public Record Office at Kew where the War Office records are located. There, after rummaging around in the vast index of documents, I requested for personal scrutiny an explanatory statement of the 99 Squadron crest and the Squadron's "Operations Record Books," 1939-41 inclusive. These record books comprised the daily log of the Squadron's wartime activities and it was with considerable excitement that I anticipated scanning their contents in the hush of the reading room. As an attendant delivered the musty, dog-eared log books, my stomach was turning over with the thought that Ernest had probably fingered those same battered tomes more than forty years ago. First, however, I examined the statement—dated 7 July 1934—describing the 99 Squadron crest. My eyes were soon met by a familiar name: the signature of Wing Commander F. J. Linnell was scrawled in large letters at the foot of the two-page document. I was hugely encouraged by that.

Next, I located some riveting confirmation of Ernest's testimony in the operations log. Here, in black and white, was the official record of the squadron's bombing of Norway, the "nickling" and bombing raids over Germany, and the anti-shipping strikes. Here, too, spread over three years, was the pattern already sketched out by Ernest, of squadron moves from air base to air base—Mildenhall to Newmarket Heath to Waterbeach. Two days before England declared war on Germany, an entry noted tersely: "Eleven aircraft were flown to Newmarket and picketed down. Sleeping accommodation was found in the Rowley Mile grandstand." Ernest, of course, had said how uncomfortable it was to sleep at the racecourse. An entry on 18 February, 1941 recorded the bombing raid on Newmarket's main street which, again, Ernest had described.

Later, I tracked down Group Captain, J. R. "Benny" Goodman, who, as a twenty-year-old bomber pilot with 99 Squadron, had shot down the Dornier DO 17 which demolished the post office, hit the White Hart Hotel and killed twenty-two civilians. Goodman, who happened to be flying his Wellington bomber on training maneuvers at the time, managed to draw alongside the Dornier so that his front and rear gunners were able to open fire on the enemy plane which crashed eleven miles from Newmarket. This incident was one of the very few times in the annals of war that one bomber shot down another. But did the Group Captain remember Flying Officer Scott? "I remember a Malcolm Scott," said Goodman by telephone from his home in Frogmore, Devon. "He was a fat sergeant who flew M for Mother."

I spent several hours in the Public Record Office, scanning page after page of the 99 Squadron log books, searching the lists of six-man bomber crews for FO William Alfred Scott. At the end of the afternoon, it was heartbreaking to admit to myself that I had searched in vain. Sergeant Scott was there, a pilot whose first name was indeed Malcolm, but there was no Flying Officer Scott, not in all the operations log books spanning three years of wartime activity. My mind rejected the void revealed by my eyes and fingers. Surely he *must* be there! But he wasn't there, nor was Harry Sergeant, a pilot whose plane was said to have crashed at Waterbeach.

Then I discovered that Wing Commander Linnell, far from being commanding officer of 99 Squadron during the early years of the war as Ernest had said, had relinquished his post on January 1st., 1936. I looked for other names supplied by Ernest and entered the same vacuum of disappointment. Neither Willie Douglas nor Derek Watford could be found in the Air Force List containing the names of all RAF personnel. I double-checked the list for FO William Scott. He wasn't there either.

I walked out into the thin February sunshine bewildered and crestfallen beyond belief. How Could Ernest's description of life with 99 Squadron be so lifelike and so accurate in part, yet so much in error? I proceeded to investigate the remaining information that Ernest had imparted, looking on with growing distress as the existence of William Alfred Scott utterly and irretrievably collapsed. At St. Catherine's House,

London, where births, marriages and deaths for England and Wales since 1837 are registered, no William Alfred Scott had been born in Brighton in 1917 or had died in Coventry in 1944. No William Alfred Scott had enrolled at Bristol University from 1935–37 and no Jonathan Langley had been a faculty member there. According to *Kelly's Directory of Bristol and Suburbs* (1926), there was no Hill Road in the city (the street where Ernest claimed to have lived) and, in further contradiction of his testimony, no Princess Victoria School; not even a Princess Victoria Street.

Compulsively, I pursued the fugitive airman still further. I wanted to play the Ernest tapes to men who had served with 99 Squadron during the war. I wanted to see how they would react to his voice and to his recall of those memorable days when the bombers of East Anglia lumbered through the skies in the cause of Britain's survival and European liberation. Fifty-five thousand of the one hundred thousand men who flew with Bomber Command were killed on active service and, in the ensuing years, old age and infirmity had killed many, many more. There were very few surviving members of 99 Squadron from the early days of the war, but I managed to locate Norman Didwell, who had served with 99 Squadron as ground crew from 1939 to 1941, at his home in Leighton Buzzard, Bedfordshire. He had formed the 99 Squadron Association in 1976 and, according to Group Captain Goodman, was "a mine of information."

Norman Didwell did not know what to expect. If he was apprehensive before he listened to the tapes, he was consumed with fascination as Ernest's voice droned through his living room. Leaning forward to catch every word issuing from my tape recorder, he puffed on one cigarette after another, his eyes flashing with recognition of much that was said. And when Ernest's voice had faded away, he declared: "He was there. He must have been there. It's very convincing. Who would have known about us sleeping in the grandstands? You'd only know that—and several other things mentioned there—if you'd been in the squadron."

Didwell confirmed Ernest's knowledge of the crashes at Waterbeach; the mention of the 4,000-pound bomb ("We were one of the first squadrons to have 4,000-pounders"); the squadron's showing at Salon, France and Ambala, India; the chasing of the German battleship *Tirpitz;* the naming of Air Vice-Marshals Cochrane and Harrison who succeeded one another in charge of Group Three between 1942 and the end of the war; the nickname "Sisky Tenants" which, said Didwell, probably came from the old Armstrong-Siskin light bomber that was around between 1927 and 1930; and the forty-eight-foot hoops of insulated aluminum attached to some Wellingtons. Flying fifty to seventy feet above the water, Wellingtons so equipped would detonate magnetic mines laid by U-boats—the Thames estuary was a favorite location—during the first months of the war.

Although Didwell knew of no Flying Officer Scott, he found the voice "very, very familiar," saying that it sounded like the "Scotty" he once knew—Sgt. Malcolm Scott. Another 99 Squadron veteran, Jim "Ginger" Ware—a rear gunner who flew with Sgt. Malcolm Scott on at least four missions—agreed. Ware, whose left leg was amputated after he crash-landed in the North African desert on 7 August 1942, flew on fifty-eight missions before being captured by the Germans. Listening to Ernest's voice at his retirement home in Barking, near London, he shook his head in wonder and disbelief. "That's right, that's right," he muttered to himself, shivering with the eerie familiarity of it all. "There's a lot there that's strikingly true and it sounds quite like Scotty. He spoke quick like that. He was a Billy Bunter type. He could always make short work of a plate of egg and beans. Scotty wasn't very pretty. He had, like, a rubber face. When he had his flying clothes on he was huge. He was a wealthy bloke. He never seemed to have a lot of worries. I think his only worry was that he wasn't commissioned."

Malcolm Scott, said Ware, had joined the squadron well after the outbreak of the war and was killed—or so he had heard—at an OTU (operational training unit). This information only contributed to my confusion, which was compounded when I pursued further Ernest's claim of being killed in Coventry. Investigation showed that, like so many other assertions, the alleged place of his death—a street called Sandrich—did not exist.

By now, I was thoroughly frustrated with my efforts to confirm the claims most crucial to Ernest's contention that he had lived in twentieth-century Britain. While much of the information could be corroborated, anything which hinged directly on the existence of William Alfred Scott was proved false. Without question, I had been lied to over and over again and I was burning to return to Toronto to confront Ernest with this heartfelt complaint.

Underneath my anger, I tried to fathom the meaning of the flaws in Ernest's testimony. If Ernest was not William Alfred Scott, who was he? My mother had an answer. It was predictable enough, I suppose, leaping straight out of years of Christian conditioning. "Demons," she said, her voice quivering a little. "You're talking to demons. And I don't like the sound of it one bit."

CHAPTER 10

An Exercise in Reincarnation

I had no idea until I was back home in Toronto that Ernest had been busy making excuses well in advance of my return. As early as the night of my departure for England, he was being politely uncooperative where once he had been eager to oblige. Asked to supply his birthdate as William Alfred Scott—a query I had left with Tony Zambelis—Ernest had replied:

> I'll have to think about that one, isn't that silly? You see, it's important things that we remember. We don't remember the cluttering information because it is not relevant and has nothing to do with forward development. Can you remember your birthdate from your last incarnation? Can you remember your death date from your last incarnation? Well, it's the same thing....

This reply might have been convincing had Ernest not already delivered a wealth of information which, in terms of forward development, must surely have been considered equally cluttering and irrelevant...like the forty-eight-foot hoops on minesweeping Wellingtons and the Latin motto of 99 Squadron. Thinking about Ernest's claim of forgetfulness, I was haunted by Russell's unequivocal statement: "We have no impediment to memory here."

Ernest had turned evasive. Quickly, this evasiveness developed into a defensiveness bordering on paranoia. While still in England, I had telephoned Roger to inform him that William Alfred Scott could not be found in the records. When Roger asked Ernest for an explanation, he was harangued at length about the "invasion of privacy" that my quest represented. Suddenly, inexplicably, Ernest had become pointedly hostile.

> I do not wish in any way for my privacy to be violated. I do not wish in any way for any surviving relatives to be contacted. I do not believe it would be in the best interests of any of those left on the earthbound plane. And I do not want them trying to contact me because that would impede me in my position here as a guide. Others may pursue this as a rather interesting thing. I do not consider it as anything other than a vast invasion. I have given you all the information that you need and, as such, it will stand....

It was then that Ernest admitted, in a back-handed way, that he had lied to me.

> He will find discrepancies for I do not want various concerns and various people knowing, literally, my business. Not all lives go according to that which we planned. And there are many things that I have had to work out here and I am still working out here. I do not wish for others to be privy to these things. It is for me to work them out. I'm not sure you fully understand what I am saying. I am saying that I am working out some major karma associated with this past lifetime. And a lot of it is involved with people still on the earthbound plane. There were many involved. There were many things that were done. These are things of impetuous youth. These are things of indiscriminate judgement. These are things that I am now working through and am not particularly fond of with regard to that particular lifetime. And I do not wish for that to be interrupted or impeded in any way because of a curiosity on the part of others. That is why I have "covered my tracks" you might say....

Ernest concluded his tirade with an ultimatum:

> If I find that there has been a violation of my privacy to anyone

involved, I will withdraw myself and my charge from these sessions.

Gone was the convivial Ernest, nostalgically harking back to his days in the RAF. In place of the genial raconteur was a peevish and thoroughly obstinate individual. Now he was saying that he had covered his tracks and was threatening to pull out of the group if I dared to check further into data that he had provided. Could the indisputably false nature of much of the material have anything to do with his change of attitude? The answer had to be "yes." But I was still at a loss to understand why Ernest, knowing that his story would not stand up to scrutiny, would attempt to deceive me. It didn't make sense.

When I next showed up in Aviva's living room, I wished only to understand why I had been misled. My fellow group members, too, were eager for answers. Angry and disillusioned, I flung myself vehemently into debate with the elusive Ernest. But when our verbal wrangle was over, I was no closer than before to comprehending what had actually transpired. If anything, I was more confused than ever.

For the first time, I was suspicious of a guide and of his motives.

Ernest maintained that he had realized only after I had left for England the potentially harmful effects of an investigation into his "revelations of personal import." As a result, he said, he had "backtracked" or changed his story. But the truth is that he had supplied names, places and events at the beginning of my conversations with him, long before I boarded a plane for England. So any intent to mislead or "cover up" must have been in place all along. But he persistently refused to admit that he had fed me with false information from the start. Throughout our debate, he kept referring to the damaging karma that would have been incurred had I managed to unearth his identity.

> At first, I was rather entertained at the idea and enthused that someone would actually go ahead and do what you are doing ....Unfortunately, the glamour of the moment got me rather caught up. Then it struck me like a slap in the face when suddenly the realization was there that this was not only going to harm me in my future life but harm my charge as well. And

not only this one particular charge here tonight but others....So, in that respect, things were kept from you. But this was not any lie, merely an omission....

William Alfred Scott, Ernest then revealed, "is not in fact a wrong name, it is not a complete name."

I was infuriated by this admission and almost shouted at Aviva's quiescent figure: "Come on, Ernest, be straight with me, can't you? Obviously you're hiding something from me and...."

"Well, actually I am not hiding as you would call it hiding. I am protecting my charge and my other charges."

"So your surname wasn't Scott?"

"My surname *was* Scott," Ernest replied.

"Then why were you not in the operations log book?"

"I was in the log book."

Yet when I repeated this question a little later, he replied: "Because, originally, I was flying as a teacher. I was not on flight crew. I was sending them up."

"Why then," I persisted, "was neither your birth certificate nor death certificate registered?"

"Oh, my birth and death certificate would have been registered but they would be under my full Christian name, I would presume."

"I see. So I was misled. Which is a shame because your case was very evidential and Russell told me that the guides would help me all they could...."

"We have tried to help you all we could. In fact, I gave you all the information you needed. You could have tracked me down and I'm rather glad that you did not because I did not want to imperil my charge in any way whatsoever. As you have guided before, I would just ask you to reach back and think—what is your priority? When you are guiding, what is your priority?"

"Well," I replied, "it has to be the welfare of one's charge."

"It must be. It can be nothing else. All else is secondary and all else—when, karmic debt is involved—is most secondary. I understand that you are combative at the moment. I also understand that you are mortally wounded and quite distressed. This has probably thrown quite a jolt in your works, as it were. I'm very sorry that you could not have just found the information that you needed without trying to pin someone to a fetter that he no longer wishes to be involved with. You see, in bringing your attention to my life, you not only increase the original karma that I incurred, but you also imperil yourself to karmic debt with me. I don't think either one of us wants debts. If we must have ties, let them be positive."

Ernest's contrariness left me quietly fuming with dissatisfaction. Realizing, however, that I could argue with Ernest all night without reaching a satisfactory conclusion, I decided to show forbearance and wish him luck in his forthcoming incarnation.

"Well," he replied, "perhaps you would like to come and see me there [in England) and then perhaps we can talk face to face. Of course, I am not planning to bring this experience as a guide with me to the earthbound plane. I am quite aware of the path that I must walk. I have a major karmic debt to relieve and I do wish to begin discharging that debt—which is my only reason for returning to the earthbound plane."

Weary from my inconclusive tussle with Ernest, I next asked to speak to Filipa. Hardly had the request been enunciated when she came crashing through Aviva's voice box, more eager and excitable than ever before.

"Yassoo! Yassoo! Harika pu se itha! Harika pu se itha!"

"Could you translate that for me?"

"I am so happy that you be back."

"It's nice to hear your voice again," I told her, thrilled by this affectionate reception. "Why are you excited? Because I am back tonight? Is there any other reason?"

"For now we can speak again. For now we can speak, you and I, for I miss so much talking with you. Ernest tells me all about your airplane. Most interesting! I don't understand one bit!"

"Is there anything tonight that you particularly want to say to me?"

"I have just wished for you be back. I wish so much to speak with you direct. I wish to talk very, very much. I'm so glad you back."

* * *

The bad taste in my mouth generated by the Ernest affair lingered on. Two weeks later, when my emotions had cooled, I consulted with Russell in the hope of gaining some insight on the matter. Russell pointed out that guides do not exchange information with one another on karmic situations as they are "strictly personal, strictly private and must, for the confidentiality of all, remain so." Then he added:

> I do not believe that there was any misleading intent until Ernest literally began to panic at the thought of overturning four lifetimes of work. That became a hazard for him and represented little danger to you. And it did, unfortunately, represent physical danger to his charge that you are in contact with, which most distressed him. We are people, we make mistakes, and I will be the first to admit that. I have made many, even with my own charge....We make mistakes that incur further debt with you or further ties with you....

Already, I was considering further expeditions to trace the lives of Russell and Filipa. Should I decide to attempt to verify another guide's previous existence, I told Russell, I needed the assurance that I was not embarking on another wild goose chase. To which Russell replied:

> The first thing that you must do is to make perfectly sure that the guide has no bad karma that could be brought up by your investigations. In Ernest's case, this was unforeseen at the beginning. At first, it was but fun. And quickly the fun turned to a little bit of terror, then a little bit of horror, then a great deal of panic. And we're supposed to control ourselves!

I was somewhat placated by Russell's words. He even made me smile in spite of my determination to resist being mollified. The guides were, after all, only human beings and human beings were prone to tell untruths, especially if they felt threatened or insecure.

On 17 May 1985, Ernest bade farewell to Tony, his charge, and the rest of us. The time had come, he said, for his withdrawal from guiding so that he might prepare for the task of being reborn into physical reality. We were all—myself included—sad to see Ernest depart. Beneath his pride and pomposity, there was something vulnerable and woebegone in his manner that struck a sympathetic chord within each one of us. Strangely, the liaison between Ernest and Tony was often awkward and trying, in spite of their obvious closeness. When Tony told Ernest that he had "woken up the past few weeks feeling quite good about out relationship," Ernest replied:

"Well, you must admit it has improved a lot, hasn't it, now that you know the old sucker is going away."

"Exactly true," said Tony.

"Of course it's true. And that is something that one could only say to one who understands. We shall always be a part of each other's lives. We've had too many close ties and debts to work out to just disassemble what we have built together. It is with great love and fondness that I will always think of you."

"Well, I guess it won't be long before you have a lollipop in your mouth," chuckled Tony.

"Oh yes," Ernest sighed. "I've got all that to go through all over again, haven't I?"

Ernest had already announced that Tony's new guide was to be a "most interesting fellow" called Bill, who was at that moment learning how to communicate via Aviva's prone form.

> I'm not leaving you in the charge of someone who cannot take care of you very well. Otherwise, I would not be going—or coming, from your point of view! I've had to accustom him to the idea that this [communication] is really happening. He is guiding many other people, none of whom he has direct contact with. So I have been alerting him and speaking with him, directing him how to absorb and use the energies of his charge to effect speaking engagements. Indeed, I'm hoping that he will not have to learn by trial and error as I did....

"As you are about to reincarnate, are you reading calendars and scouring information on the state of the world right now?" Tony inquired.

"Oh yes, absolutely. I do want to know precisely what I am getting into. I do perceive there to be quite a bit of upper-echelon turmoil. There is a lot of negativity emanating from the upper echelons of Great Britain at the present time."

"You will be pleased," said Tony, "to meet Maggie Thatcher, the Prime Minister of Britain."

"Yes," Ernest remarked, "I've heard about her."

"She's called the Iron Lady when people feel good about her."

"Oh, you know, that's what we used to call battleships…there's no correlation, is there?"

"She's a battle-axe rather than a battleship," I volunteered.

"Oh dear! I suppose I shall have to watch my politics rather carefully. Of course, I'll really not have to think about such things for quite some time."

Ernest informed us that in approximately three weeks hence he expected to be entering his body-to-be in anticipation of being born by 1 July. He spoke of entering a transition plane "where you become oriented to locality, time, dates and, once again, structuring your thoughts and making sure that you have with you the information that you need for this lifetime. You have to make sure that you have not overburdened yourself with information that you do not, in fact, need. There's so much that I regret I can't take with me—I've had to be quite selective." (Russell noted on another occasion that one takes only seven per cent of one's knowledge into the new existence.) Finally, Ernest pointed out that he had no choice whatsoever as to his forthcoming sex. "I have no idea until I enter the body what I am going to be."

"Maybe Ernestine this time?" Tony loved to tease his guide.

"Oh, I hope not! I'm sure that they can come up with something a little more colorful."

"I've heard," said Tony, "that there's grieving and remorse on your plane when you leave."

"Yes," Ernest agreed, "I would have to admit to you that there is and that I am feeling it. Speaking with you, I am feeling it. But we shall be together again. I must move on, and so must you…"

With these words Ernest receded, never to be heard from again. Five weeks later, Tony's new guide spoke through Aviva for the first time in a broad Cockney accent. Before these first words were uttered, Russell informed us that Bill had asked to be known as Harry. It was explained that, although William or Bill was his first name in the last incarnation, he had been called Harry to distinguish him from his father, William senior.

"'Allo!" Harry exclaimed,
"Hello!" the group responded.

William Harry Maddox quickly installed himself as the group's resident comedian. Harry—" Me Mum came from Wales and me Dad came from Ireland"—claimed to have been raised in London's dockland at the turn of the century, living as a youngster on Barfing Road in Millwall.

> Let me tell you, it's not exactly an open area. I mean, there were a lot o' people crammed in there. I mean, we were livin' elbow to elbow.....It wasn't nothin' to look at. It was a lot of slums, it was. But it was 'ome, y'know. It was 'ome.

After a rough and tumble adolescence spent fighting in East London's street gangs, he joined the Royal Corps of Engineers soon after the outbreak of World War I, in 1914. Sent to France, he toiled in the front lines as a "stringer," one who strung telephone cable from trench to trench. "I 'ad to run out wif them little crankin' devices what went from one trench to another," he explained. "An' I 'ad to carry messages if I couldn't get me lines strung." There he stayed until August, 1917 when he was killed in the thick of the fighting at a place called Trones Woods.

"I know it was flamin' rainin'," Harry said of the day he died. "It was bad. It wasn't no good over there—there was mud up everywhere. Yer feet would rot because they was wet an' there was no way of gettin' anyfink dry. There was men fallin' all over the place.....The horses would go down in the mud. You couldn't get 'em out. They'd die. You'd die. Fall in the mud wounded...you couldn't get yer 'ead up. You'd die. It was a bloody mess. It were awful, it were. You want to go in a nightmare, you go in one of them trenches. You try to string lines, I'll tell you, right under the noses of them...."

As soon as Harry introduced himself, Tony felt much more at ease than he had with Ernest. He told Harry that he sensed clearer direct contact and greater co-operation. And he expressed nagging misgivings about his former guide. "I sometimes felt," said Tony, "that Ernest was disappointed in me or lost patience with me. And that didn't make me want to be more affectionate in my bonds with him."

Harry, who said he had been apprenticed to Ernest over several lifetimes, believed that this feeling could be traced back to their last shared experience on Earth. Ernest and Tony, apparently, were brother and sister in Africa during the first half of the eighteenth century. "You was the little person, y'know. You was younger than 'im. And I fink sometimes that older ones get a little impatient wif the younger ones. An' they expect 'em to be doin' fings that maybe they're not capable of. And I suppose that could 'ave been brought over into your relationship after the earth-bound experience."

Harry had us laughing uproariously on several occasions, his contagious humor relying as much on his earthy Cockney accent and phrasing as on what was actually said. After Tony and I had run for eight kilometers through the streets of Toronto—a workout marked by Tony's loud exhalations—I asked Harry at the ensuing Friday night session whether he had been in attendance.

> Wot? When he was blowin' himself out? I was wonderin' if 'e was goin' to make it. I thought that I might be havin' a transition on me 'ands. It's a little better to be a little more moderate. But 'e's not at all moderate, is 'e?

On another occasion, Harry lectured Tony on his driving:

> You got t'be concentratin' when you're drivin' that flamin' vehicle of yours. Otherwise you are goin' t'be spread all over your road and that's what's goin' to happen. You've got to 'ave that concentration—don't let it lapse! You may be concentratin' but others may not be, an' if you're not quite as pinpoint as what you fink you are then when they do somethin' stupid you're goin' t'get nailed. It's a little frightenin' fer me...I sit 'ere and cover me eyes!

One day when Tony was listening to CBC radio, a popular World War I ditty—"Waltzing Matilda"—was broadcast. At once, Tony endeavored to make contact with Harry in the hope that he could share his enjoyment of the song. But when Tony later mentioned the incident, through Aviva's mediation, Harry confessed that he had heard neither his charge's call nor the song.

"Waltzin' Matilda—wasn't that the Australians?" asked Harry.

"Yes," said Tony.

"Yes, we 'ad a lot of 'em. They was fightin' wiv us, y'know, in Belgium an' in France. Oh, there was lots of 'em. They was quite good, y'know. They were quite what you would call tenacious. They wouldn't not goin' to give in, y'know. Not like those Scotsmen. They just run."

"Russell's charge will be glad to know that you have a good thing to say about Australians."

"Why is that then?"

"Because she's Australian herself."

"Oh, is she really now?" said Harry. "Well, isn't that interestin'...I've never been that close outside a war to an Australian!"

* * *

I was mindful that the time was drawing near for Ernest's rebirth. Ever in search of verification, I asked Russell to supply me with details concerning Ernest's reincarnation. I wanted a name for the newborn entity, a date of birth and a location—data that I could subsequently check against birth records in the United Kingdom. Russell said that he would endeavor to consult Ernest's guide and the guides of his parents-to-be and, if all went well, would retrieve the information I had requested.

As the weeks went by, I kept asking Russell whether there was any news. Week after week he replied in the negative. Then, towards the end of July, Russell announced that he had received notice of Ernest's reentry into the material world. His birth had taken place, he said, on 13 July, his name was Thomas Hugh Graham, his birthplace was the county of Kent in southern England, and his parents' Christian names were Hugh and Susan. Eagerly, I made a note of the particulars and longed for the time when I could justify making another trip to England. Russell suggested that the information could be validated were I to dispatch an inquiry to England "by carrier." However, rather than rely on the postal system and long-distance dealings with bureaucrats, I decided to wait for the opportunity to conduct a personal search.

Although 1986 was well advanced before I was able to make another trip to London, my eagerness to check the birth records at St. Catherine's

House had not diminished by the time I reached the other side of the Atlantic. It is always a thrill to walk through London's West End, but this time my mood was tense. Expectation gnawed at my insides as I rounded the corner of Kingsway and strode through the registry's main entrance.

I was not proud to be afflicted with such an excess of adrenaline and knew that emotionalism had no place in the cool corridors of objective research. But I also knew that this was a hurdle the guides must leap if they were to retain their credibility. My faith in them was delicately intact in spite of the disappointing climax to the quest for Flying Officer Scott. Perhaps because of that failure, I was nervous that Ernest's reincarnation data, too, would fail the test of scrutiny. That was something I didn't want to think about. My tacit commitment to Filipa and her colleagues forbade such considerations.

The births for 1985, yet to be properly bound, were contained within four plump quarterly binders, each identified by the last month of the quarter. I pulled out the September, 1985 file and riffled through its pages in search of Graham, Thomas Hugh. I was hoping to pinpoint the entry with the birthdate but no dates were given, only the full names of those born in England and Wales within the quarter. I found the Grahams quickly enough. There were five with the first name of Thomas, each accompanied by the maiden name in parentheses as well as the district of birth:

> Graham, Thomas Alexander (Crook); Hammersmith
> Graham, Thomas David (Fell); Portsmouth
> Graham, Thomas Frank (Ayling); Northampton
> Graham, Thomas Hugh (Saunders), NE Hants
> Graham, Thomas Langdon (Langdon); Hounslow

So there *was* a Thomas Hugh Graham but he was not born in Kent, as the guides had said, and there was no way of knowing immediately whether he was born on 13 July. To find out, I had to fill in an application for a full birth certificate, which I did.

Several weeks later, some time after I had returned to Toronto, the certificate I had ordered arrived in the mail. Anxiously, I opened the envelope and scanned its contents. To my great relief and satisfaction, the pink, ink-scrawled certificate was inscribed almost the way I had dared to expect:

> Thomas Hugh Graham
> Birthdate: 13 July 1985
> Parents: Hugh and Susan Graham
> Birthplace: Aldershot, Hampshire

It was all just as Russell had said—with one exception. The birthplace was located in Aldershot, Hampshire, rather than in Kent, which lay thirty-five miles away.

Triumphantly, I carried the birth certificate with me to the next session at Aviva's home and announced the news to cheers and applause. Even Aviva, who was not inclined to show much enthusiasm for matters pertaining to the guides, became quite excited at the sight of evidence supporting Russell's pronouncement. I think it made her feel that her weekly "sleeps" were well and truly justified. And, like the rest of us, she couldn't help but laugh at the thought of Ernest gurgling in a crib somewhere in the south of England.

Once the clamor and excitation in the room had subsided and Aviva was escorted into unconsciousness, I informed Russell of my success in substantiating most of the information he had provided. He accepted the news with the utmost equanimity and, after apologizing for his inaccuracy over the birthplace, added: "Hampshire is not far from Kent, is it? Projection into those areas is not our....Unfortunately, geographically, it is as correct as could be."

In terms of pinpointing a location on the Earth's surface from the next dimension it was, of course, a remarkably close approximation. I told Russell that we were all most curious to learn exactly how the information had been obtained and he obliged us with a thorough explanation.

> It took a great deal, but we had already one advantage and that was that we had come into contact with several who would be active, at least initially, in guiding Ernest. And from there it was a matter of asking each to try to elicit as much information as possible. Then we located the guide of the father who was really quite helpful and very good at being able to

understand and pinpoint pertinent information....There were several what you would call middlemen involved. Messages were relayed and brought forward before we passed them along to you.

The child's energies, incidentally, were initially quite fearful and then extremely stressed. His name was easy enough to get for the father carries it in his mind, of course, as does the mother. We were very lucky in that the guide of the father had been his guide for a number of years. If it had been a new person doing the guiding, we might not have been able to get such easy access. It wasn't as easy as it might sound. You see, we have difficulty with dates because we don't have to deal with them . . . I'm not sure if you can understand that, but it would be much the same if we dropped you in the middle of the ocean and didn't show you which way to swim to land . . . It was quite complicated and involved, but it was certainly a wonderful exercise for us.

More importantly, it was a potent vindication of the guides. Although we had no way of knowing whether Thomas Hugh Graham actually was Ernest's reincarnation, the detailed evidence of his birth—passed through Aviva's slumbering form more than 3,000 miles away—was formidable. Evidence, of course, is one thing; proof is a different proposition entirely. And perhaps Russell voiced the only certitude in this tantalizing case when he said: "I'm sure Thomas will grow up to be a packet of trouble for someone."

There is an appropriately odd postscript to the bizarre tale of Ernest and Thomas. It stems from my desire to make contact with the Graham family in the hope that I might meet their son. Confounded by Ernest's claim to having been a bomber pilot, I wondered whether young Thomas would unconsciously reveal another clue to the puzzle. There are, after all, many hundreds of documented cases of young children who have recalled episodes—and even recognized surviving relatives—from their past lives. Would Thomas, if encouraged, talk about his own once he had learned to speak? Would he register emotional recognition if I were to present him with a toy model of a Wellington bomber?

Just to establish contact with the Grahams was going to be tricky. As Filipa pointed out, were I to mention that I had been speaking to their son *before he was born* via a medium, "This might make them upset or it might making them think that you are needing medical help." I decided to seek Russell's advice as to the best way of approaching them.

"Well," he said, "if you had a horse you could break its leg right outside their house and ask for assistance, couldn't you? Or you could have your wagon wheel fall off...."

Good old Russell, I thought, beleaguered by his nineteenth-century mind-set.

"The trouble with doing something like that, Russell, is that when you finally have to state the real reason for your visit you look like a fraud."

"Well, of course," said Russell. "But if you want your foot in the door, break your horse's leg....I'm sure, however, that you'll find something a little more sophisticated and less garish. If you do run up against the little chap, give him all our regards and wish him 'Happy life.' Better him than us...."

On a subsequent visit to England—in July, 1987—I decided to approach the Grahams directly by placing a telephone call to their home in Camberley, Surrey. It wasn't an easy call to make. I had visions of either Hugh or Susan Graham slamming down the receiver in my ear on the understandable assumption that they were talking to some strange brand of lunatic.

It was a warm and sunny Saturday afternoon when I placed the call. Mrs. Graham answered almost at once, and I began, as simply and as clearly as possible, to explain who I was and what I was doing. To my surprise, she kept listening to what I had to say. But not for long. I had begun to relate the story of Ernest and was just about to describe his connection to young Thomas when she interrupted me to say: "I think you should speak to my husband."

While waiting on the line, I could hear in the background an infant's shouts and gurgles. That had to be young Thomas who, I calculated, must have celebrated his second birthday only a few days earlier. When Hugh Graham picked up the receiver, I started my account all over again. To his credit, he listened attentively to all I had to say. My heart went out to him. I tried to put myself in his shoes and wondered whether I would have been so long-suffering. I kept stressing that I was not a crank, but a published writer in the metaphysical field who was endeavoring to fulfill his obligations as a researcher.

"First of all," Mr. Graham declared, "I have to establish whether you are legitimate." He went on to say that he would endeavor to verify my claims with my British publisher and would then decide whether we should meet for further discussion.

"I'm intrigued," he said, after hearing my account of Ernest and the guides. "It cuts across my own religious beliefs. My wife and I are both Methodists and I'm bound to approach this with a certain amount of questioning. I'm going to talk to my wife about this to see whether we want to pursue it any further."

Then he added cautiously: "If we do meet, it may have to be in another location because I don't know whether I want you to meet my son."

As I hung up, young Thomas was still making baby noises.

I called Hugh Graham again three days later from Oxford. The conversation was short and Mr. Graham did most of the talking. "I spoke with your publisher and you are who you say you are," he began. "I've also talked this over with my wife and we can't see any advantage in getting involved in this. In fact, we can see a number of disadvantages so far as Thomas is concerned and we want nothing further to do with it."

I respected his decision. Besides, I had no choice. But still I wonder whether Thomas will grow up with a strange fascination for the aircraft of World War II and, in particular, the "Wimpeys" of Bomber Command.

CHAPTER 11

The Changing of the Guard

For weeks, Sandford Ellison barely said a word. Having been invited by Tony Zambelis to attend our Friday night sessions, the soft-spoken, bespectacled management consultant would sit in a corner of Aviva's living room listening intently but never participating in the discussions. There were two reasons for his reticence. First, he was naturally shy and withdrawn and, secondly, his guide emerged more slowly than most from Aviva's slumber.

The guide's name was Tuktu. Once Sandford had introduced himself, it was six weeks before Tuktu was identified by Russell and another seven before Tuktu spoke with his own voice, a brisk Asian lilt. He told of having incarnated with Sandford more than thirty times and said that they had agreed "at least fifteen lives ago" to share a guide-charge partnership.

Step by step, Tuktu's protracted awakening drew Sandford into active debate with the guides and, as time elapsed, it became clear that our discarnate friends held him in high esteem and placed considerable emphasis on his importance as a group member.

Sandford's interest in the sessions had been stimulated by his lifelong fascination with the occult, his natural healing abilities and his part-time work as an astrologer. He was said by the guides to be a different breed of entity than the rest of us, an entity who had originally been created as a soul. According to Russell, the relatively rare and difficult transition from soul to entity had been accomplished over many incarnations. Sandford's wife, Betty, however, was labeled a soul and, as such, there was no guide available for her. Betty, nevertheless, continued to attend the sessions along with two or three other souls who, although unable to speak to a personal guide, were engrossed by what they saw and heard.

The guides were still stressing that an entity was not necessarily "better" than a soul. But they were also saying that an entity's forward development could be impaired by teaming up with a soul in a business or personal relationship. In Russell's words, "Generally speaking, when an entity and a soul are contracting together, the middle ground is reached—that is, forward development for the soul and regression for the entity." Indirectly, Sandford was being told that his marriage, while a positive experience for Betty, was detrimental to his personal growth.

The guides had spoken occasionally of the web of karmic association which had drawn various members of the group together. It was said, for example, that I had served as Aviva's guide and had been her lover in a German incarnation while Tony Zambelis, having spent eleven lifetimes with myself in varying relationships, had been Aviva's mother in a primitive Armenian life of indeterminate antiquity. Yet it seemed that Sandford's karmic workload with Aviva outweighed all others in our immediate circle. Certainly, it was seen to be of greater magnitude than the burden of karma he shared with Betty.

Sandford was told that, while he had been Aviva's mother in a harmonious Siamese life of long ago, he had last incarnated as a Jewish girl named Hanna Fleischman who had lived in Czechoslovakia. Hanna was killed at the age of fifteen when German troops marched into her country during the last war. She was said to have been girlfriend to eighteen-year-old Stanislav, Aviva's previous incarnation who had been identified and explored in the early days of Roger's hypnotic experimentation.

"You must remember your feelings towards each other in that life," Russell told Sandford. "You may have been young but your feelings were very powerful. [For Aviva] the great trauma and the great fear and the great dread when you disappeared carried right into this life . . . Her concern for your well-being is always above her own because that is something she has brought with her from that lifetime."

The guides made it very clear that Sandford and Aviva had incarnated expressly to be together in this life in order to confront a tricky karmic situation which had evolved over many shared incarnations. Sandford was born in England and Aviva was born in Australia and the way that they had found one another in Toronto was a magnificent example of karmic communication, a seemingly magical process in which people make unconscious yet purposeful connections, sometimes crossing great distances to do so. Russell explained:

> Karmic communication is the communication between two or more people who, upon meeting, have a strong draw to one another. It would not really matter where you travel, you will find, in all likelihood, people with whom you have karmic debts or ties. And you will be drawn to these people by a recognition of energies. You will feel a great knowing of these people already. They are people with whom you have had very intense dealings in other lives...[In the between-life state] you plan debt alleviation, which is a very strong drive for fulfilling your karma. This will, of course, necessitate very powerful karmic communication so that you may find one another.

As Russell and Tuktu provided more and more past-life information, it was evident that Sandford—a warrior with a taste for brutality in life after life—had more debits than credits in his karmic ledger so far as personal accounting with Aviva was concerned. One shared experience in Mongolia, particularly, was cited as requiring redress. During the thirteenth century, Aviva had been a teenage male peasant living in a walled village situated in a district ruled by Sandford. When the overlord paid a visit to the village, all were expected to bow as he passed by. All did so with the exception of Aviva's past-life personality who, impulsively rebellious, turned his back instead. Infuriated by this behavior, Sandford ordered his soldiers to bring the peasant before him. Then, as an example to others, he executed the defiant serf on the spot.

Soon after Tuktu began to communicate in his own voice, Russell asked Roger to arrange a private chat between Sandford and himself. In the ensuing discussion, Sandford learned that Aviva had leukemia and that, under current conditions, she had only three months to live. There was hope, however, that her life could be saved...hope that rested entirely with himself. Russell said Sandford's energies were perfectly compatible with Aviva's and that he was the only member of the group capable of channeling healing to her disease-ridden body. Sandford was informed that he had been developing his capacity to heal over five previous lifetimes. To assist in Aviva's recovery, said Russell, would be an ideal way to work on discharging his karmic debt.

So it was that Sandford learned how to channel energy from Tuktu through his mind and into his fingertips which were placed successively, according to the guides' instructions, on various parts of Aviva's body. "It was as though my forehead was connected to my hands," Sandford said of the healing sensation. "My hands and fingers would get quite hot. I would know when the work was completed on a particular area—the sensation of heat would die away. The difficulty always lay in blanking out the conscious mind. In time, I could tell where the problem areas were. The direction was mine, but the healing energy came from the guides."

In the course of many private sessions at Aviva's home, Roger would usher Aviva into the trance state, then Russell and Tuktu would train Sandford in the art of direct healing. The group as a whole was not involved in this work, as only a few members knew that Aviva was seriously ill. Those of us who did know were aware only that Aviva's condition was apparently worsening, that she was at the hospital more frequently for chemotherapy sessions and that Sandford was being called in more and more to deal with an escalation in pain and suffering caused by the progression of the disease. Months later, when Aviva's affliction had become common knowledge, David's charge, Valerie, asked Russell in open session the precise role that Sandford played in Aviva's health care. Russell replied:

> Tuktu's charge plays a most vital role. He has an energy pattern which fits quite closely with that of my charge, which allows her to absorb his energies. We are therefore able to channel through him very specific types of energies into specific areas of the body. We change them for different reasons and for different areas up to twelve or fifteen times....This helps to eliminate pain. We are also trying to alleviate some of the problem itself. This can be done through specific types of energies. Sometimes, we find that we have to change these energies more than once because her body no longer accepts them.

Within four months of requesting the original private chat with Sandford, Russell announced that he wanted Tuktu's charge to be able to lead Aviva into trance. Russell's wishes were made unmistakably clear after Roger vacillated rather than acting at once when Aviva asked him to give her a hypnotic command that would trigger an automatic response to her pain attacks. When the group next convened, Russell ordered everybody save Roger and Sandford out of Aviva's living room before unleashing a withering attack on Roger. In the course of the tongue-lashing, Roger was told that he was irresponsible, that he didn't have Aviva's best interests at heart and that he was placing her life in jeopardy. Finally, he was ordered to instruct Sandford in his hypnotic technique and to hand over knowledge of the key phrase which facilitated Aviva's journey into unconsciousness.

From that moment, Sandford not only proceeded to conduct healing sessions on Aviva without Roger's mediation but he also, with Russell's blessing, gradually assumed leadership of the Friday night discussions. It was soon obvious to the group members that Sandford was able to bring Aviva out trance with greater ease and speed than Roger had managed. On awakening, Aviva said she felt less groggy than before.

Anything less than the most dedicated concern for his charge was liable to provoke Russell's wrath. Having been solely responsible for Aviva's safety and well-being in the trance state, Roger had taken the brunt of her guide's displeasure on a number of occasions. Once he had failed unknowingly to restore Aviva to her normal waking state after a trance session and she had spent the night floating in and out of her body.

"It was one of the worst things that I've ever gone through," said Aviva. "I felt like a helium balloon going up and down. I was terrified of going to sleep in case I didn't come back. The next morning I sat in my [ground floor] kitchen and described the tops of the buildings in the neighborhood. It was then that I realized the roofs—which appear peaked from the street—were actually flat. I also saw the tops of the nearby factories. It got sort of frightening. I started to panic and that got me back into my body."

In response to a phone call from Helen Fields, Aviva's closest friend and a founding member of the group, Roger rushed over that morning to restore full consciousness. His first move was to talk Aviva into trance and, as soon as this had been accomplished, Russell flew at him with a flurry of harsh words: "Don't you realize what could have happened?" he demanded. "In that state, she could have been captured on the lower astral planes. You've endangered my charge. Don't you ever do that again!"

Russell was proudly enthusiastic about the new, improved care that was being lavished on Aviva and he expressed a gentle affection for Sandford during the sessions. On the other hand, he appeared to treat Roger with chill displeasure whenever, as the need arose, he substituted for Sandford on Friday nights. Not only had Roger been pushed into surrendering the hypnotist's chair and relegated to ordinary membership in the group he had helped to found, but also he was being subtly yet publicly scorned by the guide with whom he had toiled for so long on Aviva's behalf. While Roger withstood Russell's barbs without complaint, Jane—the charge of Kinngalaa, the African huntsman—voiced her concerns:

"When I hear you speak, particularly to Hanni's charge," she told Russell, "I feel that you speak in a rude manner. I wonder why you do that?"

"I am not rude—and I've never been rude," Russell replied. "It may appear rude to you, perhaps, because of the difference in timbre of the voice....I come through my charge and I am the one within the body at the time, or within the mind. Therefore, there are no relay stations to weaken the signal. When I am speaking with Hanni's charge, I do not even wish to give the impression of rudeness. That is not something that I admire in others and I do not wish that thought of me. I have been told that I am exceedingly direct. I do not believe in making things less understood than they should be."

"It's a concern of mine," Jane persisted, "that a guide would not stand by, love and encourage a charge ."

"That is all I have been doing," said Russell. "That has been my motivating concern. But when someone else's charge stands in the way of the health and the very well-being of my charge on the earthbound plane, I must step in—just as anybody else's guide would step in, if the situation were reversed."

Indirectly, Russell was accusing Roger of not heeding his wishes in caring for Aviva as she wrestled with her leukemia. He went on: "When subtle messages are given and understood and not acted upon, especially when time is of the essence—as it was—things must be made exceedingly plain. And I am very, very sorry if it has been taken personally, for these things are not directed at any one individual. They are directed for the salvation of the earthbound vehicle and of the earthbound entity, as my charge is."

Roger was unaware of any "subtle messages" and, with Sandford's help, he looked in vain for evidence of these in the transcripts of preceding sessions. Their futile search didn't change anything, however, because Russell insisted that Roger was being overly sensitive. Jane accepted Russell's explanation—"I want to believe what you're saying," she told him—and the cry of protest died away. Russell well and truly healed the rift by congratulating Jane on having the courage to declare her misgivings.

"Have I not told you to challenge openly? This is what Kinnggalaa's charge is doing. In her own way, she is checking for validity and that is a step forward in development. That is a step to opening the way to learning."

The changing of the hypnotic guard had threatened dissension within the group, but the potential crisis evaporated as quickly as it had arisen. Aviva's health, after all, was of paramount concern and we were all convinced that Russell knew best. If Sandford could replenish her fragile reserves and free her from periodic bouts of pain, so much the better. With Aviva's life at stake, it mattered little whether Roger had to eat humble pie.

Months later, after Sandford had spent innumerable hours channeling healing energies from the guides to Aviva's diseased body, Russell declared that Aviva's survival could be directly attributed to Sandford's intervention. "If she had not traveled to the country that you are now in, she would not have met Tuktu's charge," said Russell. "And if she had not met Tuktu's charge, probably she would be no longer on the earthbound plane."

Sandford was not a close personal friend of mine. We never engaged in heart-to-heart discussions. But seeing him every Friday night I noticed that, although he always put on a smile, he was becoming increasingly anxious and uncommunicative. And I wondered occasionally why his lifesaving mission hadn't brought him greater joy.

Sometimes, I also wondered about my own state of mind. I was more jittery than usual, more susceptible to insomnia and nervous tension and, to my irritation and dismay, certain friends seemed increasingly concerned about my well-being. No matter how hard I tried, I could not shrug off a cloying sense of contamination which could neither be pinpointed nor explained. Life had rarely seemed so fraught with uneasiness. When I asked Filipa about this vague discomfort she said that I was the kind of person who, wanting to cross a river, would try to swim its width even though a bridge was only a short distance away. "Sometimes you make for yourself things very hard and you do not see that you have done it to yourself," Filipa said tenderly. "This is my concern for you. It is just clear mind, clear mind. It not take you long to learn. You most smart man."

CHAPTER 12

A Surfeit of Spooks

It is hard to say just when my fascination with the guides turned into an obsession. The process was subtle, imperceptible, incremental. Information from the sessions accumulated in my mind like pennies in a piggy bank while echoes of the Friday night gatherings reverberated through my head. The strengthening of my love for Filipa went hand in hand with my veneration for the *bardo*. More and more, I saw my fellow human beings as either souls or entities and—interpreting the wealth of material on the subject—practiced distinguishing one from the other in everyday life. I worked diligently on Filipa's various suggestions as to my conduct and motivation, endeavoring, most of all, to love myself so that I might be more open and giving towards others. As I told all my pals *ad nauseam*, the continuing dialogues with the guides and Filipa's touching solicitousness amounted to the most remarkable experience of my life.

Throughout 1985 and 1986, the guides were my lifeblood, my consuming passion. Every session—and particularly the rare private sessions that I had with Filipa when, alone, I hunched over the sleeping yet garrulous Aviva—was an extraordinary thrill. So honored and privileged did I feel at being granted this open communication with the next world that when I tried to express my gratitude to Filipa, tears welled up in my eyes and my voice began to quake.

Largely because of Filipa's influence, I embarked upon a relationship with a Greek woman, Sylvia Prousalis, whom I met at a party one evening. Though Sylvia doubted the existence of my guide, she did teach me words and phrases in Greek so that I could make Filipa feel at home as well as test her responses. Filipa passed each of these mini-tests easily and, often, with humor. For example, when I greeted her with *Manare mu*, meaning "My little lamb," she shot back: "I am not woolly!" Disappointingly, however, on the two occasions that Sylvia visited Aviva's living room in the hope of conversing in Greek, Russell insisted on holding "forward development" debates to the exclusion of all else. Sylvia's skepticism intensified as a result, and I tired of trying to convince her of Filipa's presence. We soon drifted apart.

My terrestrial love life was doomed. No woman of flesh and blood could hope to emulate Filipa's love and concern. No incarnate female could ever begin to understand me in the fashion to which I had become accustomed. In a sense, I was lost to the world, living in a limbo land beyond most earthly cares and considerations. It was eternity that mattered, I told myself, not the petty concerns of unenlightened beings who were blind to our infinite potential. Still, I wanted to demonstrate that this larger vision was more than a dream and, with this aim in mind, I returned to my original mandate: to venture beyond the group to see whether there was a consensus among channeled entities at large.

The channeling movement was fast expanding in North America and there were many people in Ontario and neighboring New York State who claimed to be able to enter trance in order to bring forward guides and teachers for the elucidation of all. As I made my plans to meet some of them, Russell's original warning resounded in my ears. "The first thing you must establish is whether a guide is, in fact, a guide or a playful spirit and not a guide at all."

Would guides communicating through other mediums be able to identify Filipa, make contact with her, and impart information about our last life together to verify that the link had been made? Yes, said Filipa, if they were genuine guides. If they shrank from being tested in this way, I was advised not to trust them. "Rising to the challenge of a test," said Filipa, "would be more to the liking of genuine people." Russell felt that I should challenge other discarnates by inquiring about my occupation during my most recent Greek incarnation and by asking to know where in Greece Filipa and I had lived. And he urged that I inquire about souls and entities: those who did not understand the difference between the two streams of humanity would be the fakes who would give themselves away by revealing "absurd discrepancies."

Filipa said that if I notified her in advance she would attend any trance sessions I might hold with other mediums and would later counsel me as to their genuineness. She even intimated that, if energies could be matched satisfactorily, she would be able to speak through another medium's voice box, thereby establishing beyond all doubt that she was *not* a fabrication of Aviva Neumann's mind. But I was alerted that she would not necessarily communicate as Filipa; she might have to adopt a different past-life personality for the sake of achieving compatibility with the medium's energies. No matter. She would always be able to confirm her life in Greece as Filipa Gavrilos.

With mounting excitement, I made appointments with a succession of mediums, professional and non-professional, telling them that I was conducting research into the nature and substance of our allies in the next dimension. On my list, randomly selected, was Rik Thurston, the supervisor of a small facility for the mentally handicapped, who, in the trance state, became the one-eyed Mikaal, an Egyptian teacher from 4,000 years ago; Louise Oleson, who channeled an arthritic North American Indian grandmother from the seventeenth century; Kevan Dobson, a twenty-eight-year-old ex-hairdresser who turned into the doddering Dr. Jamieson, a nineteenth century Boston "bone-setter"; Edith Bruce, a frizzy-haired Scottish Spiritualist who transformed herself into Han Wan, keeper of the sacred scrolls in China more than 2,300 years ago; and J. Lee Hall, a psychic artist from Johnson City, New York, who claimed to be able to paint her subjects' discarnate guardians as well as their past-life likenesses.

Snow was falling in Ontario's Prince Edward County as I drove to a beige brick bungalow on a rural road for a session with Rik Thurston and his guide Mikaal who was billed in Thurston's brochure as "the perfect manifestation of love and understanding." This claim aroused my suspicions immediately. Had not Filipa and the other guides told us on numerous occasions that they were only human and subject to error, like ourselves? Yes, but Mikaal, I was soon to learn, said he would not be coming back to Earth because it was "much too limiting to do such."

Thurston—stocky, balding and bearded—introduced me to his "director," Karen Lee. Then he told how the onset of fierce migraine headaches had led him to try self-hypnotic techniques, his first step towards becoming a pipeline to the next world. After detailing the development of his mediumship from childhood awareness of a guiding presence to the dreamlike experience of full trance, he lay back in a long tipped-up armchair and breathed deeply several times. A log fire popped and crackled in the living room grate as Karen Lee counted him slowly into trance.

"Ten...nine...eight...seven...six...Dear Lord," Karen Lee intoned, "we are gathered in your name to quest and seek answers...five...four...three....Violet Christos...two...one." Thurston breathed loudly and swallowed several times. His eyes could be seen moving around beneath his closed eyelids. The countdown was repeated and Karen Lee declared: "In God's name, with God's direction, the body will assume its natural forces...now. Dear Lord, please protect all entities present from all negative influences regardless of source and give us the answers we seek through this inquiring mind through the manifestations of truth, intelligence, wisdom and love. Amen."

Thurston inhaled and cleared his throat. When he spoke, his voice was utterly transformed into a quaint Irish brogue:

"Greetings, Karen Lee. The form is well in that it be in a relaxed and stable condition conducive to the trance state."

This was the voice of the Transcendors, a group of entities said to number between 30,000 and 100,000, some of whom had incarnated on Earth, some of whom had never incarnated. In 1981, they started speaking through Thurston while be was asleep and have remained with him ever since, Mikaal having appeared on the scene much more recently. Guardedly, I inquired about Filipa, without mentioning her by name.

According to the Transcendors, my guide had "walked with the Nazarene," had been a priestly healer in Egypt and had incarnated as an Indian medicine healer and chieftain. I stifled my skepticism.

"And our last incarnation together?"

"We find an incarnation where the entities were wed...in Europe...one be unattainable to the other due to that of social classing and positioning....Those of outside influences would not allow the consummation. You were indeed intimate at that time."

Close, I thought, but not quite specific enough. So I asked the Transcendors to name the country.

"We have resonance here with France. However, it could be a visitation to such..."

I remained silent.

"Is it England? Again, a visitation?"

My comment was that a visit to England or France was an extremely unlikely undertaking for European peasants in the eighteenth century. According to Filipa, the most major expedition of her life had been a five-day walk to the Greek coast. The Transcendors were guessing, it was clear, and I changed the subject. I wanted to know how many incarnations I had experienced.

"Three hundred and seventy-two within that of this aspect of the soul, and there are many aspects to the soul. Fourteen hundred and seventy-three taking in half-aspects of soul."

"That's confusing," I said.

"Oh, indeed," agreed the Transcendors, "when one gets into soul fragmentation."

Thurston rebounded from trance and, after a short break, he settled back once more into the elongated armchair. When he was comfortable and relaxed, Karen Lee instructed: "Trigger A-T-1" He breathed deeply and moved his head around. Then his hands started to flex as his feet were drawn in and his shoulders heaved. Somewhat mechanically, Thurston got up out of the chair, placed his hands together and stretched his body. Then his eyes flickered open. His left eye, however, failed to open all the way because Mikaal, I learned later, was blind in that eye during his last incarnation as a teacher who lived near Alexandria in Egypt.

Mikaal introduced himself in a voice that sounded much like the Transcendors leavened with jauntiness. "And how can we be of service to thee this day?" he asked. I explained my research mission and Mikaal declared: "You will write the book in the form of automatic writing—that was an agreement made between yourself and your guide. You will become a direct channel for such...."

Filipa had never mentioned any such thing. Although Mikaal claimed to be in touch with my guide, he was unable to bring through any information to confirm that this was so. He did say, however, that Thurston, Karen Lee and myself had known one another during the last century in a part of the central United States "which now has many wheatfields." Apparently, we shared a wagon and a negligible water supply, surviving while others in the vicinity perished. "There was a cooperativeness for that of a common purpose," said Mikaal. "It just goes to show how important it be to share."

Filipa, of course, had mentioned that I had once selfishly guarded a supply of fresh water while others died of thirst. But the time and place were vastly different and I dismissed the similarity of this incident from the days of the Wild West as mere coincidence. Generally, I was not impressed. Not because I doubted Thurston's sincerity or the genuineness of his trance, but rather because Mikaal's pronouncements directly contradicted what Filipa had told me. And there was certainly nothing to indicate that Mikaal was "the perfect manifestation of love and understanding."

* * *

Norwegian-born Louise Oleson first became aware of "Grandmother" while participating in a meditation meeting in April, 1976. Suddenly, she felt as though she was being pumped up, like a balloon. Later, she said: "I thought to myself, 'If I get any bigger, I'll explode with a big bang.' There was lots of tension and tightness in the body. It was a very powerful experience." Her body contorted as Grandmother intruded and her first words were "big" and "old."

Grandmother, an entity of few, slow words who claims to be Oleson's guide, told how she last lived during the first half of the seventeenth century as a Petun Indian in the Blue Mountain area of central Ontario. In those days, Whitefeather—Louise Oleson in this life—was her granddaughter while Oleson's common-law husband, Andrew, was Whitefeather's husband, a brave named Tauromee. Later, I was told that I had been Strong Buck, Whitefeather's brother!

Oleson, who works as a file clerk, has never charged a fee for channeling Grandmother. The humble, whispery-voiced spirit is invoked only for Andrew and certain, selected friends who accept metaphysical reality. After explaining the nature of my research, I was invited to meet Grandmother and welcomed to Oleson's suburban home in Scarborough, Ontario. We chatted for a long time and then I looked on expectantly as Oleson sat quietly, eyes closed. Almost imperceptibly, within a minute or two, she metamorphosed into Grandmother. The change became apparent when a sweet smile spread gradually across her features.

"Hello," she said, her voice, rasping.

"Are you able," I asked her, "to identify my guide?"

"Yes," said Grandmother. "I can see him. He is right behind you now. He is wearing a long robe. He can show himself as different...He has shown himself as a Chinese with funny sleeves and funny hat. Now he's changed again. Now he is white hair and big beard. Now he is laughing and he's saying 'I am one and many at the same time.' But he is always helping you and he will put you in touch with people who can help you in your work. He is now with a sword and fighting off anybody who could interfere and get you off track."

I told Grandmother that my guide had appeared to me as a woman.

"When he was first there as a monk," Grandmother replied in soft staccato, "I almost said, 'He is a woman,' but I said 'No, monk not woman.' He smiles now. He says there is much more writing for you to do and you will have to work closely together for a long time."

Could Grandmother pick up any information on the last life I had shared with my guide, I wondered aloud. That is, when she was a woman.

"She has once been your mother and your teacher.... You were little girl. She now woman, say 'Not important at this time.' Now monk is back. She was once wife to you, the monk is telling me. She keeps going away."

"Which country?" I inquired.

"There were many mountains. You run away together. It didn't last long.... She was taken back. You were found. You tried to go back. You were killed...not really killed but you sort of died. She keeps going away."

Grandmother was as imprecise and as improbable as Mikaal. My doubts only intensified when, just like Mikaal, she insisted that I was a member of her channel's reincarnation family. She told me that, in India, I had been "keeper of the elephants" for "the Princess," who had already been identified as the past-life personality of one of Louise's and Andrew's friends. Andrew and I were told that we had worked together as Tibetan priests, had known one another in Atlantis and in India, and had been cousins—"you fought very closely together"—in Roman times.

Grandmother continued, "You are in very good hands with your own guide. This book you are working on now will be more of an eye-opener to many people who have a hard time accepting and believing this kind of work."

Filipa was buzzing loudly in my ears as I left.

***

In a sparsely furnished apartment seventeen floors above the streets of downtown Toronto, Dr. Frank George Jamieson sat across from me, gravelly voiced, elderly and infirm. Only minutes earlier, his hunched-over body had been lithe and straight-backed and owned unquestionably by Kevan Dobson—a blond-haired former hair stylist. Dobson had chatted animatedly about his dissatisfaction with life in Toronto salons and told how, as a child living in Saskatoon, he had been discouraged from having anything to do with psychic development.

Now a professional medium, Dobson had traveled far in pursuing his natural curiosity about life beyond the material world. Dr. Jamieson had first spoken through him spontaneously, while he was meditating one day. His words of greeting were: "Hello, This is Jamieson. I bring my love to you. I'll be working with you. We have a great distance to travel together. I must leave you now." Initially, Dobson thought that some strange part of his mind had concocted the experience, but it wasn't long before he found he was able to leave his body at will, allowing Dr. Jamieson to fill the vacuum.

Police sirens wailed in the streets below as Dr. Jamieson related details of his most recent incarnation as a chiropractor or "bone-setter" in Boston. He said he had been born in England during the late 1780s and had been brought to America on a sailing ship while still a boy. In the New World he had proceeded to acquire a degree in chiropractic medicine as well as a wife and family. He gave me his address in Boston and the names of his four children. Indeed, the kindly doctor's co-operation in providing such verifiable information gave me hope that I might have encountered the genuine article. Then I asked him if he could see my guide.

"You do have souls around you," he said. His voice was cracked and feeble. "Looks like three and there seems to be another floating around you there."

I explained that my guide communicated with me as the woman she was during her last life in Greece and that, although she was assisted by a number of apprentices, she was my only guide. When I inquired as to whether he was aware of Filipa's presence, Dr. Jamieson responded in the affirmative.

"I see her light around you. I also see the light of more than her. This is a very energetic soul, you realize that, don't you?" [How Filipa would loathe being called a "soul," I thought.] "I had not made a connection with her before, even though I had been around you. You see, it's very much like ships passing in the night in our world. I do believe I see her light here. Did you have a sandwich for lunch today?"

"No," I answered, mystified. "I had bacon and eggs."

"She was saying something about a sandwich for lunch. Exactly what that means, I don't know. Yes, we have made a connection with her. A great deal of white light around this soul. A very special individual. Do you have a question of her?"

I told Dr. Jamieson that, as Filipa and I had had many conversations, I would like him to bring a message from her that bore the mark of authenticity.

"Give me a moment, here," said Dr. Jamieson unsteadily. "I'll just let her bring whatever she can here. She tells me, firstly, that as you continue on doing the work that you're going to do that you are indeed going to find great discrepancies in information and so forth....She has been working with you for a number of years and, indeed, there have been a number of incarnations here....Did you tell me that you were in an incarnation with her, is that what...?"

"Yes," I interrupted. "The last one in Greece."

"There was an incarnation here in which she tells me of a Greek tycoon. Are you aware of that one?"

I was not.

"Perhaps it's just wording here," Dr. Jamieson continued, "but this was an incarnation which you and her would have spent together once again....Oh, just a moment. Hmmm. I do apologize here. That is not correct....I do have an incarnation here in which, just a moment...." The doctor breathed heavily. "Yes, you were a Greek tycoon. She was not in this lifetime with you. She was a guiding spirit to you in this lifetime....She tells me that this was prior to your last incarnation."

Nothing could have been further from my understanding of the truth. Though I continued my conversation with Dr. Jamieson for another fifteen minutes or so, it was plain that he had failed my private test. Just to make sure, I asked him the name of the village in Greece where Filipa and I had lived and I asked him about the difference between souls and entities, all to no avail. The question remained: If Dr. Jamieson wasn't in touch with Filipa as he claimed to be, what was he up to? It seemed that the doctor had few qualms about lying to people who came to see him for advice. He admitted as much:

"Quite often," he said, "I will tell souls that they are on their last incarnation because if they heard of anything less they would be sorely disappointed."

"Doesn't that build up karma for you, though?" I asked.

"No," he replied. "Not at all. You see, it's not so terribly important. What is important is that when [these people] come back into our world they'll realize what the true picture is. It's not so much a lie, I would say, as just smoothing the fire, shall we say."

Dr. Jamieson concluded our conversation by saying that he would provide proof of his existence by appearing to me in my home late at night.

> You will see me as a man who is somewhat receding of hairline, full face....I will also have glasses. I will have a physical body that will be shorter than this instrument's, approximately five feet seven, five feet eight, somewhere in that neighborhood...somewhat of a plump character and I shall be fairly well dressed, I can guarantee you that....Have the lights off. Make sure that you are sitting and I shall ask that you stare into a corner. Start in a few days and do it every night for the following week. And if you do not see me by then, I'll appear in your dreams instead.

I looked in vain for Dr. Jamieson in the dark recesses of my apartment. And I never saw him in my dreams.

* * *

Edith Bruce spent thirty-five years as a Spiritualist minister in Aberdeen, Scotland before emigrating to Canada. Petite and white-haired, she's also fiery, tough-minded, practical and in constant communication with the spirit world. "I've been aware of my guides since I was very young," she told me. "I'm closer with my guides than I am with my fellow human beings. My guides are ambassadors of love and compassion. I give thanks every day for the divine guidance of these unseen forces."

Bruce is aware of having an Arabian guide, Nadi, and an African guide, Sibu, but her principal guardian is Han Wan, who makes his presence known by taking forceful charge of Bruce's body. Han Wan is said to have held the sacred scrolls of the temples of China before his assassination more than 2,300 years ago by forces who wanted to use the teachings against the people. Bruce believes that she was Ti-Fu, Han Wan's daughter. Han Wan, said Bruce, does not have to reincarnate.

In company with three other people, I watched as Han Wan commandeered Bruce's tiny frame. The transformation was rapid and complete. Gone was her Scottish accent and her reserved, self-effacing manner as she suddenly became bloated with self-assurance and lordliness. Dogmatic and authoritarian, with a taste for oratory and prediction, Han Wan stood up, gesticulated proudly with his arms and spoke as though he were addressing an assembly of thousands. Strangely, he sounded more East European than Chinese.

"Greetings to my sisters and brothers!" he declaimed. "As I come into your vibrations, I give you the blessing of the Father/Mother God, to enrich you in body and spirit and also that you may go forward upon your journeys to have faith and also courage to enjoy and to know that God, the divine parent, is at the helm of your pathways, giving you also the strength and also the incentive to plough the field and to scatter the good seed on the land."

Han Wan spoke with a preacher's rhetoric and he was not a good listener. Once he had completed his introductory address, be spoke benignly to the other people in the room and then turned to make a swift survey of my life, claiming to know the peaks and valleys of my existence but offering only vague substantiation of such knowledge. He would name a year or a range of years, speak of "difficulties" or "changes" and I would be expected to fill in the specifics. When I was finally able to ask a question about Filipa (though I didn't mention her by name), Han Wan replied long-windedly that I had first made contact with my guide "in a family life" in the Egyptian temples of the sun.

There was much respect and dignity and in that time you were also attached to devotion. It was devout meditations and also, too, working with colors and also mantras which were of that time to the healing of mental disorders and emotional stresses. You understand? The colors were bathed in essence, but the essence was flowers....But remember that the people of that time believed faith removed the mountain so that they did not cloud their minds in a negative vibration. They came to the temples to receive because they knew the power that the initiates of that time held, could you understand me? And this is where you worked with your hands and there were sacred oils that were also poured upon the heads to relieve the stresses.

Filipa had said that our first encounter had taken place on a tribal battleground—a far cry from a life of religious devotion in the temples of the sun. Yet again, I had happened upon disturbing contradictions. Little wonder, then, that I was hounded by confusion, and not a little buzzing in the ears, all the way home. The "truth," it seemed, was more elusive than ever.

* * *

As one who had always been sensitive to unseen influences, artist and sculptor J. Lee Hall, of Johnson City, New York, found it quite natural to slip into trance and sketch people as they had been in their past lives. In time, she discovered another innate ability: she was able to sketch the dominant guiding presences of her subjects.

During a rare visit to Toronto, Hall agreed to tune into my vibrations in search of my guide. The granddaughter of a Spiritualist, Hall is a large, gentle woman with sad eyes. She started by holding my hands and envisioning both of us in a crystal ball filled with white light. Then she visualized her energy travelling through her hands into mine and curling back through her head and returning to her hands. Out loud, she asked Almighty God to direct her in rendering the most appropriate and beneficial images on paper. Then she turned to the easel at her side and started to draw with a selection of colored chalks.

"I'm a channel," said Hall. "I never know what is going to appear on the paper. It's a constant battle to remain detached—to work in a prayerful state and leave it in the hands of the supreme being."

Sketching, at times, with her eyes closed, Hall was perspiring profusely. As she applied purple, gold, yellow, pink and blue chalk, a face slowly but steadily emerged from the dark paper. To my disappointment, it was the face of a man, a man with wise, keen eyes and a third eye which shone brilliantly from his forehead. He was wearing a most unorthodox, conical turban.

"Do you get any sense of which country he's from—or is that an unearthly hat?" I asked her.

"That's an unearthly hat. Definitely. For a while, I thought he was a swami, the way that the face was beginning to build with the turban. In fact it's a very unusual, perhaps ancient, kind of head ornament. Sometimes, I even relate some of these to Atlantis...."

"What does the hat mean to you?" I wanted to know.

"If I just glanced at it, I would immediately relate it to a master teacher. That's what it would tell me."

"Rather than a guide?"

"A master teacher is a guide."

Hall said that, as she worked, she repeatedly offered a prayer to my guide saying, in essence, "If you're really there, let's put you on paper." Then she shunted the chalk back and forth across the sheet of paper until the face developed of its own accord. "If it isn't correct," she said, "it never works. It refuses to work." Before she applied pink chalk to the drawing she said that she heard, clairvoyantly, the words, "Now send him my love."

So many claims, so little substance. Disconsolately, I took the painting home and left it lying in my attic, gathering dust. Filipa told me later that, while she was aware of Hall being in my vicinity, she had neither inspired the drawing nor communicated with the artist in any way. "I could not make thoughts in that person to tell anything," she said.

So from whence came J. Lee Hall's inspiration? An overactive imagination? A playful spirit? A telepathic ability to tap into my deep unconscious? Or—a faint hope—was she contacting an ascended master who had transcended the cycle of death and rebirth? All I knew was that something was amiss with the channeling of J. Lee Hall and the other mediums who claimed to be in direct contact with wise and benevolent beings in the next dimension.

Ragged with disillusionment, I was ready to relinquish all experimentation with other channels when I encountered a "spiritual teacher" who reached out and clasped me to his discarnate bosom. His name was Dr. Samuel Pinkerton.

CHAPTER 13

Can We Trust You, Dr. Pinkerton?

Toronto's New Age community was rife with gossip about an English surgeon from the last century who spoke convincingly through an Italian woman with long, blonde hair. Comments such as "he's adorable!" and "wise old owl" reached my ears and left me curious. Still nursing a hangover from a surfeit of mediumistic gibberish, I felt compelled nevertheless to seek out one last channel. On locating Claire Laforgia at the Kentwell Personal Awareness Center in Toronto, I was delighted by her acceptance of my intent to probe the shadowy depths of the trance state. Saying she was keen to learn more about her mediumship as well as Dr. Samuel Pinkerton's "world of spirit," she offered to work with me as a research subject.

Claire seemed an unlikely vessel for a surgeon from Victorian England. Stocky, with bright red fingernails and flowing blonde hair to her waist, she liked to chew gum and wear high heels. Having been born in Milan, her Italian accent was unmistakable and I wondered whether this would inhibit or otherwise affect the doctor's elocution. Claire, a former nursing assistant, had been aware of non-physical presences since the age of four when she had a vision of her father immediately following his death from a heart attack. At convent school in Italy, she felt comforted by a guiding presence and in her teens was once again "visited" by her dead father. But it was not until her thirties—after being told by a psychic reader that she had the ability to communicate actively with the other side— that she developed her latent ability as a medium.

Upon joining a psychic development class at the Kentwell Personal Awareness Center in the summer of 1985, Claire began to experience strange sensations during group meditations. "I felt very numb and I seemed to be choking," she said. "I felt as though I weighed 250 pounds. It was as if some force had taken me over." Three meditative sessions were plagued consecutively with this nagging discomfort and, during session number four, Claire paused to remove the ever-present chewing gum from her mouth—with startling results. As soon as the gum was gone, the "force" swept into her larynx to announce: "My name is Dr. Samuel Pinkerton." The invading presence later explained that he was Claire's spiritual teacher, that he had guided her in previous lives, and that he had been trying to communicate through her for some time.

Claire not only began to channel Dr. P., as she came to know him, but she also perceived and chatted with the discarnate surgeon during private meditation. He appeared to her as he was at various stages of his life—in his thirties, in his fifties, and as an old man with a white moustache and beard. Sometimes he would be wearing a suit, sometimes a white lab coat. In his later years—the time of life he adopted as a channeled communicator—he would be seen peering over his spectacles and leaning on a cane placed always on his left side. A cigar and a glass of brandy were never very far away.

As thrilled as she was to be a conduit for Dr. Pinkerton, Claire realized from the start that she must establish guidelines for her mediumship. She told me: "I said to Dr. P., 'You may use my physical body only when I ask you to do so—not in a public place where I could be embarrassed.' In reply, he hugged me in meditation and said: 'By all means, Young Lady.'"

Several weeks after Dr. Pinkerton had announced himself, Claire became a professional medium based at the Kentwell Center. As word spread of the doctor's sagacious and penetrating counsel, his ability to contact friends and relatives in the next world and his talent for prediction, a steady stream of clients paid $65 an hour for the privilege of conversing with the venerable gentleman. "I have always looked upon my ability to channel Dr. Pinkerton as a gift from God," said Claire. "I see Dr. P. as an ascended master. My mission is to be a messenger who can help people."

The arrival of Dr. Pinkerton helped Claire to understand why she had chosen her earlier career as a nursing assistant. She said of her former occupation at Toronto's Doctors Hospital: "I felt that I knew exactly what I was doing from the moment I entered that hospital. Mentally, I knew exactly what to do in the operating theatre. I could have taken over. Dr. Pinkerton has said that he was working through me in my job."

It was of no consequence to the other discarnates of my acquaintance whether, when they held forth, the sun was high or the artificial lighting was bright. Dr. Pinkerton, however, preferred to conduct his business in a darkened room with the door closed and only the muted light of a shaded table lamp for illumination. Such was the setting—a small room at the Kentwell Center—for my first encounter with Dr. P.

Claire sat in a chair across from me, a tape recorder activated on the table beside her. Ten feet away, I crouched next to the lamp in order to write and consult my notes. Claire closed her eyes and folded her hands in her lap. Twice, she breathed deeply and then recited a blessing. "Heavenly Father/Mother God, we thank you for bringing us together today in thy tender care and love. Father, I ask that you place the divine light of protection around Joe, myself, and the Center. Father, I ask you to place a special blessing upon Joe and his loved ones. Father, guide him, guard him and protect him. Lead and teach him always...."

The blessing had only just passed Claire's lips when a strange bleating, like a troubled car engine turning over, escaped from her throat. It was an old man's garble, high-pitched, unsteady, and wordless. Next, Claire's right leg crossed over as her body hunched forwards into a stoop and leaned over to the left side. There was much smacking of lips and some wringing of hands before Dr. Pinkerton had made himself comfortable.

"Can you hear me?" His voice sounded strained, as if he were pulling on a rope as he was talking. He was unquestionably male and undeniably English.

"Yes I can, Dr. Pinkerton. Pleased to meet you."

"Blessings to you, Son. I've been waiting for this day. Finally, we've both made it. Greetings. I trust you're well.... I didn't give her a chance to finish, if you noticed. I'm quite excited."

Dr. Pinkerton—who referred to Claire either as "my instrument" or "this young lady"—explained that he worked with "numbers of souls" who assisted him in searching for answers to people's questions by delving into the Akashic Records. Seers and mystics have long regarded these records as a non-material warehouse of memory said to contain the indelible impressions of everything that has ever happened. Dr. Pinkerton's most dedicated helper was someone he called Master Nathaniel and, as I was to hear, he sometimes audibly conversed with this invisible assistant as the consultation proceeded.

"My, my, they're saying 'Blessings to you, Joe' and they're linking quite well with your voice vibration. Of course, you're well-known in our world. What can I do for you, Son?"

I explained my mission as concisely as possible, telling him that I was looking for earthly corroboration of messages relayed by various "guides" as well as for commonality among the guides' testimony about themselves. I began by asking Dr. P. to provide me with as much detail as he was able concerning his own most recent past life. He obliged by recounting his life from the day he was born in London on 29 January 1801 until his death in a Sicilian village called Gela on 3 February 1895.

Leaving England at sixteen years of age, the youthful Pinkerton traveled to Italy where he studied medicine in Milan and Bologna, graduating in general surgery from the University of Bologna at the age of twenty-nine. Subsequently, he moved to Rome, where he established a practice, and then, on turning fifty, traveled to Catania, a small city on the east side of Sicily. There he lived and worked — "they still talk about me; they used to love me," he said—until retiring in Gela towards the close of his long life. He married twice, his first wife dying of cancer at a young age. Dr. Pinkerton was a huge man—six feet four inches tall and 300 pounds in weight.

> Son, let me tell you that if it wasn't for my weight I would have lived to be 200. Ahh, but I was quite careful what I ate. And drank. And I was quite a healer on my own. Self-healing. I used to heal myself through the mind. Through meditation and concentration I would rejuvenate myself. People would say to me when I was about seventy-five, "How come you never age, Doctor?" And I would only smile and bless them. I was prepared. Crossing over was just like going to another home. Indeed, this is home.

Having been careful not to mention Filipa to Claire, I told Dr. P. that I was in touch with my own guide and asked whether he could see her from his vantage point.

"Your guide's name....I have the light of a young lady. She's greeting you with love. You've linked with this young lady, haven't you, on the Earth plane?"

"Yes."

"And the information that they're giving me...you were related as brothers...."

"Yes, she's told me that."

"She's also a master teacher to you, Son, isn't she? This is how she's presenting herself. Her light has been with you for several years...early 1980s. Do you have any message, Madame? Perhaps you will understand what she is telling me, Joseph...."

I told Dr. Pinkerton that I would be most interested in any information that he could bring from my guide about our last incarnation together.

"She's saying, 'Isn't there anything else you want to ask? Always the same question.' They're bringing me 17...60."

Thus far, the information supplied by the reedy-voiced doctor concerning Filipa had been stunningly accurate. I congratulated myself on having stumbled, at last, upon a genuine source of discarnate intelligence.

"Yes, we were incarnate in 1760. As what?"

"As brothers."

My heart sank with disappointment.

"That's different," I replied.

"Perhaps," said Dr. Pinkerton. "Let me tell you something, Joseph. What you're doing here, Son, is a form of testing, isn't it?"

"Yes, it is."

"May I be very open with you?"

"Please."

"You see, spirit knows, we know, that we're being tested. And sometimes we do not like the idea, Son. Therefore, we give you a hard time. If your guide says to me that she does not want to give me this information, what do you want us to do?"

Mindful of Filipa's words that genuine guides would not object to being tested, I explained that Filipa knew exactly what I was doing and had agreed to co-operate with me in providing information about herself, wherever possible, via other mediums.

Dr. Pinkerton reacted by changing the subject. He proceeded to give me the names of some descendants of the Pinkerton line who were currently alive on Earth—great-grandsons living in London and Brussels, both doctors, and a great-granddaughter in Vienna who had married a Polish refugee. I made notes of their names and steered the elusive doctor back to the slippery question of Filipa. Why, I asked him, would he bring me information different from that which my guide had already provided?

"That's what they brought me, Son. That's what I'm bringing you.... She's playing games with me, even with her name....She's saying 'You should know my name.' She's given me her first initial. It doesn't help me at all."

"What is that?" I asked.

"P. Like Peter."

Dr. Pinkerton was right, of course, if Filipa was spelled as the anglicized Philippa. He continued as if he were talking to her:

"Are you going to give me the last initial perhaps, Madame? What do you mean, my dear?" Then, to me, he added: "She says that perhaps another time she wouldn't mind coming through this young lady."

"Really? She could come through your instrument?"

"Ah—hmm. But not today, Son."

Finally, I raised the soul-entity concept with Dr. Pinkerton. He chose to avoid the issue by stating that he agreed with whatever Filipa had told me on the subject.

"Let me tell you one thing, Joseph. I never disagree with anyone's guide. With Madame P. I must agree." And then he excused himself, saying that he must return his instrument to the workaday world. Before leaving, he promised to bring Filipa through Claire's voice box the next time we met.

"God be with you, Joseph," he said. "We shall see you very soon. I shall be expecting you."

Seconds later, Claire raised her hands to her face and whispered faintly, as if heavily sedated, "Thank you, Dr. Pinkerton." There was no trace of the forthright English accent. Claire Laforgia had returned. Her Italian inflection told me so.

Dr. Pinkerton left me intrigued but unsure. He had given me enough to demonstrate that he knew something about my connection with

Filipa, yet not enough to inspire full confidence. Was he merely an astute guesser or a genuinely knowledgeable entity? Within two days, I was sitting on the floor of Aviva's living room checking with Filipa on the surgeon's credentials.

"This individual is a guide, the guide of an entity is he?" I inquired.

"I think I am knowing of who you speak," said Filipa. "He calls to you 'doctor'?"

"He said that he was a doctor in his last life and he's given me information on himself that I can check."

"I knowing him. Only in the name of Albert. This guide was naming Albert to me. I am Filipa to him."

Now I was really baffled! *Albert!* I went over my time with Dr. P. to confirm that Filipa was not confusing the session in the darkened room with any other recent episode of my life. Then I told her that Dr. Pinkerton had said she would proffer only the initial P as a token of identification.

"I think that is all *he* is giving to you," she said.

"Well, I wondered that myself," I told her. "He said that he could see the light of a young lady and described you as a master teacher."

"I am just guiding, no more. You ask him which incarnation he was Albert. This must be the one I know as Albert. It must be the same one. Ask him what was your name when we were together in Theros—but do not tell him Theros. And I will tell Albert and he must impart that to you. Then we will be knowing."

I told Filipa that Dr. Pinkerton had said she would be able to speak through Claire.

"The energies are very difficult. Perhaps we can try. However, if it is not possible you have many things you knowing of you and me so that you can verify."

It seemed as though I was closing in on a situation laden with potential. Filipa was aware of Claire's guide whom she knew as Albert rather than Dr. Pinkerton. Presumably, Albert was Dr. Pinkerton; he was simply identifying himself as a different past-life personality. Unfortunately, this developing state of affairs was hampered by Aviva's imminent departure for Australia where she was to spend several weeks with her ailing father. Without Aviva as intermediary, it was going to be hard, perhaps impossible, to share with Filipa my conversations with Dr. Pinkerton. My mind-to-mind contact with Filipa had not advanced beyond habitual buzzing and the occasional reception of a lone word or phrase. I would have to wrestle with Dr. P. on my own.

Meanwhile, Roger Belancourt had regained his original position as group leader and hypnotist. Sandford Ellison, it was rumored, would not be returning to our sessions. There was talk of personal antagonism between Aviva and himself; there was even talk of Sandford's mental instability. I knew that Sandford had not been feeling well for a long time and that his marriage was under tremendous strain. Yet he was closer to the guides than anyone and it was hard to imagine the sessions without him. Moreover, I wondered how Aviva would survive without his healing hands.

Sandford's abdication of the group's leadership spoke more loudly than words of a serious rift within our family circle. Fearing involvement in a petty squabble, however, I chose not to seek out Sandford to ask why he was no longer with us. Instead, I accepted Russell's explanation. Sandford, he said, had opted for negativity and backsliding rather than forward development and the group would be better off without him.

* * *

Aviva had left for Australia and the month of May, 1987, was only a few days old when I telephoned Claire to arrange another chat with Dr. P. By this time I had inadvertently disclosed my guide's name and, during our conversation, Claire told me that Filipa had contacted her several times, both in her dreams and through her innate ability to hear my guide's voice. She also said that Filipa was working on regulating her body chemistry so that she would be able to channel her at the forthcoming session, as Dr. Pinkerton had promised. Claire described Filipa as "radiantly gorgeous" with long black hair, big eyes and perfect breasts. She was dressed, she said, in a silk robe and the light around her was gold.

"I could be wrong," said Claire, "but I think Filipa resents the fact that she had to stay behind. I know she's helping you more there than she would be able to on Earth. But there's so much pain in her, the pain of love. She didn't have enough time in another life to express this love to the fullest and the highest."

Several days later, Claire wrote to me giving more details of her communication with Filipa. Her letter included a message which, she said, Filipa had asked her to pass on to me. It went like this:

> Remember our promise
> The eternal love that we promised each other
> The many times you whispered in my ears
> "I love you."
>
> Your eyes were full of fire
> Your love was very vibrant
> Your touch made my skin shiver
> And your arms gave me the comfort
> that I needed then,
> My eternal love.

Would my guide really have composed such awful poetry, I wondered? Perhaps...perhaps, Filipa *was* trying to contact me through the mediation of one who was psychically sensitive. On the heels of the poem, Claire presented me with a framed portrait of Filipa drawn by a psychic artist named Margaret who, she insisted, had not been told my guide's name. The picture showed a young woman with long black hair, dimpled cheeks, pursed lips and a broad nose. A message in brown chalk was scrawled across the top of the illustration. It read: "To Joe from Phillipa. You must accept what life gives you and know that love is all around you. I bring you love and healing. Think of me every morning and I shall help you overcome your daily problems."

In my heart, I knew the picture wasn't a likeness of Filipa and, consequently, I never hung it on my wall. The strange thing was, aside from the hair color, the drawing looked remarkably like Claire.

Meanwhile, time was running out. I was on the verge of leaving for a newly-purchased rural retreat some 180 miles from Toronto. I had told Claire that less than three weeks remained in which to conduct the all-important sessions with Dr. Pinkerton. In her letter, Claire brushed aside my concerns.

> I don't see this move as causing a problem because your Guide

definitely would like to communicate through me in regards to your book. However, if this is the will of God and Phillipa's choice, to communicate through me, I am willing to come to your new home to help you twice a month, if that is convenient for you. I know in my heart, as your Guide told me, that this book is very, very important for you. I chose to be a medium and [because] your Guide loves me and cares for me, I am very delighted to help you.

My next session with Dr. Pinkerton was held in the bedroom of my apartment, the room that provided most shade from the light of day. In accordance with the doctor's wishes, I closed the blinds to make the room as dark as possible and, for the sake of my notekeeping, equipped myself with a flashlight. As an afterthought, I poured a glass of port—the only liquor I possessed at the time—and placed it at Claire's side just before her identity was consumed by the trance state. When Dr. P.'s infirm yet commanding voice superseded the deep breathing of his instrument, I told him:

"Dr. Pinkerton, I have some port for you. I don't know whether you can drink it. I just thought that you might like to taste some."

"Are you teasing me, Son?"

"No. It's the real thing. I'm told that you like brandy. Port is the closest that I have."

"Do you like brandy?" he asked me.

"Yes, I like the occasional glass."

"And a good cigar?" He paused. "Well, well, well, is it testing time again, Joseph?"

I replied, reluctantly, in the affirmative.

"I'm quite stubborn, you know, when someone wants to test me."

Acknowledging this fact, I told him that I wished to know about Claire's alleged communication with my guide.

"One thing I must guarantee for this instrument of mine is that she never lies," said Dr. Pinkerton. "Secondly, she's quite concerned about her work and she needs a lot of answers for herself. More than you do, Joseph. If she tells you that she has been contacting your guide, I can assure you that she's telling you absolutely the truth."

At this juncture, Dr. Pinkerton announced that he had to leave his instrument because Claire wasn't letting go and relaxing in trance. "She's fighting me, Son. I think what she needs is a bit of confidence from you to make her relax a little more." He raised his glass of port and said, "Joseph, to you."

"And to you," I said. "Cheers! How does it taste?"

"It could pass. It's all right. It makes no difference for us." And with that he was gone.

Several hours later, when Claire slipped into trance for the second time that day, I told Dr. Pinkerton that he was known to Filipa by the name of Albert.

"And who's Miko?" he wanted to know.

Miko? Refusing to be drawn any further into a tangle of meaningless names, I asked him whether he had been known as Albert in one of his other incarnations.

"What else did she tell you about this Albert? Did she say anything about Barbara?"

"What does the name Albert mean to you?" I persisted.

"It's quite a nice name. Do you want to know whether it applies to myself?"

I confirmed that this was so.

"Perhaps."

"That's not much of an answer," I told him.

Dr. Pinkerton's response was to change the subject. With difficulty, I drew him back to the main thrust of my questioning to explain that Filipa had said he could prove his genuineness by one simple act, that is, by supplying my name when I last incarnated as a Greek.

"Mm-mmm. Your name? All right. First of all you had something else to ask about my instrument?"

He was as devious and as exasperating as he was endearing. And he had a knack of clambering into my personal attic of suppressed fears to see what he could find.

"There's quite a lot missing in your life, My Boy. What stops you? Your fears? When are you going to get rid of them? What do you fear the most, Joseph?"

He would tell me to let go, relax, and tune in to my inner self.

"Did you ever ask Joseph if he likes Joseph? Did you ask him, did you ask Joseph? Did you ever go in front of a mirror and look at Joseph and say, 'I really love you, Joseph. You're the greatest man in the world,' Did you ever....?"

As valid as Dr. Pinkerton's psychological insights undoubtedly were, they seemed to be thrown at me as a tactic of diversion. I knew I had to keep the evasive surgeon on the topic and did my best to do so without resorting to rudeness.

"All I need to hear," I told him, "is one shred of information that I've learned from my own guide to know, truly, that you are in touch with her."

"And I did not give you any reason at all in the last sitting that you and I had together that I have contacted your guide or her light?"

"You said that she gave you the initial P, and that makes sense but...."

"Well, well, well, well, well. You're talking to a very stubborn spirit here."

"What reason do you have to be stubborn?"

"Because I like you, Joseph. I want you to trust us a little more. And because I have a lot of proofs to bring you, but only in my divine time, if you stop pushing me.... I don't want to be like the others, Son. I want to bring you true facts. You're going to have to be patient."

Once again, I steered the conversation back to the subject of Albert and told Dr. Pinkerton a second time that my guide knew him by that name.

"Didn't she tell you what relation we had?"

"No."

"Why not?"

"I don't know," I told him. I was getting more and more frustrated. "We're in the dark in this world of ours, and you have all the cards in your hands."

"There's certain information that sometimes we don't like to bring through, Joseph. We don't want to be reminded of certain things. It can be quite painful. So, if I am being a little stubborn about this Albert, it's because I have my own reasons."

"So he was an incarnation of yours?"

"Indeed."

"Can you tell me anything about him?"

"It's quite painful. That is why I cannot see the light of Filipa. Because when we open that book, Son, there is pain. And I do not wish, right now, to talk about it."

Without any fanfare or coercion, Dr. Pinkerton had mentioned Filipa by name. But there was no time to savor the moment. To my surprise and consternation, Dr. P. was breaking into muted sobbing.

"All right.... You must forgive me. I'm quite sensitive too, you know. I'm quite sure that you also have feelings and pain from the past, perhaps, those sad times—" He sighed bitterly, "—and if I would talk about this now I would definitely leave that sorrow with my instrument."

I had no option but to change the subject. Dr. Pinkerton's earlier promise that Filipa would speak through his instrument was postponed to another time and the session was brought to a close with a stream of endearments.

"I truly love you, Joseph. I have my reasons to love you. You are very special to me. And don't ask how much. Perhaps one day you will find out the love that I have for you, Young Man. There is no ending...."

I did not want to discount Dr. Pinkerton. Personally, I found him charming, entertaining, and quite likeable, despite his elusiveness. I felt there was a chance that he was authentic and that there might be sound reasons for his reluctance to declare himself. But I was disconcerted by—and mistrustful of—his lavish show of affection towards myself, Filipa and especially Claire, whose unimpeachable character and unconditionally loving heart were mentioned at every opportunity. I believed Claire when she said that she had no conscious knowledge or recall of her trance state, but I wondered whether she had any unconscious stake in the proceedings. I could not help wondering, too, whether Dr. Pinkerton had named Filipa because I had disclosed her identity to Claire.

In the next three sessions, my shaky faith in Dr. Pinkerton was taxed to the limit. While failing to supply my Greek name and to bring Filipa through his instrument as promised, he told me that Claire—who was said to be enjoying her final incarnation—would be my guide when I next reincarnated in company with Filipa. Further, I was informed that Claire had been brought into my life as a forthcoming substitute for Aviva who, said Dr. P., "will have to come to my world one of these days."

Dr. Pinkerton leaned forward. The wise physician's voice grew even more benevolent than usual, as if he were prescribing a healthful practice for a favored patient.

"Filipa's got so much to give," he said, "and when there's a female vibration that is sincere around you, she trusts that vibration and she feels the same as if she's touching you, Son. Especially through a medium. Making love to a medium who pours out love. It is a wonderful, wonderful journey."

At first, I couldn't believe my ears. Was he really suggesting that Claire and I become sexually involved? In the long pause of disbelief that followed, I stared at the unsighted blonde "instrument" while my ears buzzed like a swarming hive.

The session resumed when Dr. P. announced that, having shared several incarnations with him, I had intended to become his son back in Victorian times.

"What happened, here is…you changed your mind at the last moment. You were supposed to be my son. We had plans, As you know, we choose to do what we want when we come to the Earth plane, who to become, a doctor or a bum…and you were to become a doctor, just like myself. And my name was supposed to be Albert."

"Your name was supposed to be *Albert?*"

"Was supposed to be. And you were supposed to be Albert junior. But you chose to remain in the spirit world." He smacked his lips loudly. "So, we link once again here."

In conclusion, he said: "When I tell you all you want to know about Albert and all you want to know about Madame P., you will be touched. You'd better have a box of Kleenex with you because I know you're going to be needing them."

What I needed more than anything was Filipa's counsel. But Aviva was still far away in Australia and so instead I discussed Dr. Pinkerton with one or two friends. One of them, Alexander Blair-Ewart, the publisher of Toronto's New Age monthly periodical, *Dimensions,* whose metaphysical learning I respected, had already expressed his uneasiness over my communication with the guides. But then he hadn't experienced Filipa's love and concern and, accordingly, I forgave his cautionary stance. We were eating a meal together in Toronto's Chinatown when I told him about Dr. Pinkerton being fond of a good cigar and having taken a sip or two of my port. Alexander reacted with undisguised alarm.

"You say he lived in Sicily?" he said. "Don't you know that Sicily is one of the homes of black magic? One day, Joe, I trust you'll get beyond these so-called guides. Spirits like Pinkerton get a rush by swooping into a body and gratifying themselves with the sensations of physical life—sensations such as drinking alcohol, for example, This is contrary to the teachings of all the great spiritual masters. This is forbidden. This is possession, not true spirituality."

Although I was by no means convinced by Alexander's argument, I raised the issue with Dr. Pinkerton.

"Mm- mmm," murmured Dr. P. "Did I ever smoke a cigar?"

"Not yet. I was thinking about lighting one up for you."

"I would not have accepted it, Son. Did I have the drink?"

"Very little."

"I wanted to prove to you that this is how I greet my instrument when she comes to my world—with a glass in my hand. It reflects my thoughts, you understand. I would not ever drink the whole glass or ever smoke a cigar. Are you sure this young man knows what he's doing? I do not want to end up in a dark corner, Son."

"But this craving for physical sensation is felt by some discarnates, is it not?" I demanded.

"Yes, indeed. They get very possessive and...Let me tell you something else, My Dear. If you've noticed, I do not take her over unless she calls upon me. That's an agreement we had from the beginning and I will stick to it. If I was truly possessive I would take her over at any time. You spend enough time with this young lady to realize that I am telling you the truth....In the name of love, in the name of Christ, she calls me from the pure light."

According to Dr. P., Filipa was "hiding" and yet she was buzzing my ears whenever I consulted him and I longed to be able to discuss with her the host of peculiar claims. Mercifully, Aviva returned at last from Australia and I sat earnestly by her side as Roger eased her into trance. As usual, Filipa knew my concerns before I gave voice to them. Her first words confirmed my worst fears:

"Albert does not talking into her."

"Then what is going on, *Laluda?*"

The answer I received was that Dr. Pinkerton was merely one of Claire's many past-life personalities. Albert, her guide, had no input whatsoever. Filipa explained:

> This is someone [Claire] who can call other existences to mind with much readiness....This person [Pinkerton] was she. Very, I would say, flamboyant in making of self-importance....This Dr. Pinkerton I believe not to have been a real doctor, but one who established himself as such, treating people when he had little formally in education. He was someone who was eager for others to adore him. He craving respectability. This does not change. This personality is still there. Because you have gone on to another life does not change what your past life was. What she is doing is using another, whom she was at that time, to deliver messages of his intent....It is easy to do this...any time you wishing to satisfy for *drachma*.

I told Filipa that I had been concerned about Dr. Pinkerton's evasiveness.

> When they cannot answering, they will do this. But when they are seizing on something they will take it and go as far as they can. In that state, prediction is very easy and can make them seem very powerful.

Filipa denied having had any communication with Claire. She said that she had not visited her in her dreams and meditations and had not made contact with the psychic artist who claimed to have tuned in to her vibrations in order to execute her portrait.

"You must telling me of it, Gideon," she said, when I mentioned the picture. My description of the illustration and reading of the accompanying message evoked a response of gentle derision.

"This sounding like all Greek girls, but not sounding like me," she said. "And I would never call you...*Joe*."

"And what does Albert have to say about all this?" I asked.

"He does not saying much. It is her [Claire] that wishes to be doing this. In time, she will go into transition and be shown what she has done and will making her plans for the next life."

When Claire next visited me, I played her the tape of my conversation with Filipa. She listened in silence, raising no protest, even when the tape recorder fell silent. "I want to talk to this Albert," was all she said. Claire had come to believe in Filipa as much as in Dr. Pinkerton and I knew that she was mortified by what she had heard. Without saying another word, she tossed her long hair over her shoulder, climbed into her car and wept. Later, I learned that she had cancelled Dr. Pinkerton's appointments for several weeks to come.

CHAPTER 14

Dressing for Yesterday

The unmasking of Dr. Pinkerton brought Filipa and myself even closer together. Experience had shown our relationship to be sturdy, well-founded, and divorced from the apparently widespread dissemblance in the world of channeling at large. In three years of communication we had come to know and trust one another. Now the time was fast approaching when I would travel to Greece to dispel any lingering twinges of uncertainty about Filipa's identity.

Plans for my pilgrimage to the past had been gathering momentum. Countless times, I anticipated the thrill of walking down the main street of the remote village where Filipa and I had lived and loved more than two hundred years ago. My musings revolved around a precise image of the little place…a cluster of shuttered and whitewashed houses in various stages of disrepair, flanking a curve of wide, slabbed steps. I visualized a pastoral assembly of inhabitants—men leading donkeys laden with panniers of olives or bundles of sticks, women in shawls, ragged children with smudged faces, scrawny dogs with haunted eyes and goats whose necks were strung with tinny bells that echoed against the walls. The village would be hot and dry and dusty, thriving early in the morning and settling into somnolence at twilight.

Filipa had told me that Theros (which means "harvest" in Greek) was, in the eighteenth century, a tiny community nestling in mountainous terrain in the region of Thrace, which extends to the Turkish border. The village was inhabited by about one hundred people and at its center stood a church—big enough to hold half that number—named after the Emperor Constantine. In vain, I had looked for Theros in a Greek gazetteer which listed even the smallest communities. Yet this was no reason to be disappointed. Thrace had endured centuries of guerilla warfare with the Turks and, since Filipa's death in 1771, there was every chance that the village had been either destroyed or had undergone a change of name. It was even conceivable that the village had been razed to the ground *after* having its name changed. The Greek Tourist Board in Toronto confirmed that, in the wake of Turkish occupation, there had been widespread re-naming of settlements in the region.

Nevertheless, the place must still be there, I told myself, even though it might be a heap of rubble. And, with luck, I would stand once again in "our spot," the hideaway near the river where Filipa and I had held our trysts. As Filipa had said, "We would walk away from the village, going in the morning with the sun to our right. It was rocky. It was much scrubberies. Not very beautiful, but for us it was beautiful. You would sing eight or nine soldiering songs and we would be there."

"So it was quite close to Theros?"

"On thinking about it now, it was too close. We were seen too much by others. It is not possible, in small places, to be discreet sometimes."

The ultimate test was drawing closer. If Filipa could succeed where Ernest and the discarnate communicators of five other mediums had failed, then all doubt would be erased. My love, my intuitive belief and my intellectual appreciation would be fused in delicious certainty.

My preparatory efforts for the trip to Europe were redoubled now that I had withdrawn from the discouraging exercise of seeking evidential testimony from other channeled voices. Before leaving, I needed as much detail as possible about my former home in the mountains and I encouraged Filipa to pass on everything she knew in the course of several private sessions at Aviva's house. I obtained a serviceable map of north-eastern Greece and, at the next session, unfolded the map beside Aviva as she was being talked into unconsciousness. After exchanging with Filipa our customary greeting of *Yassoo,* I asked her to describe any landmark that might be close to the village.

"There was a big or tall place called *See-Oh, Shee-Oh*. I am not of spelling so very well. It was the tallest place. It's not far from Komotini."

Komotini was clearly marked on the map, a provincial town in western Thrace.

"Which direction from Komotini is Theros?"

"In the morning you would walk to Komotini and the sun would be at your back. In the afternoon, it would be in your face."

Meaning, of course, that Theros was east of Komotini.

"And this tall place is near Theros?" I asked her.

"It is one-half day in walking from the village. It is rocky with tangly but not tall trees."

Poring over the map, I started calling out place names between Komotini and the Turkish border, which was said to be three days' walk from Theros. I was counting on happening upon something familiar to Filipa.

"Ariana?"

"No."

"Souflion? Sapai?"

"No."

Then I spotted a name that made me yelp with excitement.

"Did you say the name of that height was Silo?"

"Yes."

"Then I've found it! It's a mountain and, according to this map, it's 3,494 feet high....What about Aisimi?"

"*Aisimi?*" Filipa's pronunciation was quite different from mine and redolent with recognition. "That I can remember. It was two, maybe three, days away."

"What about Kirki? Or Nipsa?"

"Those are going in the wrong way."

I was closing in on Theros, like a hunter who had chased his quarry into a confined area. I was gratified—and not a little stimulated—to have found Silo, or "*Shee Oh*" as Filipa pronounced it. What I needed now was a large-scale map showing every nook and cranny of the landscape around that mountain. At the University of Toronto map library I found exactly what I was looking for—a map produced by the British War Office in 1944, scale 1:100,000. The density of contour lines and the paucity of place names confirmed what Filipa had already told me, that the landscape was sparsely inhabited and riven with ridges and valleys.

There was no place called Theros but there was a village called Kotronia in roughly the position where Theros should have been. It was hard to measure a half-day's walk simply by looking at a map of exceedingly steep and alien territory. Also, a half-day's walk was not a morning's excursion, as I had supposed. Filipa insisted that a half-day's walk lasted roughly from sunrise to sunset. In those mountains, with no knowledge of the Greek language, it was not going to be easy. But Filipa urged me on:

> My village will still be there. There is much pavement of stones in the town, all made to go together so that people could walk easily, and animals could be made to go down the streets easily to go to the fields, and soldiers, like you, could march and took beautiful. And there were places of eating. And you would sit sometimes inside if it was not very pleasant and outside if it was warm....We were an agricultural village. Prosperous enough, but there were many who went to war....I can only suppose it is still the same. There are different dialects, almost, for each village....If we were to travel to a large city very far from our village we could not understand them very well. They could not understand us very well. We would speak very slowly, draw lots of pictures, wave our hands....It takes much time to go from one place to another, so many people just stayed for all their lives in one place, never seeing others than those who came through bringing spices and foods and fine materials and not-so-fine materials. While we were some distance from the trade route, we would be influenced by the travelers, for they would spend night lodgings in Theros. Mostly, people were born, they grew up and they died right in Theros. They never went outside except to the soil.

"Were there records kept of people who lived there?" I asked.

"I'm not sure I'm understanding."

"Now, when you are born, a record is made. Your name is written down and it is kept permanently. And when you die, there is also a record."

"There was nothing of this. If people dying they would be taken down to the valley and made in the earth."

"What was the name of the river?"

"It was small, very small. *Tik-ay-on*. This is where the creek or small stream would finish."

Filipa spoke of having once walked for several days to visit Alexandroupolis, the port city to the south where, in awe, she had watched the "big, big, floating housings." But she hadn't heard of Kotronia, which, I thought, could possibly be Theros under a new name. When officials at Toronto's Greek Consulate were unable to trace whether Kotronia had been re-named, I was even more determined to travel to the area and ask my own questions of the local inhabitants. First, however, I wanted Filipa to speak "our language" into the tape recorder. Eager to discover whether the Greeks of Thrace understood her, I asked for a description of the walk from Theros to "our spot" in her native tongue.

"This is hard," she replied sadly. "That would not be fair. Thinking of this is very...difficult. I would rather thinking of happier things."

"Could you talk about something else in Greek?"

"I am wondering if some of our families would still be in Theros..." These words led into several sentences of guttural Greek, at least it *sounded* like Greek, a language that was incomprehensible to Aviva who had never set foot in Greece. "There," Filipa said at last. "I think that would be very nice if you could find relatives that are still living there. They would be knowing right away."

"From what you've just said?"

"Yes. You know that this is how we were speaking where we come from...."

"This is our dialect."

"And I know that in Komotini they speak very differently."

I soon learned that modern Greeks, especially modern Greeks from Athens, speak very differently, too. I took the tape to the home of Athenian Pedros Benekos, an officer of the Greek Consulate in Toronto. He and his Greek wife, Nota, listened over and over again to Filipa's linguistics before saying that Filipa sounded like a native Greek who was splicing their tongue with words from another language, or maybe two other languages, to form a local dialect. They were able to translate only brief snatches of what she had to say. When I told Filipa of their confusion, she bristled defensively, especially upon learning that Benekos hailed from Athens.

"I would never understand someone of such pomposity," she said. "Peopling in these big cities are always thinking that they know everything that is good for us in the villages. They know nothing of growing. If not for us, they would starving. They cannot telling us how we must speakly—we communicate enough to make children."

"But do you happen to know what other languages are mixed in with your dialect?" I inquired.

"It was our language," was all Filipa would say. "It was Hellenica. Hellenica is Hellenica. There will always be some wordlies that are the same. I going to Alexandroupolis, I not hearing hardly any wordings that I can understand. I going to Theros, I hear and understand it all."

Filipa reminded me that in returning to our homeland I would be revisiting the scenes of much fighting with the Turkish foe. "You must be mindful," she said, "of those who were your enemies." She recalled how the Turks strove unceasingly for religious conversion ("Always there was someone trying to make follow Allah") and how the Greek soldiers would conceal themselves in the hills and in the isolated villages, such as Theros, and conduct rearguard action in the form of surprise raids. "The Saracens would come in the main roads. They could not find the Hellenic armies hiding in towns like ours . . . and then you would go and hunt them away."

Filipa was confident that I would find Theros once I made my way into the neighborhood of Mount Silo. In my mind, I was there already. I could hardly wait to walk on Greek soil.

"Your feet will be taking you right there, Gideon. When you are in our village you will sit and I will be sitting with you. Maybe we can laugh together or cry together."

As for locating "our spot," Filipa was certain I would be drawn to the location. Once there, I would know exactly where to place my feet. "*You will feel it,*" she whispered, her voice trembling with emotion.

"I am hoping," Filipa said wistfully, "that it is all just the same."

* * *

On my way to Greece, I planned a stopover in England in order to investigate Russell's previous incarnation. My file on Russell's last life was already well stocked with information from a lengthy question-and-answer session conducted earlier. Born in Harrogate, Yorkshire, he had grown up to become "a dashing young man," a farmer who tended a flock of thirty to fifty sheep and "other sustaining animals" on twenty-five acres of land in the Yorkshire Dales. His property, he said, was bordered on the north side by a stream called the Burn Gill which ran into the River Nidderdale (pronounced "Nitherdale" by Russell). In fact, his farm was situated in the crook of land shaped by the confluence of the two watercourses. On this farm called Hetherington, Russell and his wife, Mary, had raised a family of three children. A fourth child had died as a tiny infant.

Heatherfield was said to be the name of the closest village. "There is only one street. There is only one church, five houses surrounded by farms, the Black Lion, and that is all." Harrogate, the nearest town, was "a good day's ride or a little over a day with the carriage." Russell would also travel to Skipton, a little farther afield, where he would purchase dry goods and fruit and vegetables "when they were available." Wool and meat merchants journeyed to Hetherington Farm twice-yearly from the city of York and, on one occasion, from Cumbria on the far side of the Pennine hills.

Russell told of landmarks in the area—a prominent ridge called Great Whernside (which he pronounced Great Wernsey) and a Druid's Temple, made of stone, which was half a day's ride north-east of his farm.

> We used to call it the Druid's Place. That is all it was ever called by any of the locals. The children would like to go there and play, though it was a little far for them. At the time, there was a great deal of suspicion and superstition around that area and children were not encouraged to go out there very often, if at all. I would try to discourage mine from going there, just as others would. It was said that if children were left there unattended then evil things would happen to them. Of course, we know now that that is not so.

The farm north of Hetherington was called The Glen and owned by Walter Smyth. ("I may not have been able to read and write," said Russell, "but I do remember he spelled his name with a 'Y'.") To the south, closer to the town of Pateley Bridge, lived Angus Fellows who fell from his horse and died a lingering death seven years before Russell himself passed away. Russell's death, which he did not want to discuss, was brought on by consumption combined with chest diseases and a minor farming accident. The accident caused him to be "confined to my cot," as he put it. As his condition worsened, he was carried into Heatherfield for medical help, death taking hold after he was laid on the floor of St Mary's Church.

I was intrigued that Russell was reluctant to talk about his death. Filipa, too, had shied away from discussion when I inquired about the manner of her passing. Knowing that they were immortal, why were the guides so touchy about death? Russell answered my question with a trace of irascibility:

> It's not being touchy about death. We function now, as you have done, always looking towards the future and always working uninterruptedly with our charges. When anyone speaks of a highly emotional earthbound event—and death is usually *the* most emotional earthbound event you'll ever discuss—it can actually distract us.... Filipa and I would not want our charges for one moment not to have absolute vigilance on their side. We must maintain objectivity of a fashion with our charges and anything that can blindly lead us from that or distract our energies for one moment from any charge, well, that is not right. You may be sitting quite comfortably in one room. Other charges are not; other charges may be in danger. And so we will try at all costs to avoid any topic that has to do with a great deal of emotion.

I was very fond of Russell. In three years of conversations, he had become a good friend and I was almost as excited about searching for records of his life as I was at the prospect of re-experiencing the environs of my earlier incarnation with Filipa. Although he was often brusque and occasionally abrasive, Russell had a heart of gold and a wry sense of humor. I admired the no-nonsense way in which he handled the sessions and respected the tireless care and concern he showed for Aviva. And if I was still somewhat wary in the wake of the Ernest episode, he dispelled any lingering doubts by remarking in avuncular fashion: "I will attempt to provide you with a little more accurate information than Ernest did."

Following the same line of inquiry that I had taken with Filipa, I went searching for a detailed map of Russell's native Yorkshire and returned to Aviva's house with a one-inch-to-one-mile Ordnance Survey chart of the Pateley Bridge area. As expected, I located Great Whernside and the Druid's Temple. Then, closing in on Russell's home turf, I picked up the broad, meandering line of the River Nidd or Nidderdale and—there it was—a tiny squiggle identified as the Burn Gill running westwards from the Gouthwaite Reservoir, which had flooded a large section of the Nidderdale valley.

Russell said that it took about an hour and a half to ride from his farmhouse to the Burn Gill. "It's boggy. Very slow going. You would never want to try to walk over there." Heatherfield by horseback was said to be another ninety minutes in the opposite direction, I looked for Heatherfield on the map. South of the reservoir by a thumbnail was a tiny village called, not Heatherfield, but...Heathfield.

"I've found *Heathfield,*" I told Russell. "But not Heatherfield."

"My sons used to tell me that all the time," he replied. "I couldn't read—it sounded like Heatherfield to me. You look around when you get there and tell me that it isn't Heatherfield. It *looks* like a Heatherfield."

I mentioned that, when I had located Hetherington Farm, I planned to take photographs of the farmhouse so that members of the group could see for themselves exactly where he lived.

"Ahh, the magic lantern. My farmhouse would still be standing, would it?"

"I hope so."

"I hope so, too. I wonder if my wall is still there? A lot of toil and effort went into that wall. Yes, I spent a great deal of time in getting the stones and matching them and putting them around the property. I would hope my wall has lasted....The house itself was built on a base of stone."

"Was it a wooden house?"

"It was basically stone. There was wooden construction as part of it."

"How old was the house?"

"I would have believed it to have been at least fifty or sixty years old when I brought my bride to it."

When I reminded Russell that he had given 1852 as the date of his death, he moved to correct me.

"I think that's too soon."

"Why would you give 1852 if you weren't sure?" I asked.

"Dates, dates...the bane. Oh, the young queen was on the throne...." [Queen Victoria was crowned in 1837.] "Let me clarify something. I didn't bother bringing dates with me, not from any of my incarnations. I generalize, yes. I have to. But dates are not important. They're of no value to me. They're of no value to you either. You are also one who discards them completely. All I can tell you is that I believe that I was around forty-eight to fifty-two years of age. That I *do* know. I was beginning to feel a little under the labors of that....Probably, though I couldn't swear—I could nithee swear—my death would have occurred around the early 1870s. Oh, days, weeks, dates...." (Interestingly enough, in the earliest days of communication, before Russell spoke with his own voice, the alter-consciousness had relayed Russell's dates as 1823–1871.)

Russell went on to explain that, although his name was Parnick, he might appear in the records under either Nichols or Parr because his name had been formed by fusing his father's surname, Nichols, with Parr, the surname of his mother. "She and father decided that the children should have both names. I'm a Parnick, as far as I'm concerned."

"But at your death, would you be known in the records as Russell Nichols or Russell Parnick?"

"That I don't know. I'm sorry, but I didn't get to read the certificate. I couldn't read anyway. I never did learn. We never got a lot of schooling, you see. There were schools—Yorkshire had very good schools—but not for the children who were not of the town."

"You were buried at St Mary's, Heathfield were you? In the churchyard there?"

"Well, providing the churchyard is still there, I certainly hope that I am."

As an afterthought, I felt that Russell should know about the reservoir that had been constructed in the Nidderdale valley. In fact, the Burn Gill now ran into the reservoir rather than the River Nidd. Russell was shocked to hear of such a thing.

"Really!" he exclaimed. "You mean, they've backed it up?"

"They've filled it up with water," I said. "There's a lake there now. Not for the entire length of the river. The river still goes...."

"How big is the lake?" Russell interrupted.

"I would say it is about two miles long, judging from the map."

"And how wide?"

"About half a mile wide."

"It wouldn't have taken my house, would it? And my wall?"

"How close were you to the Nidderdale?"

"We were a lot closer to the Nidderdale than to the Burn Gill. No! They couldn't have...they wouldn't have. We were too high. There were a lot of hills."

"If you were south of the Burn Gill, then it certainly wouldn't have affected your farmhouse," I assured him.

"Well, let us hope not. Why did they do that? There's enough water. It's always very wet."

The thought of a massive reservoir so close to his old homestead left Russell clearly unsettled and I apologized for having caused him distress. He dismissed my regrets as if he had not heard them, giving me leave to return to the question of the church in Heathfield. On closer examination of the ordnance survey map, I noticed that the village was not marked with the usual symbol denoting a church. So I asked Russell again:

"Are you sure the church was in Heathfield?"

"Yes."

"So it's probably still there."

"And there should be a graveyard too—unless they've put that under water with the Nidderdale."

* * *

Miraculously, Aviva seemed to be overcoming her leukemia. With each passing week, she was looking increasingly robust. This delighted me but I also found it surprising, if only because Sandford's withdrawal meant that she had not undergone a healing session in well over two months. Aviva herself was counting on having entered remission, hoping beyond hope that it would last. When I next spoke to Russell, she was looking particularly healthy. I commented on her rejuvenated appearance.

"Yes," he said, matter-of-factly. "She's done very well. I think we've certainly broken the back of the difficulties."

Having booked my flight to England, I was able to confirm that I would be heading for Yorkshire the following month.

"What month would that be?"

"July."

"Oh good! You're not going to get bogged down then."

Russell made frequent references to the wet and boggy conditions of his home pasture. Mud and ooze had had to be confronted, it seemed, every time he set out for either Harrogate or Skipton. I asked him for the names of traders he had dealt with in both towns.

"There's only one place worth frequenting in Harrogate," he said.

"What was that?"

"The Black Lion."

"There was a Black Lion in Harrogate as well as in Heathfield then?"

"Heatherfield didn't have a Black Lion. That was in Harrogate."

"You told me before that Heathfield had a Black Lion."

"There was an establishment for the consumption of comestibles of beverage nature."

"What was its name?"

"Yes, you're quite right in that we often referred to it as the Black Lion—more for its manager than anything else. But the Black Lion in Harrogate was the largest establishment of its kind within the part of the realm in which we lived....It was a rather remarkably wonderful place to frequent when one had the luxury of time, and the weather be willing and the plowing be done. It was a most relaxing place."

Russell had already mentioned that "the Herrons" ran a dry goods shop in Skipton. I pushed for the names of other merchants with whom he had dealings, in either Skipton or Harrogate.

"Oh, of course, in Skipton there was that Scottish couple, wasn't there? The MacDonalds. They were there for a while."

"What kind of store did they have?"

"Actually, their kind of establishment was prepared meats. There would be some that would make sale of their meats to the MacDonalds. However, most of us preferred to deal with the Yorkshiremen. There was, oh yes...."

"Is it coming back a little?"

"Oh, it doesn't have to come back. I'm trying to come up with the important ones that might have established an ongoing lineage that you could trace."

"Any merchants should be in the record books," I said.

"Oh yes. Undoubtedly. Of course, there was the Fells."

"What did they do?"

"They constructed farm equipment that you would need. Wooden farm equipment. We relied on them for such as handles for perhaps axes and things that might have broken. They would manufacture these. They would have the wood and carve it for you and it was all very nicely done. Skipton wasn't very big, you know.... There was a family in Harrogate that you might still find in the books. Their name was Taylor and they had a shop where women could purchase all manner of things that women liked...bolts of cloth, bonnets, unmentionables, this type of thing. Now they were quite large. I would imagine that the Taylor family has gone on to bigger and better things."

I told Russell that I had a friend who hailed from Bingley in Yorkshire.

"Now you have mentioned to us that it takes only a short while to go from one end of Great Britain to the other. And if I said to you that Bingley were quite an adventure you'd laugh, so I won't."

Assuring Russell that I would try to suppress my mirth, I offered him my thanks for the wealth of information and bade him farewell.

Harry Maddox had already provided some basic facts about his short-lived existence during World War I. As well as travelling to the Yorkshire Dales, I intended to search the Royal Corps of Engineers' records of war dead for confirmation of the Cockney humorist. Indeed, I was now ready to explore bygone eras in England and in Greece and would have left for Europe earlier than July had I not postponed my flight on the advice of Dr. Pinkerton. Before Filipa had exposed his unworthiness, I had bowed to his interpretation of a dream.

The dream was Claire Laforgia's. Early in June, two weeks before I originally planned to leave for Europe, Claire arrived at my country home to tell me that both she and a friend had had the same dream on the same night. More a nightmare than a dream, it was set in a warm European country and I was the central character. Apparently, I was seen remonstrating with a woman in her early sixties who was dressed in black. The argument had followed the woman's refusal to accede to my request for information and I was later seen walking along a beach in company with another individual. Once the companion had left my side, I was approached by five men who proceeded to attack me. They left me lying in the sand, face down. Claire said that both she and her friend had been awakened by the violence of the images.

At my request, Claire had entered trance so that I might consult Dr. Pinkerton on the matter. I had drawn the curtains, but the afternoon was bright and Dr. P. lasted for only a few minutes in the shade of such a flimsy veil. When evening came we tried again.

"Are you upset, Son?" he inquired in his infirm and reedy voice. "Joseph, do you have fears in yourself...?"

He asked for details of the dream and asked, also, that I supply him with the itinerary of my upcoming trip. I told him that I would be travelling to England, then Greece and, if time allowed, Sicily—all in quest of past-life information.

"Are you going to be asking questions, Son? To whom, for example?"

Anyone, I explained, who could provide information on the lives of Russell, Filipa, Harry and himself.

"Joseph, are you sure you want to go on this journey now?"

"I feel it's important for my work."

"You could not postpone it, could you?"

"It *could* be postponed."

"From what I have researched here, these people [in the Greek village] will not be able to tell you much. They will be quite frightened of you, My Dear. They will probably think, some of them, that there's definitely something wrong with you mentally. Or they would see you as a witch doctor....There's going to be a couple of people there who will start problems for you, Son. There could be a chance, indeed, that they will come after you, thinking that you were practicing witchcraft. They are quite ignorant, do you understand me?"

"This is going to happen *whenever* I go there?" I asked.

Dr. P. was spooking me. Although I did not care to admit it, I was afraid of him. And, if I was not mistaken, he was a little frightened of me, too.

"There's one lady there," he went on. "She's in her late eighties and she's quite a troublemaker.... She is like a princess in that little town. Everybody listens to this individual. I'm going to be quite honest with you. In exactly five weeks she will be here with us and things will be better, Son. I'm not saying to you not to go at all. Just wait a little longer. If you want to go on the 24th., then go right ahead and do it....You have a choice.... But they say here that there is a strong possibility that it could happen exactly like the dream, My Dear. This means that, to shield you, Son, we must do extra work around these people in the village. Are you disappointed, My Dear? You might encounter a lot of disappointments, you know."

I told Dr. Pinkerton that I doubted very much whether the Greek village I was heading for would hold records from the eighteenth century. "It's not England, after all," I added. "It's a backward part of the world."

"What makes you so sure that they have the records in England, Son? Let me tell you, Joseph, if I could see that any harm could come to you that would leave you on the ground like you've told me, I would say 'No, Joseph, don't go at all.' I'm saying postpone the trip for a short while."

"OK. " I said. "I'll postpone the trip."

"It would be wise."

"Are you picking up a name for this village, incidentally?"

"Don't rush me, Joseph. Do you have another question in the meantime?"

It was only a few days later that Filipa informed me that Dr. Pinkerton was merely Claire's past-life personality and not a guide at all. But the decision to postpone had been made, the travel itinerary re-booked, and I made ready for a July departure. Filipa was amused by Dr. P's description of the elderly Greek "princess" holding power in the village and scoffed at the idea of a sandy beach near Theros. She had this to say about the doctor's observations:

> In Hellenic villages women have no power of such kind nor did we ever have power of kind, only of children. Always the men were the heads of villages....I would not consider anyone in black to be disturbing for all women in Hellenica are wearing black once they are no longer husbanded. And there is not anything beachy near to Theros. It is a long way from Alexandroupolis or the Black Sea or any placing where there is beaches. Much walking. Much, much walking.

So much for Dr. Pinkerton and so much for the nightmare. But there was another nightmare to come in which, again, I was the central character. Had I known of it at the time, I would have found its dreadful image infinitely more disturbing, especially as the dreamer was a stranger to me. She was a patient of Dr. Joel Whitton and knew only that I had written *Life Between Life* in partnership with her psychiatrist. Dr. Whitton had never spoken of me to her and she had no idea that I had a Greek guide, much less that I was about to leave for Greece in search of evidence of that guide's former incarnation.

Nevertheless, only a few days before I set off for Europe, she dreamed of me in Greece in times gone by. More specifically, she dreamed that I was arguing with my lover, a woman dressed in period costume. Then she was startled into wakefulness by the violent act that followed. In horror, she watched my lover plunge a long-bladed knife into my back.

By the time Dr. Whitton learned of the nightmare, I was already in England. Disturbed by what he considered to be its premonitory symbolism, he decided against telephoning me for fear of creating unnecessary alarm. Consequently, I traveled to Greece oblivious of the dream and the implicit warning it contained.

Another warning did reach my ears, however, a warning which instilled plenty of misgiving about my forthcoming journey. It so happened that I ran into Sandford Ellison at a house party only days before I left Toronto. He looked awful. Drawn and defeated, he exhibited all the signs of physical and emotional exhaustion. I was not inclined to spend much time in Sandford's company because Russell had left us in little doubt about his regressive behavior. Besides, the party's hubbub forbade serious discussion. But one comment made during our brief chat was to remain with me all the way to Greece and back again:

"Any time you are ready to hear about the other side of the guides," Sandford said, somewhat cryptically, "I'll be glad to tell you all I know."

CHAPTER 15

Misadventure

St Catherine's House in London was packed with genealogical detectives—lawyers, amateur historians, family tree researchers, executors, students, and people of all ages and intentions in quest of their own or someone else's ancestry. The summer holidays meant that the ranks of the inquisitive were more swollen than usual and I was soon in the thick of elbows and briefcases, jostle and intensity. All around me, above the din of conversation and the sound of fingers and thumbs flipping through days, weeks and months of births, marriages and deaths, I could hear the *thump-thump* of heavy registers as they landed on the desk space between the shelves.

William Harry Maddox (with an X, he had stipulated) was on my mind. Of the three guides who now commanded my research interest, he was the most recently incarnate and, theoretically, the easiest to locate. I squeezed my way through the crowd in search of the ledgers for 1917, the year he was killed. Harry had given 17 August as his date of death but on another occasion had expressed the possibility that he might have died in October. Such a minor variation was unlikely to pose any difficulties, however. August to October inclusively could be scanned within a few minutes.

I retrieved the several volumes which bore the dead of 1917 and the births for 1895, the year Harry said he had appeared in the world. First, I made directly for the dates Harry had given. To my disappointment, there were no listings in his name and so I expanded the search progressively until all four quarters of 1895 and 1917 had been scrutinized. Still nothing. My stomach clenched in remembrance of Ernest and, fighting off frustration and anxiety, I turned to consult the *Wartime Directory of Deaths, Other Ranks, 1904-1920*. William Harry Maddox was not there either.

I could hardly believe it. Harry, I protested inwardly, was so candid, so disarming, so lovable, so obviously a World War I veteran. How *could* he? Perhaps, I told myself hastily, he had ended up in a mass grave and his death had never been registered. But even if that were true, his birth should have been recorded.

I could feel my agitation growing and I knew that, no matter what the emotional cost, I must face the worst, the very worst, that these mute registers could throw at me. I pushed through the throng to the shelves which carried entries for the last century and pulled down volume after volume in search of confirmation of the death of Russell Parnick or Russell Nichols. 1870, 1871, 1872, 1873…the years fell to my fingers without yielding a glimmer of familiarity. The sheep farmer had said that he was nineteen years old at the time of his wedding and I looked all the way through 1842 and 1843 in the hope of finding a record of his marriage. Once more, my eyes searched in vain, and my innards screamed in protest.

Even now, although the thought suggested itself, I could not accept that Russell and Harry had deliberately misled me. Nevertheless, a chill passed over my heart as I walked out into the firm July sunshine. There was no telling how or what I was feeling as panic nipped at my heels all the way to the British Library, a short walk away. There, I filled out retrieval requests for London street directories dated around the time of World War I. I was searching for a record of Barfing Road, the street where Harry said he had lived in the slums of London's dockland. Nervously, I scanned alphabetical listings in three reference books—*The London County Council List of Streets and Places within the Administrative County of London* dated August, 1901, *Kelly's Street Directory of London, 1913* and *A Dictionary of London* pertaining to the city's streets and buildings, which was dated 1918. Barfing Road was nowhere to be found.

The records were incontrovertible, but still my mind ferreted for a loophole. Could it be that Harry had carelessly given us the street's nickname rather than the official version? Had he gone missing in action and been passed over by the army's amanuenses?

I traveled to Maidenhead, Berkshire to inquire of the Commonwealth War Graves Commission. A clerk made a note of Harry's particulars then left me waiting after saying it would take "about three minutes, hopefully" to find him in the records. Eight minutes later she returned empty-handed to declare that the Commission had no record of a William Harry Maddox. She said she had tried a number of options, all of which had drawn a blank. "If he died in Europe in World War I," she told me, "we would have him."

I was being forced to face up to the hard fact that Harry did not exist, at least not as William Harry Maddox. Yet his tale was not without a certain validity. A visit to the library of the Royal Corps of Engineers at Brompton Barracks in Chatham—where Harry's name was markedly absent from a volume entitled *Soldiers Who Died In The Great War 1914-19, Part 4: Corps Of The Royal Engineers*—revealed that there had been heavy fighting at Trones Wood between 1916 and 1918 in the battles of the Somme.

Furthermore, the Eighteenth Division, which Harry had named as his division, had captured Trones Wood in July, 1916, although the territory had later been surrendered to the advancing Germans. Without doubt, Royal Engineers lived and died at Trones Wood: a unit of the corps was attached to every brigade of every division in World War I. Today, a memorial obelisk to the men of the Eighteenth Division stands at Bois des Trones beside a healthy young forest bearing scant resemblance to the quagmire of mud and shattered trees known by the troops.

Harry's description of the perilous work of the "stringers" who laid cable from trench to trench was fact, not fiction. In a book titled *The Work of Royal Engineers In The European War 1914–19: The Signal Service (France)*, R.E. Priestley tells how by 1914 the buzzer telephone was essential to mobile signals operations and how brigade signal sections were issued with pack cable-laying apparatus. Priestley writes that, in the heat of battle,

> Almost always, by one means or another, signal touch would be kept. Runners, for instance, could always be found who would make the effort to cross the shell-swept, corpse-strewn barrage zone....Casualties amongst battalion signalers and runners were normally heavy and at times fifty per cent and over fell in a single battle....Ground lines, even if they escaped the enemy's shells, could not be expected to survive

the constant stream of walking wounded, reinforcements, orderlies, limbered wagons, stretcher bearers and other miscellaneous traffic. A well-worn track appeared at once and momentarily expanded in width. Along this, feet and wheels would rapidly trample and churn out of existence the strongest cable.

Driving north up the Ml motorway to Yorkshire, I felt confused and apprehensive. The unsuccessful search for Harry and the failure of preliminary inquiries into Russell's past had revived unpleasant memories of Ernest and left me distrustful and vexatious. I did not even want to think about my feelings for Filipa. Reluctant to confront my worst fears, I felt locked into an extended process of betrayal even as I hoped that everything would turn out all right, that there had been some colossal oversight on my part. In the meantime, I resolved to check against the records and registers every statement made by the guides that lent itself to verification. Flagging optimism notwithstanding, personal and professional curiosity demanded that the pathway I was treading be followed until the end.

After an overnight stay at the village of Lutterworth, close to the

Men of the Royal Engineers carry telephone cable along a dunkboard track in Flanders, 1917. Harry Maddox said of the task, "It was a bloody mess." (photo courtesy of the Imperial War Museum, London)

motorway, I arrived in Harrogate by lunchtime and headed directly for the reference room of the Harrogate Public Library. I was fortunate enough to find an Ordnance Survey map, drawn in 1850, of the area around Pateley Bridge and Heathfield. It was a magnificent map, six inches to the mile and crammed with detail—every field, trough, well and shed was marked and every farmhouse mentioned by name. Even sheepfolds were designated, an inclusion that confirmed sheep farming as the predominant farming activity.

The Nidderdale—unadulterated by the Gouthwaite Reservoir which was to be built towards the end of the century—curled fatly in a south-easterly direction, fed on a large S-bend by the slender Burn Gill. On land south of the confluence where I assumed Russell's farmhouse would be (though there was no hint of Hetherington Farm) stood Gouthwaite Hall, presumably the local landowner's mansion. Heathfield lay further south by a good six inches—a village conspicuously without a church.

I made a photocopy of the map, then sought out Yorkshire's commercial directories published during the middle of the last century. I looked in

The Gouthwaite Reservoir. In his former life, Russell Parnick claimed to be a sheep farmer near the area now covered by the reservoir. He was shocked to hear that the Nidderdale valley had a man-made lake. "They couldn't have...they wouldn't have," he protested. (photo by Joe Fisher)

vain for the Herrons, the MacDonalds and Harrogate's Black Lion public house. But I did find the Taylor family, whom Russell had said "brought in women's clothes," listed under the sub-heading "Milliners and Dress Makers" as "Taylor, Bessy, High Harrogate." I also found the Fells of Skipton—"Robert Fell, Lead Merchants"—a firm that Russell had said manufactured and repaired wooden farm equipment, such as axe handles. Later, in seeking further information concerning the 150-year-old family business that still exists today, I received a letter from director Harry Fell who noted: "It's not beyond the realms of possibility that we could have repaired wooden axe handles as I know we did have our own lathes, etc., but…our main industry was lead."

In late afternoon sunshine I drove deep into the Yorkshire Dales, past signs pointing to Fountains Abbey and Mother Shipton's Cave. The countryside was exquisitely beautiful. Sheep, lots of sheep, grazed on green hillsides and there was an abundance of old stone walls and old stone houses. Despite the cars, tractors and the occasional jet fighter screaming overhead, the prevailing mood was nineteenth-century pastoral. I shivered involuntarily as I drove into Pateley Bridge and turned left down the steep incline of the town's main street.

Had Russell, I longed to know, ridden his horse along this very thoroughfare 130 years earlier? He asserted and I dreamed that this was so. But something was dreadfully wrong and whatever it was checked my romanticism at every turn and forced me to consider other possibilities. Was Russell Parnick a name of convenience for a real historical individual who knew the area intimately? Or was Russell a complete impostor who was drawing on someone else's knowledge? It didn't make sense that Russell could be both brilliantly accurate and hopelessly wrong about historical and geographical information. The more I learned about the Nidderdale Valley, the more I was confronted with this maddening dilemma.

On a precipitous sidestreet across from the police station stood the Nidderdale Museum, a shrine of local history in glass cases. Owen Brown, the white-haired, bespectacled custodian, led me into a back room where he rummaged through the contents of an antiquated filing cabinet containing family records of the area. I supplied him with three names—Hetherington, Parnick and Nichols—but each one, in turn, failed to raise a reciprocal echo from the stacks of handwritten white cards. So I was referred to Eileen Burgess, a local historian with the Nidderdale Museum Society, who lived down the hill and around the corner.

Mrs. Burgess had been poring over family records from Pateley Bridge and district for the past five years, but she had never heard of a Parnick or a Nichols in the locality—or a Parr, for that matter. Hetherington Farm was entirely unfamiliar to her. Moreover, I was assured that there had never been a St Mary's Church in Heathfield, although in Pateley Bridge there was a St Mary's which had fallen into ruins. "The church was closed in 1826—and it was in a bad state of repair then," said Mrs. Burgess, who then recommended that I consult another local historian, 84-year-old Ginny Calvert. Ginny, I was told, had studied local history for fifty years and knew everything it was possible to know about the area in days gone by.

Next morning, I drove along narrow, winding country lanes and into the village of Heathfield. There was no St Mary's Church and no pub, but otherwise the village was as tiny and as unspoiled as Russell had described. Whatever the inconsistencies in Russell's story, it was exciting to be standing at the heart of the little settlement that had been discussed with such eagerness and intensity in Aviva's living room thousands of miles away. Birdsong and the *baa-ing* of sheep in the distance were the only sounds to be heard.

Not far from Heathfield I found Ginny Calvert and her little dog Judy in a secluded stone farmhouse called Low Wood. To reach the house I crossed a bridge beside the road and passed through four old wooden gates which had worn deep grooves in the stones that secured them. I skirted dilapidated, overgrown outbuildings and spied rabbits frolicking in the wet fields. Ginny, youthful and spry for her age, welcomed me inside and I made myself comfortable on a settle—a stout wooden seat from the last century—before beginning my interrogation about the enigmatic Russell Parnick. As I talked, Ginny walked over to a cabinet and pulled out a stack of papers which, she explained, were hand-copied registers of the district reaching back to the year 1551.

Ginny had never heard of the names Parnick, Nichols, Parr, Fellows or Smyth in the Heathfield area. But I was fascinated to learn that Russell's predilection for calling Heathfield Heatherfield could well have been rooted in reality. "Nobody called the village Heathfield," said Ginny in her broad Yorkshire accent. "It were '*Eerfield*." Later on, I was to discover that Heathfield had, in centuries past, been spelled Harefield and then Hearfield. And while there is no sign of a public house in Heathfield today and nobody living there had ever heard of such a thing, Ginny revealed that there was a pub in the village during the last century. The tavern had been situated in a house, run by a family called Moors, and named—in recognition of local lead mining—the Smelter's Arms. In the 1880s, said Ginny, the pub had been closed by the Methodists.

High above Heathfield, at the end of a steep, uneven road, I found farmer Ned Simpson standing, windswept, in relief against a glorious panorama of the Dales. He, too, looked blank when I recited the litany of supposedly local surnames and gave me a quizzical glance when I told him that my research subject used to ride for about an hour and a half from Heathfield in order to reach his farm, which backed on to the Burn Gill.

"But it's only half an hour's walk from the village to the Burn Gill," he said. That remark sent me back to the detailed Ordnance Survey map of the area. While westerly reaches of the Burn Gill might entail a ninety-minute journey on horseback from Heathfield, Russell had said that his farmhouse was "much closer to the Nidderdale than it was to the Burn Gill." That assertion placed his farm to the south of the easterly end of the stream and, consequently, well within half an hour's walk, or slow trot, from the village.

It was while I was uncovering this obvious discrepancy that I happened upon another hole in Russell's testimony. He had said that it would take approximately ninety minutes to cross his farm of twenty-five acres. Only, I reasoned, if the land were rank with thick, shoulder-high brambles!

I drove back to Pateley Bridge and the ruins of St Mary's Church on the hilly outskirts of town. Despite the abandonment of the church itself, burials had continued in the churchyard until the end of the last century. So, conceivably, Russell could have made a mistake about the location of the church in Heathfield and maybe, just maybe, his remains were located somewhere beneath this preserve of leaning and eroded gravestones. In hindsight, it seems strange that part of me was still bending over backwards to make Russell's story conform to my findings, a tendency which shows just how convincing the guides' testimony had been. I trampled around the outside of the ruined nave, examining gravestone after gravestone in search of a familiar name. And though I encountered some families over and over again, all the names were alien.

Gloomily, I trudged further uphill in the fading light and turned to look back over the rooftops of Pateley Bridge. The wind had dropped and the little town was cloaked in a pall of mist thickened by slow trails of smoke rising from nests of chimneys. Higher and wider, the torpor of dusk spread across the valley, swallowing up occasional shouts, traffic noises and the bleating of sheep. It was all so magically melancholic that my taut emotions were coaxed from hiding. I felt like crying for the group of believers in Toronto, for the guides themselves, whoever they were, for the elaborate deception in which I had become entangled, and for the all-enveloping, myopic struggle of incarnate life. Now that Ernest, Harry and Russell had fallen at the hurdle of rigorous scrutiny, only Filipa, my Filipa, was left.

Always, it seemed, there were more avenues to explore whether or not I believed they would eventually turn into cul-de-sacs. Returning to Harrogate Public Library, I spent an hour scrutinizing the 1851 census records of Stonebeck Down, which encompasses the entire Burn Gill area. Names such as Metcalf, Hullah, Pounder, Newbould, Moor and Raw cropped up repeatedly but not once did I come across a Parnick, Nichols, Nicholls, Smyth or Fellows. I traveled to the County Hall at Northallerton, a large institution which houses the County Records Office which, in turn, holds the microfiched parish registers of Pateley Bridge. If Russell had been buried at St. Mary's, Pateley Bridge, his death would have been recorded in these registers. Arguably, his marriage and the birth of his children should have been there also.

For more than three hours, I scanned the registers all the way from 1820 to 1876. After squinting at a seemingly interminable procession of penned baptisms and burials, many of them faded and some of them nearly illegible, I came away without running across any of the names Russell had supplied, his own included. There was a Grace Pennock of Dredging Box who was buried on 5 June 1846 at the age of ten and a Robert Pennick of Stock Plain who expired on 17 June 1871, aged fifty-nine. But Parnick? Definitely not. Absence of evidence may not be evidence of absence, *but* I now faced the unassailable conviction that Russell had lied to me. With ill-concealed bitterness, I dashed off a postcard to Aviva and the group telling them my quest for evidence of the authoritarian sheep farmer had been abandoned in failure.

Regretfully, there was now no question in my mind that Russell, Harry and Ernest had not lived the lives they had claimed as their own. In vain, I had searched for confirmation in every conceivable corner.

Yet even as I suffered the pangs of betrayal, the Druid's Temple at Ilton stood mutely eloquent in support of Russell's testimony. I drove there one afternoon as respite from the incessant pursuit of documentation. As

The Druid's Temple at Ilton, Yorkshire: "It was said," Russell declared, "that if children were left there unattended, evil things would happen to them." (photo by Michele Hawkins)

eerie as it is picturesque, the temple with a sacrificial slab at its heart is a scaled-down replica of Stonehenge and was built as a makework project at the beginning of the nineteenth century by William Danby, the local lord of the manor and patron of the arts. According to other visitors I met, the temple is suspected of being used for witchcraft ceremonies and Russell's words came back to me as I strolled among the sculpted limestone slabs: "It was said that if children were left there unattended evil things would happen to them." Today, the land is leased to the Forestry Commission and a wood of larch trees has grown up around the temple, accentuating the spectral atmosphere.

Returning to the Nidderdale Valley from the heights of Ilton, I sought out one last historian—Mrs. Eileen Crabtree of Boggledyke, Ramsgill, a village situated at the north end of the Gouthwaite Reservoir. I lounged on a wooden bench on her front lawn as she obliged me by checking a list of all burials at St Mary's Church, Ramsgill up to 1874. After failing to find any sign of Russell, she shook her head when I asked whether she had heard of Hetherington Farm. An evening onslaught of mosquitoes then drove us into the protection of Mrs. Crabtree's home and, sensing a sympathetic ear, I told the story of the guides over a cup of tea. I repeated Russell's claim of having lived as a sheep farmer in the locality during the last century and then I played Mrs. Crabtree a tape of Russell's voice. She listened carefully as he expounded on the trials of life in Yorkshire more than a hundred years ago and then offered in agreement:

"He calls the Nidderdale '*Nitherdale*,' which is the pronunciation used by the locals in the last century. And yes, it must have been grim. He's right when he speaks of the boggy conditions here. My house isn't called Boggledyke for nothing! Naturally, he would be surprised at the construction of a reservoir in such a wet area. But the reservoir wasn't intended for our use—it was built in the 1890s, to serve the growing city of Bradford. He'd be dead by then, I suppose."

I was intrigued by the way Mrs. Crabtree accepted Russell's existence even as she questioned his authenticity. Then she made a suggestion:

"You could ask him some questions to find out how much he really knows about this area in the last century. Ask him about local industry—as you now know, there was lead mining at Heathfield. And there was a brewery at Pateley Bridge—the Nidderdale Brewery run by J. Metcalfe and Sons, established in 1796. Ask him about that. And you could also inquire about the hunting that went on here long ago. Before the reservoir was built, they used to hunt for otters with hounds."

I was grateful to Mrs. Crabtree for her contribution and I vowed to turn the tables on Russell by interrogating him just as she had suggested. Unfortunately, there was no overturning the distasteful fact that my investigations had caught Harry and Russell in several flagrant lies. Worse still, there was now every reason to fear that Filipa was another dissembler in this prolonged charade. Like all victims of duplicity, I was ashamed of myself and, despite my initial determination, was tempted to abandon my mission and bury my folly. I was not looking forward to the trip to Greece. I would be traveling with the heaviest of hearts and the smallest of expectations.

* * *

I was the first client of the day at London's Greek Tourist Office, having walked in just as the grille was being drawn back at 9:30 A.M. Hoping to be steered towards an organization or institution in Greece that could assist me in researching and locating the village of Theros, I was absorbed in explaining my quest of "archaeological research" to a raven-haired assistant at the main desk when a large and imposing woman walked in wearing a colored shawl draped around her shoulders. "She's interested in cultural matters," said the assistant, nodding in the woman's direction, and I was introduced to Margaret Tyrrell, personal assistant to the director of the tourist office.

"Now what *exactly* is it that you're interested in?" she demanded.

"Well, actually," I told her, lowering my voice, "my research involves reincarnation."

"Come downstairs," she said conspiratorially, adding as we entered her basement office: "You have to pick your moment and your person. Otherwise you'd be in a psychiatric home in no time."

It so happened that Margaret was keenly interested in metaphysics and even had a copy of my book *The Case for Reincarnation* at home. I explained, as briefly as possible, the nature of my mission to Greece and Margaret responded by telling me that she was a great believer in synchronicity. Events, she said, happened *for a reason* and she was convinced that she had walked into her workplace at that very moment so that we could meet. Margaret advised me to take a flight to Thessalonika and call there on two establishments in the city that might well be able to assist in my search—The Society of Macedonian Studies and The Institute for Balkan Studies.

The buzzing in my ears was thin, sporadic and not altogether welcome as Flight 9A 2964 from London Gatwick to Thessalonika drew close to its destination. After negotiating customs and eluding a taxi-driving brigand who was demanding eight times the going rate, it was one o'clock in the morning before, assured of fair play, I was settled in the back of a cab bound for the city center. The driver deposited me at the door of one of Thessalonika's many decaying marble palaces, the Hotel Kastoria, where I was given a shuttered room high above the restless traffic and blaring klaxons.

The next morning, I moved to a quieter hotel not far from the waterfront and, having plotted Margaret's addresses on a street map of the city, poised myself for a friendly assault on the respective institutions. Only days earlier, Greece had emerged from its harshest heat wave in living memory: many had perished as temperatures soared higher than forty degrees Celsius and even the sea itself had become uncomfortably hot. Now the sun was strong but by no means oppressive as I walked along the ocean promenade sniffing the pungency of Greek tobacco from the outdoor cafes and counting eight tankers tethered at crisscross angles in the Gulf. The Aegean sparkled magnificently all the way to the door of The Society of Macedonian Studies, which was locked against me: a sign proclaimed that the offices were closed until 31 August, three weeks hence. Undaunted, I walked inland to John Tsimiski Street in search of my second option, The Institute for Balkan Studies, which occupied the fourth floor of a concrete high-rise building at the heart of the city.

The librarian, Mrs. Thomy Verrou-Karacostas, was extraordinarily helpful once I abandoned my pretence of archaeological concern and told her why I was in Greece and where I was bound. To locate Theros before heading into the wilderness of north-eastern Greece was, she agreed, of prime importance and she spent two and a half hours picking through the Institute's large collection of books, maps, directories, reports and sundry records for any sign of the village's existence.

Mid-way through the search, in hopes of bolstering her resolve, I played a tape of Filipa speaking discursively in both English and the local dialect about Theros and Mount Silo. Mrs. Verrou-Karacostas was clearly moved by what she heard and, although she could not understand Filipa's "Greek," she said the vernacular sounded like a mixture of Greek, Bulgarian and Turkish. Ultimately, however, Theros could not be traced. When Mrs. Verrou-Karacostas had exhausted the library's resources she told me that her husband, a neurologist, had a friend who used to talk with discarnates. "It drove him crazy in the end," she said. Immediately, I thought of Sandford Ellison, his fatigue and desperation, and his abstruse message: "When you are ready to hear the other side of the guides . . ."

That same day, I took a bus to Alexandroupolis, Greece's most easterly metropolis situated just forty kilometers from the Turkish border. With the exception of Kavala, a city dominated by a superb aqueduct, the bus ride was a monotonous drone through six hours of wide open, barren countryside scattered with rudimentary farming settlements. Komotini—a town Filipa had mentioned in our geographical discussions—came and went in a blur of low-rise concrete. Herds of goats invested the rural landscape with a certain timelessness, but I felt sure that eighteenth-century Thrace must have been quite different from the dust and metal-shine seen from the bus window. Yet, in one respect, Filipa's Greece had changed little in 230 years: tension between the old enemies, Greece and Turkey, was running high. Tanks, jeeps and trucks crowded with soldiers often swung into view along the highway. Once we passed a plot of ground crammed with thirty or more tanker trucks, all camouflaged.

Having imagined Alexandroupolis to be an ancient city, I was disappointed by its shabby, neoteric appearance, its lines of unremarkable shopfronts and tenements housed in stacked concrete oblongs. Alexandroupolis reminded me of the shanty-styled modern cities of Peru—similar architecture, similar climate. The same small cars and scooters buzzing around; the same dryness and glare and honking horns. Had Filipa really trekked for days to reach this port city of "big, big, floating housings?" It hardly seemed worth the effort.

I searched for a cheap hotel of fading grandeur and found the Hotel Majestik, whose proprietors raised heaven and earth among themselves in a gallant effort to help me find Theros. Although they had never heard of

The Greek port of Alexandroupolis where Filipa said she saw "big, big floating housings." (photo by Joe Fisher)

the place, they were soon gesticulating and shouting responses. Unable to offer any contribution, I repaired to the bar downstairs for a glass of *ouzo*. I did not have the heart to tell them that Theros might be no more than a figment of discarnate imagination.

Also staying at the Majestik was Christoph Löhr, an archaeological student from Munich who spoke both English and Greek. I confided in him about the nature of my quest and, the next day, he joined me in quizzing the locals for evidence of the mythical village. A clerk at the city hall regretted that there was no record of village names in the Evros district and recommended that we talk to the amateur archaeologist who ran the photography shop across the street.

The shopowner shook his head at the mention of Theros and pointed towards the city's cluster of ecclesiastical buildings. In the square outside St Nicolas' Cathedral we apprehended a bearded Greek Orthodox priest in full black box regalia. Our conversation soon drew four other priests who listened impassively as Christoph interpreted my dilemma: how do I find my "mother's relative" from the eighteenth century? They, too, had never heard of Theros, but one of the priests reacted enthusiastically when I mentioned the relative had been named Gavrilos. He said that Gavrilos was a family name in a village called Dadia situated little more than an hour's drive up the Evros valley. Moreover, he said that his grandmother hailed from Dadia and that, after the last war, some thirty people had moved there from nearby Kotronia, the village I had always suspected of being Theros under a new name.

The following day, I boarded a northbound bus for Soufli, a town of six thousand people lying just 500 meters from the Turkish border. It felt like a war zone: military vehicles and soldiers in green fatigues were everywhere. After checking into the Hotel Orpheus, I traveled the remaining thirteen kilometers by taxi to Dadia, a name which is also bestowed on a nearby forest renowned for its eagles. I asked to be dropped on the outskirts of the community and, despite my anxious state of mind, walked into the village feeling like Clint Eastwood in a "spaghetti western." It was almost noon, the sun was high and there was nobody on the street.

My alien presence temporarily halted the hubbub of conversation among groups of men seated at shaded tables outside the two tavernas in the main square. The babble resumed as I selected a table and proceeded to ask around awkwardly for anyone named Gavrilos, being careful to pronounce the G like an H. Sadly, my entreaties were met with dumb stares from all except a drunken, white-haired man who kept shouting, "'Allo!" When I resumed my walk through the hot, hushed village I met a young woman in a striped dress who knew enough English to be able to state unequivocally that no-one named Gavrilos lived in Dadia. Hardened to such setbacks, I accepted her statement calmly, if disconsolately.

Back among the tiled roofs and iron balconies of Soufli, I visited the town hall where I was led to an English-speaking official named Tolis Bakaloudis, the twenty-six-year-old legal consultant to the mayor. Like everyone else thereabouts, he had never heard of Theros but said that his father, a forester, had spoken of a place dubbed "the holy ruins" which lay deep in the hills in the direction of Kotronia. Tolis beckoned me into his office where he made a phone call to the Forestry Commission. The voice on the other end of the line said that the settlement dated back to Neolithic times and confirmed that the ruins were located under a mountain ridge called Bukate. It was felt that a new village was built during the seventeenth or eighteenth century and that the Turks later occupied the site, abandoning the habitation during the early 1900s.

As Tolis was speaking, I retrieved my War Office map of the area and eventually found the name Bukate marked in tiny letters. I was encouraged to discover that the site matched precisely Filipa's old-world efforts to pinpoint Theros' location. The holy ruins lay approximately one-half day's walk "towards the rising sun" from Mount Silo and roughly two days' walk from Aisimi.

Tolis said that either he or his father would gladly drive me to the ruins but pointed out that Bukate lay within a controlled area for reasons of national security (the Turkish problem, again) and forest fire prevention. Only recently, he said, two Netherlanders who wanted to travel to the forest of Dadia to observe the eagles had to submit to an approval procedure lasting two days. Apparently, my intended excursion required authorization, first by military personnel in Alexandroupolis and then by police and Forestry Commission officials.

To appease the bureaucrats I took another bus back to Alexandroupolis first thing the next morning. At the city's military HQ I learned that I had first to obtain authorization from police headquarters and, minutes later, I was standing in a utilitarian office under the distrustful eyes of two Greek plain-clothes policemen. My request for a signed slip of paper to present to the military authority was greeted by the same vacuous expressions I had seen in Dadia the day before yesterday.

"We cannot just give you a piece of paper," one of the detectives replied truculently. "We have to request permission from Athens."

I fumed inside at finding myself trapped in these machinations.

"How long will it take?" I asked.

"Two days approximately, if we send a telegram."

Then came the question l had been expecting:

"Why do you want to go to Bukate? There is nothing there."

I produced an old *Toronto Sun* press card and told the policeman that

Bukate overlooked the remnants of a village that fascinated me, as a writer and journalist, from the standpoint of archaeological interest.

"Then we must send a telegram to Athens. Come with me—get out your passport."

I was led into a little room where an elderly pen-pusher made a note of my particulars while the detective looked on distractedly. Distracted he most certainly was, for as I was leaving the police station he said to me, as if we had never conversed:

"You want to go to this place to see the eagles?"

Returning to Soufli to await authorization, I related my difficulties to Tolis Bakaloudis who said: "They are suspicious of you. They don't understand why you, an Englishman living in Canada, should want to go wandering about in a controlled area." In my absence, Tolis had been asking around about the village at Bukate and said that, while no-one knew the name of the old settlement, he had learned that the Forestry Commission demolished its abandoned buildings in 1923 before christening the remains "the holy ruins."

"Perhaps," said Tolis, "they were looking for treasure."

As I waited, I tramped around the town, danced under a half-moon to Thracian folk songs at the Club Oasis, wandered into fields of charred sunflowers beyond the municipal boundary, took a side-trip up the Evros valley to see the ancient Turkish ruins of Didimotiho, and was refused permission to take photographs of the Greek-Turkish border by tense, rifle-bearing sentinels standing beside a limp Greek flag. Not that I really cared about taking pictures. Everything I did was undertaken to distract myself from the wretchedness and confusion I felt inside. As much as possible, Filipa had been banished from my thoughts. Here in the land where we were said to have lived and loved, to think of her, to sensitize myself to her presence, was exquisitely painful. Especially now that I sensed confirmation of her betrayal was close at hand.

One evening, I met the dapper and loquacious Lambros D. Calfas, Soufli's premier silk merchant, as he presided over his store of fine wares on the main street. He spoke in cleanly-picked English and, as we chatted, we were joined by the mayor, Paulos Fillarides, a butcher, who offered to use his contacts with the prefecture in Alexandroupolis to accelerate the permissions procedure. Even more graciously, he said that, once authorization was granted, be would allow Tolis to drive me to the holy ruins during working hours.

So accommodating and congenial were these fellow Soufli tradesmen that I felt sufficiently at ease to explain, over cups of Greek coffee, my metaphysical mission. Taking the news of my unorthodox inquiry in stride, both men lowered their heads over my tape recorder as I played them a sample of Filipa's "Greek." One or two of the words and phrases were identified, but the substance of the dialect was dismissed as unintelligible and Lambros Calfas smiled when he learned that I was planning to explore the hinterland in hopes of finding the lost village of Theros.

"There is an ancient Greek proverb," he said. "'Only fools go to the forests.'"

Leaving Calfas and Fillarides, I retired to the Hotel Orpheus to peruse some tourist leaflets on Thrace and, in particular, the city of Alexandroupolis. I had always supposed that Alexandroupolis was founded by Alexander the Great and had persisted in this belief despite the city's surprising modernity. But as I sat on my bed scanning an awkwardly-translated brochure the distressing truth broke over me suddenly and serendipitously:

> *Alexandroupolis is a new city* inhabited by many merchants who left Eastern Thrace and settled down here, in 1850, so it was them who gave a great evolution to the district. The very first name of the city, Dedeagats, was inspired by a Turkish monk, Dede, who had lived and been buried under a huge oak tree in the middle of the central square. The street layout of the center of the city to the promenade was planned by some Russian military architects during the Russian-Turkish war in 1878. The city became Greek (as well as the whole of Thrace) on the fourteenth of May, 1920 *and the residents named it Alexandroupolis to honor the King Alexandros who visited their place....*

Several seconds passed before the significance of what I was reading exploded in my dulled mind. How could Filipa have walked for days to see "the big, big floating housings" at Alexandroupolis if

Alexandroupolis had not existed in the eighteenth century? Why, the city was even named after a twentieth-century monarch! I had caught Filipa in a devastating anachronism and, even though I had expected disappointment in Greece, such outright dishonesty left me sick at heart and brimming with resentment.

My reaction was to throw the pamphlet across the room and yell "Bitch!" at the walls. But the word sounded hollow and constrained, sad rather than angry. As much as I had been anticipating this moment, my senses rejected what my mind was forced to accept. I could not believe that Filipa, my Filipa, had joined Ernest, Harry and Russell in blatant falsehood. I just couldn't believe it.

But I had to believe.

There and then, I scrapped my plans to travel to Bukate. Nothing could be gained from such a trip. Not now…I left the hotel and strode through the darkening streets of Soufli, torn between grief and rage. I felt about as worthless as the Greek coins in the pockets of my jeans. And as I agonized over the knowledge of my irrevocable estrangement from Filipa, I craved understanding as once I had craved intimacy. Rather than prolong the agony by travelling to Bukate, I decided to spend my last three days in Greece in a state of studied escapism on the island of Samothrace. It seemed the perfect place to lick my wounds. A short ferry ride from Alexandroupolis, Samothrace had been a center of mystical initiation in ancient times.

On my return to Alexandroupolis, morbid curiosity demanded that I collect my permit to visit Bukate from the police station. Then I carried the unintelligible document—it was all in Greek—to military headquarters for the required stamp before boarding the ferry for Samothrace. Dolphins chased the ship out to sea

The author returns from Samothrace to the Greek mainland, the scene of his final rejection of the guides and their claims. (photo courtesy of Cristina Fedrizzi)

and I sat astern in a state of mental and physical exhaustion, basking in heat haze all the way to the port of Kamariotissa. My lassitude masked my inner restlessness. Thoughts rose and fell in fitful reconsideration of the past. Just as the sunflowers of Soufli were blackened by sunshine that had once made them tall and strong, so I had been nourished by the "guides" only to wither, at last, in their false embrace.

Yet their lies failed to leave me disillusioned with reincarnation. Rather, I felt that the guides, like all adept confidence-tricksters, had fed us largely with the truth so that their lies would appear all the more convincing. They had used and abused the doctrine of reincarnation for their own ends, whatever they might be.

Nevertheless, my metaphysical framework for living—lovingly and painstakingly constructed in recent years—was buckling under pressure. I no longer knew what to believe. Years of research had shown, finally, that mediumistic communication, for all its persuasiveness and plausibility, was fraught with duplicity. How clever, I thought, for the guides to warn me from the outset about "playful spirits." What an astute gambit for control, to divide human beings into souls and entities. Come to think of it, Russell had spoken out harshly not so long ago about the evils of manipulation. If I was not mistaken, he had equated manipulation with murder.

As lovely as the island was, Samothrace afforded no refuge from the guides. Luxuriating in the sulphurous hot springs of Therma, I mulled over three years of claims and counter-claims. Climbing the heights of Saos—the tallest peak in the Aegean, from which Poseidon was said to have watched the strife on the battlefields of Troy—I brooded on Filipa's betrayal and my own gullibility. The pain accompanied my hard runs along the beach and would not be soothed by flagons of *retsina* gulped down on restaurant patios as the sun sank beneath the horizon.

Late at night, as I fretted over the possibility that my contact with Filipa had been a farce of self-delusion, her buzzing returned to plague me. Once so comforting and reassuring, the noise in my ears took on a shrill and sinister aspect, leaving me sleepless. And as I stared at the darkened ceiling of my rented room I recalled the Thessalonika librarian's comment about the man who spoke with discarnates: "It drove him crazy in the end." Yes, I thought, insanity is an option—if I choose to take it.

Two thoughts swam relentlessly through my head. Firstly, after centuries of unsuccessful endeavor by minds far more enlightened than my own, how could I have been so arrogant to suppose that, with the guides' help, I was actually unraveling the mysteries of life and death? And secondly, if the guides were not guides after all, *who were they?*

PART FOUR
Reappraisal

CHAPTER 16

Back to the Fold

Returning to Toronto, I was in a volatile state of anxiety and exasperation. An acrid aftertaste was all that remained of yesterday's knowledge, insight, trust and acceptance. I blamed myself incessantly. Self-loathing clung to every minute of every day and my future seemed impaled on the necessity of arranging a confrontation with Russell and Filipa, even though I knew that my book on our so-called allies in the next dimension must he scrapped. Notwithstanding my huge investment of time and energy, the project now had all the appeal of a rotting carcass. How could it be otherwise when the guides I had known and loved had metamorphosed from beings of light into masters of deception?

I was angry at Russell, Filipa and their cronies. But, for the first time, I was also afraid of them. If they knew us all so intimately—as they had demonstrated on countless occasions—who could say what power they wielded over our lives?

In the wake of my disturbing discoveries, I had expected to receive some support from other members of the group. I wanted the group to present a united front in challenging the duplicity I had uncovered. But when I approached selected individuals with my findings, few seemed to take me seriously and no-one rallied to my side.

While some group members were shocked and saddened to learn of my disillusionment, others held steadfastly to the status quo, refusing to accept that the guides could be wrong. Aviva, who had come to believe in Russell and the other guides in spite of her entrenched cynicism, listened impassively to my tale of woe and frustration without passing comment. Later, however, she suggested that my research methods might not be as rigorous as they could be. Helen Fields, meanwhile, urged me to persist in searching for evidence of the guides. "You'll find them, Joe," she said, "if you keep on looking."

Roger Belancourt, clearly wounded by my discoveries, muttered that he had "always left room for skepticism" and Tony Zambelis, who confessed that he had expected the guides to be vindicated, asked rhetorically: "Now who knows what they might be?" Nevertheless, nobody in the group—even those who accepted the painful message of my European misadventure—wanted to draw the inevitable conclusion: that the guides had lied to us many times in fielding questions on their alleged earthly existences. No-one seemed unduly concerned about the consequences these untruths held for the five years of taped sessions that had gone before. I felt alone in my understanding that every claim and conjecture, every utterance about life here and hereafter, now had to be regarded with grave suspicion.

I was left with the realization that my challenge had served only to intensity the group's belief.

Mercifully, my dark mood lightened once I regained the serenity of my house overlooking Lake Ontario. I sat at my desk and gazed at the water under a cloudless sky, watching a steady breeze push lines of ragged surf across the mile-wide estuary. I worked in the garden, absorbed the smells and the stars, reveled in birdsong and the shrilling of crickets, observed the morning light scaling the cedars behind the house. My hysteria was ebbing away and I was coming back to earth. It seemed that I had been away for a long time, living vicariously in the non-material world between incarnations. I was fascinated, incorrigibly fascinated, by the world of spirit and yet it was good to be reminded that planet Earth was my home. *This,* I told myself, is my world and this is where my energy must be invested.

In the course of several days' brooding and reassessment, my prolonged disillusionment was transformed into a reinforced sense of self, a sense of self that I had long ago surrendered, albeit unconsciously, to Filipa, Russell and the others. Little by little, I reclaimed my personal identity, realizing all the while how much I had lived a shadow life since becoming a member of the group. With developing clarity, I saw how subtly and how stealthily I had become dependent on Filipa, how in questioning my every move and motive I had deferred again and again to what I believed she expected of me. The buzzing in my ears—so harsh and abusive in Greece—gradually retreated and I stoically avoided any attempt at making contact with Filipa, whoever she was. I was beginning to feel strangely re-confirmed in my humanity. While there was much healing still to be done, I was managing to extricate myself from the guides' gentle tyranny.

In reclaiming my self-determination I came to realize that my book project on the guides was not the rotting carcass I had supposed. To a blinkered believer, it might be a rotting carcass but to an objective observer—a role I was busily recreating for myself—it was a treasure-trove of revelation. From my dealings with unbodily entities and my quest for verification of their past lives, much could be learned about the nature of channeling. My ordeal had not been in vain if channelers, their clients, and the New Age movement would heed the implications of my research. Invigorated by this change of perspective, I braced myself for the all-important confrontation with Russell and Filipa.

I had wanted to challenge the guides at a full Friday night session, if only because my findings seemed crucial to the life of the group. Aviva, however, declined my request. She said that she did not want to awake to dissension among the group members. Because much of the past-life information was gathered privately, she insisted that the guides also be consulted *in camera* about the results of my investigation.

My plan of action was simplicity itself. Once Aviva was ushered into trance, I would present my findings as clearly and as dispassionately as possible before demanding an explanation for the various discrepancies. Whatever you do, I lectured myself, do not get excited. But as Aviva stretched out on the sofa and I sat down beside her on the afternoon of Sunday, 13 September 1987, my inner equanimity was mightily threatened by rumblings of tension and vulnerability.

What was I up against? Waiting for Russell's sharp, emotionless voice, one thought would not be denied: *Perhaps I am talking to demons after all.* But there was little time for such fearful rumination. I glanced at the two other group members present—Mi-Lao's charge, Helen Fields, and Sonji's charge, Ruby Beardsley—and then back to the sofa where, under Roger's direction, Aviva was sinking swiftly into oblivion.

As soon as Russell indicated his presence, Roger announced that I had returned from my travels in Europe and wanted to discuss my findings. Nervously, but with a show of boldness, I plunged in.

"Hello, Russell and *Yassoo*, Filipa," I began. "I'd like to speak to both of you."

"Yes, of course," Russell responded tersely.

I started by explaining that my inquiries abroad had shown that much of the past-life information provided by the guides was wrong and misleading. I told of not being able to find Russell and Harry in the records, of discovering that Alexandroupolis did not exist at the time Filipa had claimed she was incarnate, and of unearthing a host of inaccuracies and discrepancies concerning names, places and distances.

"What we gave you was what we have," Russell replied. "If you could not find the relevant information I would be extremely surprised.... Documents were relatively well-kept in the cities, moderately well-kept in other places.... But there *has* to have been documentation of some description of myself.... Someone must have registered me somewhere. That has to be. It must be there."

Russell was so arrogantly self-assured and so convincingly outraged at his apparent omission from the records that, for a moment, I doubted my own painstaking efforts. All I could do was press on as though I had not heard his protestation of innocence.

"Let me just give you an example of the errors I'm talking about, Russell. I went to your village of Heathfield, which you call Heatherfield, and there is no St Mary's Church nor has there ever been a St Mary's Church in that village. And yet, when I noticed there was no church symbol on the map, I asked you twice before I set out from Canada: 'Are you sure St. Mary's was in that village?'"

"Yes, indeed."

"There has never been a St Mary's Church in that village, Russell."

"There most certainly was. There was a travelling pastor who would come to that church once every month and in that building—which was also operated throughout the month as the residence of one of the local families—there most certainly were services. We made sure that our children received all the rites of passage into the church itself. And the pastor would come once every month unless the weather was extremely bad and he was unable to get through on the roads."

"But you said that you were laid on the floor of the church. Not a house, a *church*."

"That was our abode for our church."

"And you said you were buried in a graveyard. According to local records and local historians there has never been a graveyard there. There's a St Mary's Church in Pateley Bridge, Russell, but *not* in your village."

"We had a traveling pastor who would come and give services in that abode which was our church."

"While I was in Heathfield I found out that it takes only half an hour to walk from the village to the Burn Gill. Yet you said it took one hour and a half to walk from your farmhouse to the Burn Gill which marked the boundary line of your twenty-five-acre property. Such a statement is just ridiculous. There's no other word for it."

"Well, perhaps the time in your aspect is out. Time is something we don't have and have no knowledge of here. But I'm trying to judge when I would leave my house to tend to any of the flock on the way and be over at the Burn Gill and to give you as accurately as I can—"

"Your name didn't come up once in the parish registers where baptisms, births and deaths were recorded. Nor did the names you gave for the farmers on either side of you—Angus Fellows and Smyth with a 'Y'...."

"Angus Fellows, he was a well-known area resident."

"They're not there, Russell. And there was no Barfing Road in London, there was no William Harry Maddox who died while serving with the Royal Corps of Engineers in World War I and there was no birth registered for William Harry Maddox at the time given...."

"I don't have Harry here so I can't do anything about that." (The absence of Tony Zambelis, Harry's charge, automatically excluded Harry's presence and participation.) "Furthermore, you have to understand about dates and our difficulties with time. We've stressed this with you before. You would have to move, perhaps, to another year on the same date or to other dates within that particular month."

"I accept that, Russell. And that is what I did in your case and in Harry's case. But still there was nothing to be found. This makes me very suspicious about everything, as you can understand...."

"Well, of course it would. However...."

"Because if this past-life information isn't standing up, Russell, everything else stands to fall as well....The same thing happened with

Ernest. Then, when I returned from England, there was a big song and dance about karma...."

"He was returning to the earthbound plane. That's quite a different situation."

"But the end result is the same, Russell."

"He was also a far different character in type. Don't forget that we don't cease to be beings in any way. We are still as much beings as you are. We just don't have a physical body."

"Yes, I realize that."

"There are many things that, perhaps, are not accurate. For that, I am very sorry. I have tried to be as accurate as possible with you in every detail. There should be records and I know someone must have registered my death...."

"But Russell, it's not just the occasional thing that's wrong....You say you've tried to be accurate but if, for example, I go back to an earlier statement of yours when you said: 'In Heatherfield there's one church, five houses surrounded by farms, the Black Lion and that is all.'"

"Well, the Black Lion was in Harrogate."

"Exactly. When I came back to you the next time you said that the Black Lion was in Harrogate. But I looked for a Black Lion in Harrogate and there was no Black Lion there either."

Russell continued to uphold the existence of the Black Lion. He also claimed that Gouthwaite Hall—marked clearly on my map of 1850—was "a long way from Heathfield" although I knew it to be only half an hour's distance on foot and very near to where his farm was supposedly located.

At this juncture, Helen Fields spoke up to ask whether I had any idea who had lived at Gouthwaite Hall in those days.

"I don't know," I said. "But everybody in the locality would have known that hall. It was the home of the local landowner."

"There's a possibility," said Helen, "that it was a heavily-treed area at the time Russell was living there."

I could hardly believe my ears. In siding with Russell on this issue, Helen was attempting a defense of the indefensible. Countless sessions in Aviva's living room and the hundreds of hours she had spent conscientiously transcribing the guides' pronouncements had converted her into a slavish apologist. I sympathized with her. Before my awakening in

Europe, I had been afflicted with the same contagion.

"Helen," I told her, "I have before me a detailed map of the area for 1850—the time Russell said that he lived there. That hall is very prominently marked and it lies within a mile of where Russell claims to have lived."

I turned back to Aviva's reclining form and pressed on with the interrogation.

"I'm sorry, but what you're saying just doesn't make sense. I'm trying to find the reason why, Russell. I've had to step back. Because of the frustrating nature of my search, I've had to step back from the guides and have been forced to look at you more objectively than I have in a long time."

"The only way you're going to be able to utilize any of the information," countered Russell, "is to step back and look objectively and find out what exactly is going to work for you and what isn't. That's what we have been telling you all along, is it not? When one becomes too embroiled . . ."

"In Heathfield," I persisted, "there was a pub in a house, just as you said, and it did have a name. Do you remember what the name was?"

"Yes. I thought it was the Black Lion but that was on Richmond Street in Harrogate."

"What was the name?"

"My goodness! The things you want us to bring. Are you going to keep all this when you go into guiding?"

"I hope not, Russell. I hope I discard it."

"Exactly. That's what we've all done."

There was a long silence and, at last, I broke in to say, "Well, if you can't remember...."

"Wait!" Russell commanded testily. "No, don't, don't, don't.....It wasn't Ram's Head. It wasn't Ramsgate. Ramsgate was a town, wasn't it? Oooh, my goodness, I don't recall. I can see.....I've walked in there. It's not the Shepherd's Crook, is it?"

"I'll give you a clue, Russell. There was industry in Heathfield during the last century. Do you remember what industry was going on at the time?"

Russell failed to identify the Smelter's Arms and the lead mining that was being carried out nearby. He was unable to name the Metcalfe Brewery in Pateley Bridge ("I'm not concerned where it comes from just so long as I get to drink it," he commented) and he was similarly unsuccessful in identifying otter hunting as a local pastime. He proceeded to justify his lack of knowledge by saying that one remembered in the *bardo* only what "touched you for learning and what you chose to bring with you."

He maintained that it was in reference to "a vast learning experience" that he had given an hour and a half as the walking time from his farmhouse to the Burn Gill. In atrocious weather, he had carried over that distance, so he said, a very sick ewe who was trying to give birth. "I don't believe, under that circumstance, that I could possibly have done it in half an hour."

"But presumably you would remember your name, would you not?" I demanded.

"Of course."

"And you would remember the names of the people in the farms next to you?"

"Yes. Those two I remember."

"And Filipa would know whether Alexandroupolis was there, or not?"

"She would, certainly...She says that Alexandroupolis was a port where there were floating houses. There were ships that would come there with fruit and they would take away meat."

"But even these things haven't checked out, Russell, these very basic things....We spent a long time discussing this past-life information. It wasn't as if it was just dashed off in a hurry. I came back to you many times to double-check the data you and the others were giving. I'm very disappointed, I must say."

"Well, I'm a little shocked myself. More than disappointed. I don't feel that disappointment would be gaining anybody anything other than to stultify growth, unfortunately. When one closes one's mind, Filipa's charge, one must be very careful that one doesn't lock out all the good along with everything else."

"I'm not closing my mind, Russell. I wouldn't be here if I were. But I *was* expecting to find this information and when I learned that Alexandroupolis didn't exist when Filipa was supposedly alive, I thought: 'That's the last straw.' Maybe there's something Filipa wants to say about this?"

"No." Russell was adamant. "You've shut her out. You've quite completely shut her out. I don't think she'd have the energies. She says, "If the value of that truth and love that you've had between you is to be undervalued because you cannot find Alexandroupolis, what basis is your life being lived on? Is it being lived only on the superficial 'I can touch, I can see, I can feel,' or is it being lived in your heart, where the truth resides?"

Russell, it seemed, was withholding Filipa from me in the hope that I would cease my opposition and plead for direct communication with my beloved guide. But my disillusionment ran far too deep. Besides, I wasn't going to give him that satisfaction. When I next spoke, my words were slow and tinged with sadness.

"The whole idea of my research was to go deeper. By finding earthly evidence of the information you had provided, I was expecting to confirm what I already felt inside."

"Filipa's charge, let me tell you one thing." Russell was adopting his professorial demeanor. "The only way that you can ever go deeper is to go into yourself, not out of yourself. The truth lies within you as the truth lies within all. Why do you think that billions on the earthbound plane still attend church? It's a deep and abiding belief with no proof. Less proof than you have of reincarnation, less proof than you have of us.... You cannot prove the existence of guides, for we are not there on the earthbound plane. All we can hope to do is to keep you intact until your transition and, in this manner, to impart to you the knowledge we have for your own lives....

"I really don't know that any of you really grasp what it is to guide someone. We don't sit here with puppet strings and pull you this way and push you that way. We still have our own forward development to get on with, and we must ensure the safety of our charges to the best of out ability at all times.....Do you understand?"

"Yes, I do, Russell, But I'm forced to step back and I'm forced to think about possible alternatives."

"So what are your alternatives? I'd like to hear this."

"Well, that instead of being a real guide you might be just a part of your charge's subconscious mind, that you might be a past-life personality as you have indicated that other so-called guides are. And I think about people such as Emanuel Swedenborg, the great Swedish clairvoyant, who warned very specifically about communicating with entities in the next world. He warned about the dangers of evil spirits who will use all manner of subtlety, brilliance and affection to reach you."

"To what end?"

"I don't know, Russell."

"You must dig further if you're a true researcher as you say. To what end would someone give you the information of the type that has been given? To what end would someone open the learning to you that you have been given? To what end? What would that end entail?"

"I don't know, Russell. The universe is so huge and so wondrous that there's so much that we don't know. We just don't know. We're in this physical body. We have a mind to reason and to check and to ask questions."

"You unfortunately cannot do this outside the earthbound framework. Now when you say this man, Emanuel…what?"

"Swedenborg."

"Swedenborg. What was he warning against?"

"He was warning about evil spirits."

"Lower astral individuals."

"He would warn about the influence of evil spirits who only wanted your downfall. They spoke about love and they spoke about goodness and they ostensibly wanted the best for you, but really they didn't."

"But how could you be downfalled if you are free to choose, free to challenge?"

"Well, we are free to choose but, of course, the guides have influenced everybody in this group. The guides have exerted influence to a great degree. You know that."

"We work only with our charges."

"But having been here week after week talking to everybody, you well know the influence that you have over people."

"We give you information. I do not think we give you influence whatsoever. If you choose to allow it to influence your behavior, that is your choice. We do not offer anything to you that is not asked for."

"But inasmuch as you say you are our guides and you want the best for us and you are working with us to help us do better, for forward development….if we accept what you are saying then of course you're going to influence us."

"I have told you all along not to accept and I don't have to justify my existence against your existence."

"You said to me a long time ago, 'Research your research.' I have researched my research and I have not found anybody."

"You have not found concrete earthbound evidence. But if I were to meet you, Filipa's charge, at your transition, would that convince you?"

"Yes. I would love you to meet me, Russell, and I hope you do."

"Well, I can't because I'm not your guide."

Helen spoke up once more in Russell's defense.

"Joe, if Sonji's charge here gave me the address to her house and I drove into that particular part of the city and couldn't find her house, can I blame her for my inability to find the house?"

"No," I replied. "But if you have the address, you'll be able to find the house."

"Not necessarily."

"If she gave you the wrong address or if she didn't give you an address, that's different. But if she gave you her correct address you would find that house by following directions and, perhaps, asking the way."

"Possibly. But maybe not on the first try. My second point is that you have some evidence of the guides that you can't totally discount. You have experiential evidence."

"But I'm wondering about that now, unfortunately. I wish it wasn't so, Helen. I wish it wasn't so."

"I'm thinking of experiencing Mi-Lao's love and knowing that it is not earthbound, that it doesn't fit into anything here. That *is* love. Do you have any doubt in your mind about what you have experienced with Filipa?"

"I do now, unfortunately."

"But how can you go back and doubt what you already know to be true?"

"Because, perhaps, I feel that I've been self-deluded. Look at all the people who come under the sway of a guru or some other charismatic individual and say to themselves: 'This is marvelous. I'm in bliss.' And then they find that the feeling is short-lived and they realize they were somehow self-deluded...."

"But," Russell interjected, "they are not thinking and the guru doesn't help them to apply thinking."

"No matter. It's very easy for people on the earthbound plane to be deluded. Very easy. You know that, Russell...."

"Incredibly."

"I have a rational mind. I have to step back."

"Listen, Joe," urged Helen, slapping her hand against the carpet on which she was sitting. "You know this is a floor. You've stepped on this and you know it's a floor. You've proved it to yourself. Once you've proved something to yourself, how can you go back and say it isn't so?"

"He has to come to his own conclusions, Mi-Lao's charge," offered Russell.

"Filipa knows me," I responded. "That much I know and that has not changed. But I have to wonder now because certain information hasn't checked out, I have to wonder, 'She knows me but is she really my guide? Or is she a part of Aviva's mind or is she possibly...?' I hate to say this about Filipa because we've had such a wonderful relationship, but does Filipa *really* want the best for me? She knows me, but does she really want the best for me? I have a rational mind and I must use it. I'm a researcher, I'm a writer. I must pursue that path. And if that which I am investigating doesn't check out, then I have to face facts."

My voice was rising steadily until I almost screamed with the pain of disenchantment and futile endeavor. "I DIDN'T WANT TO FACE FACTS! But I had to face them—in Greece and in England. I had to face facts. Emotionally, I didn't want to do it. But I had to do it and it was hard for me. But that's simply my experience."

"Let me interject," said Russell soothingly. "How many years of relationship have you with Filipa?"

"I've been speaking to her for about three years."

"And how long have you spent in Europe doing the work?"

"Well, I was working on this concentratively for about two weeks in England and ten days in Greece."

"If I had had two weeks of talking to Filipa, I might have spent three years until I found her. What I am saying is that you perhaps have overlooked many things...."

"But I spent three years, Russell, preparing for these trips...."

"Preparation makes no difference. I can prepare for a year for the pancake race, and yet I can still make a mess of it on the day."

Now Ruby spoke for the first time. She had a question for Russell.

"Do you realize the importance of this for Joe and for the rest of us?"

"Yes, I do realize the importance of it. I do realize the importance of it...for this life."

"Out of the vast amount of material that you have relayed to us, past-life information is all that can be verified from where we stand," I told Russell. "Which is why I've spent all this time gathering material from you, Filipa, Harry and Ernest."

"If people would spend as much time on forward development as you have spent on checking us out, perhaps your world would be a more inviting place for some of us to wish to return to."

"We're not doubting that for one moment," said Ruby.

"Don't give us red herrings, Russell," I added. "You know that I research and write about reincarnation. I happen to think that it's rather important that people should understand the process of rebirth...."

"You spend a very tiny amount of time earthbound, an extremely tiny amount of time earthbound. You spend the majority of your span non-earthbound where you *know* these things. Why would you choose to destroy some of the learning procedures by living an earthbound existence as though you were not in an earthbound existence? That is what I'm having difficulty understanding."

"Because this is what I'm doing with my life," I replied vacantly. Once confirmed by Filipa as entirely in accordance with my between-life intentions, my life's work was now being cited as the destroyer of my learning procedures. It did not make sense.

"That's what you're doing with *your* life," said Russell snidely. "I've cautioned all of you before about trying to organize the world to your view with your knowledge."

"Then, Russell, why would *you* bother telling us about reincarnation?"

"You asked."

"Well, a lot of people ask me, too, because I'm writing about it. They're eager to know. I'm in the same position as you are, Russell, when I go and talk to fifty people in a hall about reincarnation. The only difference is that it's all happening here on this plane. They ask me, 'What is reincarnation? Where do we go when we die?' And with your help, among others, I've been telling them."

"But reincarnation exists in every major religion. It's already there."

"Yes it is," I agreed.

"We are taking away the cloth of religion and the fantasy of religion," said Russell. "That is one thing you might want to think about—people do not like to have their fantasies dashed."

As we drifted far from the main thrust of the interrogation I remembered the damning words that Russell had used about manipulation. Was Russell, I wondered, so heavy-handed in condemning manipulation because he himself was an astute manipulator? Do we not always hate in others those faults we find most difficult to conquer in ourselves? I decided to ask Russell point-blank whether his harsh censure sprang from culpability. But when I tried to form the question, he interrupted me. It was as if he knew what was coming next.

"One of the things that you railed heavily against was manipulation and I wonder now...."

"No, we didn't rail against it, we gave you all the information that...."

"But you equated it with murder, if I remember rightly."

"It wasn't equitable in that sense. It engenders karma. Now karma is neither punishment nor reward. What is karma?"

So saying, Russell embarked on a long lecture on the nature of karma, simultaneously regaining the high ground of debate while skillfully deflecting the question on manipulation. Later, when I again attempted to express the view that he might be a master manipulator, he interrupted once more. Frustrated, I returned to the attack, reminding Russell of the inconsistencies, the patently wrong information, the changes he had made in his own personal history. Even as we spoke he maintained that he had been born in York when earlier he had given Harrogate as his birthplace. But he denied that he was being inconsistent and blamed me for failing to verify his existence.

"You have more than two thousand lives of experience on the earthbound plane and many millennia in between. Draw on that, Filipa's charge, instead of two weeks and ten days. The information is there. You can find it ...when you have the definitive information, you may come back, of course. You may speak with Filipa or anyone at any time. However, the fact that you have not found one person or four people does not negate anyone's experiences. You see, what you're doing, Filipa's charge, is negating our lives, our experiences, our karma and our learning from those lives and that is a very negative thing to do."

Russell then accused me of excavating trivia that served only to distract the guides' attentions from their earthly charges, adding: "I don't want to seem harsh because you and I have been very good friends."

"We have...."

"And I don't see that that should change. I am simply saying: 'There are other ways to look. Yours is not the only way.' The information that was given to you is there. If it were not there, we would have said so."

Had we talked all night Russell would never have admitted any intent to mislead. He was as slippery as the proverbial eel and a master psychologist to boot. Knowing that he would continue to blame me for my failure to find evidence of the guides, I left the field of battle.

"For my part, I will endeavor to remain open-minded. I've been totally honest with you today, as I've had to be."

"Course you have," Russell agreed magnanimously. "How else does one engender respect unless one is honest? If you lie, deceive and cheat there is absolutely no respect and, therefore, no confidence. But you also have to respect us, that we have told you what we know to be true and, for myself, I'm really rather upset on one score because I would have thought someone would have had the courtesy to at least acknowledge . . ."

I began to laugh, abruptly tickled by the absurdity of the conversation and Russell's professed agitation.

"...my existence by registering my death. They cannot negate my karmic experiences, my life, the lives of my children and my grandchildren and whoever was begotten from there....I don't know quite what I can do about that. However, I do know that *you* can do something about it. You can go out there and find the records and that will put me more at ease."

Cleverly, Russell had wriggled out of being interrogated as a mischief-maker who had lied shamelessly on many occasions. And in no time at all he had mounted a soapbox as an aggrieved citizen whose good name and well-being, sullied by my negligent dabbling, required that I exert myself further on his behalf! I could only marvel at his brilliance.

The session ended with Russell and me expressing our mutual dissatisfaction. As Roger hauled Aviva up the mineshaft of the trance state, I was left with no greater understanding than before of whom or what the mysterious voices represented. If I was sure of anything, however, it was that Russell was devious, manipulative and potentially dangerous. But I failed to understand why Russell and the others would have given me information that they must have known would fail to check out. If they were so well informed, why didn't they supply the names of real people who had died in the respective areas they knew so well? It would have been devilishly difficult to call their bluff had they masqueraded as individuals who *were* to be found in the records. There were still so many unanswered questions.... Why, for heaven's sake, would a discarnate sheep farmer—if that much could be accepted—apply himself so devotedly to the task of pulling the wool over our eyes?

The sight of Aviva stirring drowsily on the sofa interrupted my musings. She had been "away" for close to ninety minutes and, as usual, she looked thoroughly disoriented as she fumbled for her spectacles on the coffee table. Next, she greedily drained two tall tumblers of mineral water and, gasping in the aftermath of her thirst, inquired as to the outcome of the session. I explained that Russell had firmly resisted my findings: a stalemate. Yet, on one level, I was forced to concede defeat. Called upon to choose between my credibility and Russell's credibility, the tiny audience of group members was backing the Yorkshireman.

Meanwhile, Russell's staunchest supporter felt sure that I would find the necessary verification if only I kept on looking. "I have faith in you," Helen told me. "You'll get there. You'll find the information."

"But Helen," I replied, as gently as possible, "what I'm saying to you is that the information may not be there."

"Of course it is," she said. "And you will find it."

"Helen, you're not hearing me. I think you must be open to the possibility that the guides are not who they claim to be."

Helen answered with a look as blank as day.

* * *

The way in which Russell had handled my questions revived vague memories of an earlier session. Had not Russell, in examining the nature of manipulation, unwittingly described his own behavior, his own motives, his own *raison d'être?* Without knowing quite what I was looking for, I scanned transcripts of previous sessions until, with a leap of recognition, I came upon one of the sheep farmer's monologues woven loosely around a succession of questions. Back in February and March, shortly before Sandford Ellison left the group, Russell had maintained that Sandford was being severely yet subtly manipulated by his wife, Betty. With these words, he had proceeded to analyze the insidious process:

> Manipulation means overwhelming another with your energies. To do that, you have contempt for that person; you have disdain for yourself. You have no self-love and therefore cannot love another human. There is genuine desire to control, genuine desire to overwhelm and to have the manipulatee take on your energies to form, in essence, almost another "little you"....
>
> If you close the door to love and open the door to control, you are a manipulator. If you close the door to self-esteem and self-love, you open the door to being manipulated....How manipulators do it is by altering their own core energies to fit, as much as a key would fit into a lock, the energies of the person that they want to manipulate. As that fit takes place, they draw the energies of the other person to them. Very slowly and carefully, they work on those energies and then project them back once they have been worked on and brought into the same type of energy pattern that they themselves have. Once that key is fitted into the lock, it is very easy to turn it at any time. And if the other person is not co-operating in being manipulated then they simply turn it a little more until they do ...The manipulator simply supplants his own energies within the victim who begins to think, act and function very much in the mode of the person who is manipulating. However, the manipulator will often appear to be compliant, which gives the

manipulatee the illusion of having some control.

Manipulation is subtle and is, at first, very rarely picked up on by the person being manipulated. Often, it takes some event to show the victim that he or she is being manipulated. And even then the control can be very difficult to break and can be very painful if it has been going on for a long time.

Manipulators tend either to embellish or lie outright when challenged. Even if caught with their hand taking the bread, they will somehow explain it away in falling back on the skills from which they first learned to manipulate...that is, lying.... They have a variety of tricks in their bag that they will pull out to use as weapons for control and they will rotate those weapons, as needed....You will often find that manipulators are most vehemently defended: a manipulator has staunch allies who are unwilling to believe that this dear, sweet person is using them.

Although he was lecturing as proudly and as assuredly as ever, Russell might as well have been on his knees in a confessional. I re-read the transcript several times, stunned by the prescient analysis that inadvertently revealed the guides' nature and intention. Not only had Russell spelled out the formidable ingenuity employed by the guides in impressing and persuading their respective charges, but also he had outlined, well in advance, my painful disillusionment prompted by an "event," his own lies and embellishments countering my subsequent challenge, and even the dependability of the "staunch ally" who sprang to his defense. But if the guides' manipulative skills had preyed on myself and other members of the group, I was soon to learn there was another who had been victimized much more severely than ourselves. Belatedly, I sought out Sandford Ellison.

CHAPTER 17

One Man's Nightmare

Sandford Ellison was restless with recrimination as we sipped coffee in a downtown Toronto restaurant. At my request we had arranged to meet in order to discuss, in detail, his close collaboration with the guides and the reasons for his departure from the group. Thus I learned, for the first time, that his unrivalled intimacy with Russell and Tuktu had dragged him into despair and pitched his family into a long and nerve-racking ordeal. My own disillusionment by no means diluted the effect of what Sandford had to say. Rather, his experience opened my eyes still further, confirming my fears that the guides, more than being simply mischievous, were prone to malevolence. All I could feel was overwhelming compassion as he blamed himself for his family's plight and the near-collapse of his management consultancy.

Having left his wife, Betty, under tremendous pressure from his discarnate "friends," Sandford was about to be reunited with her and their two sons. Encouragingly, his neglected business was steadily recuperating. The extended nightmare had begun to recede as soon as he regained his will, his decision-making ability, and the control over his destiny that had been so trustingly surrendered. Five months had passed since his last chat with Russell and Tuktu and he was looking much healthier and happier than the last time we met.

Listening to Sandford's tale of trauma, I could see how the guides had traded on his weaknesses and good intentions and coaxed him into a pit of wretchedness and despondency. He was like a moth that, drawn perilously close to a flame, had somehow managed to veer away from a deadly fascination. Certainly Sandford had known the guides more intimately than any of us. But then, no other member of the group had been pursued with such ardor. Our restaurant rendezvous was like a meeting of veterans who had fought different battles in the same campaign. No matter how unpleasant the conflict, we had both emerged with an enhanced sense of self. We had survived the fray. Sandford spoke without bitterness or rancor. He told his story with a strong sense of having learned an important lesson the hard way.

The lesson might have passed him by had he acted on his initial reluctance to accept the guides as the loving and attentive discarnates they claimed to be. On his third visit to Aviva's living room he expressed the opinion that the mysterious voices belonged to lower astral beings and, ironically, it was only Betty's fascination with the sessions that caused him to return. Within a week or two, Tuktu was announced as his guide and the seduction of Sandford Ellison began in earnest. "Undoubtedly," he said, "getting a guide of my own changed my mind and kept me interested."

In a matter of weeks, Sandford was drawn in further when Russell confided that Aviva had only three months to live and, because of his natural ability as a healer, he alone could help her. His self-image was somewhat low and the task at hand, combined with the guides' solicitousness and encouragement, gave his life new meaning and purpose. Told that he was deeply in Aviva's debt because of his hostile and selfish actions towards her in previous lives, he toiled incessantly under Russell's and Tuktu's direction in a bid to relieve Aviva of leukemia's most troubling symptoms.

At first, Russell didn't want Aviva to know that healing was taking place and, at his request, Sandford pretended that the increasing incidence of trance sessions was for reasons other than the one intended. When Sandford eventually told Aviva of his therapeutic intentions she resisted, saying that she didn't want to be beholden to anybody. Sandford then found himself beseeching and cajoling her to allow him to continue. Soon after Aviva grudgingly accepted his offer, the disease flared with new virulence.

"It was like fighting a brush fire all the time," Sandford told me. "Every time I thought that I had managed to keep the leukemia in check, problems would open up in different places—in a leg, perhaps, or in her back. There was no respite. I would often spend at least four nights a week channeling healing energies. When Aviva hit pain, I'd get a phone call and go straight to her house. There was never more than a few days at a time when Aviva wasn't coming apart at the seams. My life was not my own. I was constantly on call and if I was considering going away for a weekend with my family, Russell would say, 'You can't go away. This will happen and that will happen.' At least three times I was told by Russell that Aviva had only one week to live if I didn't work especially hard."

There was no question in Sandford's mind that he was channeling life-saving energies to Aviva's entranced form. He was impressed by the guides' obvious knowledge of her physical condition and his fingers would register varying degrees of heat or coolness according to the various types of energies which he was told Tuktu was transmitting through his hands to different parts of Aviva's body.

"Following Tuktu's instructions, I would place my hands on specified parts of the body," said Sandford. "After a while, the part in question would get hot and no hotter. Or it would cool down and get no cooler. I'd know precisely when to stop working on a particular area by this stabilizing of temperatures. I remember that one type of energy was said to freeze marrow in the bone. Aviva would wake up trembling—her teeth chattering with cold—to complain bitterly that she felt as though her bones were made of ice."

Sandford's unorthodox attentions appeared to be making inroads as Aviva discovered that, despite occasional flare-ups, she had progressively less need of conventional treatment and medication. But if Aviva was showing signs of winning her battle against leukemia, Sandford found that the act of channeling energies left him feeling extraordinarily depleted and ill-at-ease. "It was as if my mind and my emotions had been totally scrambled," he said.

This sense of depletion created an opening which the guides hastened to fill. When Sandford complained of his adverse reaction, Russell and Tuktu would offer to replenish his energies—with remarkably restorative results. In this way, Sandford gradually became dependent on their intercession. The more healing that Sandford accomplished, the more conversations he had with the guides. And the more conversations he had with the guides, the more influence they exerted upon him. Towards the end of 1986, he noticed that his moods would swing wildly between euphoria and depression when he was away from Aviva's living room. Russell and Tuktu explained this see-saw of emotion by insinuating that his environment—and Betty in particular—was creating the condition.

Slowly and stealthily, the guides talked Sandford into believing that Betty was cruelly yet subtly manipulating him. First, they merely suggested that he pursue his own interests to a greater extent. Sandford agreed. Then he was told that he should stand up to people more. Again, Sandford agreed. He knew that he was easy-going and gave in more than he should to the initiatives of others. Then the guides stated that one of the people he should stand up to was Betty. He was reminded that Betty was a soul whose energies could be devastating to an entity such as himself. Next, he was told that he was being overwhelmed by the energies of others and that Betty, especially, was smothering his energies with her own and manipulating him according to her wishes.

From January to March, 1987, Sandford was in crisis as his dependency on the guides became all-consuming. Having hired Aviva as his company assistant, he would talk her into trance daily during business hours, sometimes spending as much as two hours in conversation with Russell and Tuktu. The consultancy suffered as Sandford languished in the throes of emotional turmoil. "It wasn't just that the guides were telling me that I was being overwhelmed," he said. "When I was close to Betty I would feel fatigue and this really made me paranoid."

For months, Betty had taken pleasure in preparing and serving snacks for the regulars at the Friday night sessions. But once the slurs and insinuations began, her attendance diminished as she fretted in silence over the guides' disapproval and her husband's growing impatience and irritability. Having been designated a "soul," Betty had no guide to consult about her difficulties. Moreover, the guides' anti-Betty propaganda had left few members of the group sympathetic towards her and she was effectively shunned by the weekly gathering. Singled out as a manipulator, she could only look on helplessly as Sandford was mesmerized by the guides.

As Betty watched from the sidelines she began to notice alarming changes in Sandford's disposition. The metamorphosis, it seemed, proceeded in tandem with the increasing amount of time he spent chatting with the voices.

"Sandford was right out of his mind," Betty recalled. "This was not the person that I knew. I was doing all I could to avoid him. It was a relief when he left the house. There was a total change in his personality in a very negative way."

It was little wonder that Sandford bore scant resemblance to his former self: he was sinking into a deepening depression. The worse he felt, the more pressure the guides exerted. "They kept telling me stories about Betty," Sandford continued. "They said that she was having affairs with lots of different men. They said that she was a pathological liar. They said that she was trying to kill me by projecting powerful negative energies my way. They even warned, on three separate occasions, that I would die unless I left her. Each ultimatum was different—they put limits of six months, nine months and three years on my life if I chose to stay with Betty."

Simultaneously, the guides gently suggested that Sandford and Aviva had close reincarnation ties, had been drawn to one another by their shared karma and were meant to be together. "Tuktu was trying to convince me," said Sandford, "that if I wasn't working with Aviva continuously, we would both come to an untimely end. And Russell kept telling me that Aviva and I had to express our love for one another and that she could take care of my physical needs. But the only feelings I had for her were those of duty and responsibility. That's how I got sucked in—by being told that she was going to die and that I was the only one who could help her."

Tapes that Sandford made of private sessions with the guides reveal the heavily persuasive tactics that Russell employed in a concerted effort to bring Sandford and Aviva closer together both physically and emotionally. Maintaining that they were making a "lifetime commitment" to one another, Russell urged:

> Speak of your feelings with her and make her speak of hers with you. Sit together, look at each other, touch each other, and talk of them. It is very difficult to be honest where there are the slightest barriers between you. You have no barriers now except the barrier of distance, the barrier that neither of you has trusted another person to this extent in your entire earthbound lives. We are asking you to meet, look, mix your energies together by touching so that you are trusted by one another...When one wishes to communicate depth and understanding, that person is close to you and looks at you and touches you. Is that not so?

"Yes," Sandford acknowledged.
"Do it!" Russell commanded.

Russell declared on another occasion:

This will be the only relationship that you will have at this level. You must know each other, not just obliquely pay lip service to knowing each other. You must be able to confide and talk and be open and honest with each other. Now I recognize that it is invariably frightening to be told that you are going to have, and that you must have indeed, such a close relationship. You have sought to keep distance between many people in your own way. So has my charge. But you two cannot do that. It is like water flowing downhill. Eventually it will reach the sea. Well, if you are the sea, my charge is the river and she is going to have to go downhill to meet the sea. It is inevitable....You are already feeling great guilt feelings about this with regard to your family. These thoughts are running through your mind. It is not the same relationship as you have with your family.

Aviva felt an uncomfortable sense of obligation as she learned, second hand, of the guides' exhortations. Through Sandford, she told Russell and Tuktu that she was "drowning in expectations I can't meet" and asked why the guides were exerting such pressure on them both. Choosing not to answer her question, Russell merely acknowledged that the guides had strong expectations of their mutual commitment. He even went so far as to warn that he and Tuktu would withdraw as their guides if they shrank from making a loving pledge.

You can no longer be frivolous with one another. You either love each other and trust each other enough to tell very bluntly your feelings for each other and to each other—or you do not. And if you do not you will not complete and accomplish the success of that which you have started. And this not only goes for my charge but it goes for yourself in all your ventures. You two—dare I say it?—stubborn people have two equally stubborn guides and if you will not recognize the way in which you must work together, not just for her health but in all other facets that will bring you success, achievement, learning and knowledge...then we will simply turn you over to some others.

Tuktu, meanwhile, impressed upon Sandford the inestimable value of his advice thus far.

Without any guidance you would have lost your business, you would have lost your own family, you would have completely lost it all...and many other things of a negative nature would have happened to you.

So far as Betty was concerned, Tuktu's counsel was ostensibly sympathetic even as he told of the parting that must surely follow.

It is very difficult for her [Betty] to come to the realization that she must let go of you, that you have passed way beyond the soul planes which she inhabits. That is not reason enough for her to...wish to undergo a transformation. She just wants to stay with you. But one must move on to the areas where one is capable of functioning as an entity. It will not be uncommon for her to begin to cling very hard and very tenaciously....

As Sandford's desperation grew, the guides introduced new hope of salvation to their foundering victim. Tuktu told Sandford that his problems were compounded because his emotional centers were shut down. With the guides' help, they could be opened in the cause of his well-being. "Wherever I could feel heat under my skin," said Sandford, "the guides said that an emotional center was not open, that is, was not functioning properly. Once I felt thirty or forty of these 'hot spots'—like hot walnuts—all over my body." So it was, in private sessions, that Russell and Tuktu proceeded to "help" Sandford by prying open these emotional centers, alternately counseling him and feeding him with energies channeled through Aviva's entranced body.

"Tuktu got quite vicious at times. He would tell me that I was useless, that I couldn't make decisions, that I didn't stick up for myself and so forth. These derogatory remarks were made so that I would express anger, so that my "anger center" would be opened up. I was battered so hard that I didn't know what was going on, but it was said to be all for my own good—they were supposedly breaking down my resistance to emotions held in the body. Much of the time I felt intensely hot all over the abdomen and groin area and, whenever a center opened, I felt a great rush of hot wind within, a blast of warm energy. When this happened, I would feet very calm, confident and in control. My insight was enhanced. I'd fly high—but then I'd come crashing down again.

"The more my centers were supposedly opening, the worse I felt, in spite of the periodic highs. I was feeling things I didn't realize could be experienced with such intensity. The emotional swings were phenomenal. At times, I would be totally broken down. I underwent raging storms of emotion—nostalgia, crying fits, great highs, depressive lows. One session lasted fourteen hours. I took Aviva in and out of trance so that I could stay as close as possible to the guides throughout that time.

"I see now that they were brainwashing me. It was magnificently done. They would scramble my thinking and feeling processes so that I wasn't able to function properly. And then they would be the ones to make me feel better. Practically every day I would get what you might call a maintenance shot which would make me feel better for a while. They turned me into a psychic drug addict. The guides were out to create enormous dependency—and they succeeded."

Early in March, 1987 Sandford's enfeebled resistance could hold out no longer and he capitulated to the voices' demands. He packed his bags and left home. "It was the worst point of my life," he said. "I was feeling God-awful about everything. My whole life was a mess."

Shortly afterwards, Sandford had a row with Aviva at his office and she stormed out, never to return. His relationship with Aviva had been strained for some time and he was exhausted from expending untold effort in the cause of her recovery. Nevertheless, he made an effort to resolve their differences only to find himself in the middle of another fierce argument. So Sandford withdrew and, in the peace and solitude that followed, he thought long and hard about what Russell and Tuktu had been telling him. The more he dwelled on their advice, the more he questioned who they were and what they were up to.

In the absence of any contact with the guides, Sandford made a startling discovery. He began to feel better, a lot better. Days passed and the fierce emotional fluctuations and bouts of muddled thinking steadily ebbed away. The passing of weeks only confirmed Sandford's new-found equanimity. The guides, he discovered, had not been helping him in the slightest. In fact, they were one of his biggest problems. He came to believe that his prolonged proximity to their communicating "vehicle" and his willingness to channel healing energies had left him vulnerable to discarnate designs about which he could only wonder.

Towards the end of April, Sandford received a telephone call from Roger, who had been reinstated, in Sandford's absence, as the group hypnotist. It was 11:30 in the morning and Aviva—who was due to fly to Australia in a matter of days to visit her ailing father—had been stricken with a massive pain attack. Roger had rushed to Aviva's aid to administer hypnotic anti-pain suggestions and, once his subject was in trance, Russell had demanded to talk to Sandford. Obediently, Roger had dialed Sandford's number, holding the mouthpiece to Aviva's lips as Russell barked into "the invasive instrument" that his charge's leukemia was running rampant and that the rift between Sandford and Aviva must be healed.

Sandford was unbending in his determination to have nothing further to do with the guides and, once this was communicated, Russell resorted to intimidation of the most blatant and desperate kind.

"Russell told me," said Sandford, "that he had just been handed the next installment of my life and that if I didn't tell Aviva how important she was in my life she wouldn't come back from Australia and she would die there without my healing. He also said that, in Aviva's absence, I wouldn't be able to keep my energies balanced through contact with the guides and that my business would collapse. Finally, he told me that I would commit suicide in a fit of depression."

Russell, however, had misjudged Sandford's ability to cut through the puppet strings and regain his sense of self. Such desperate threats no longer held menace for the one-time channeling junkie. In fact, Sandford now found Russell's bullying tactics preposterous.

Aviva, not surprisingly, did return from Australia notwithstanding Sandford's refusal to declare his love. Furthermore, despite not having received any channeled healing since the spring of 1987, at the time of writing she is healthier than ever. Her leukemia has been in remission since Sandford spurned Russell's last-ditch matchmaking efforts. Meanwhile, Sandford's survival, and the recovery of his business, has exposed the emptiness of the threats made against him.

In June, 1988, Sandford and Betty celebrated their twenty-fifth wedding anniversary in the knowledge that their relationship has ultimately benefited from the trials precipitated by their involvement with the group. "It was as if we shoved our hands into fire," said Sandford. "Without knowing it, we found ourselves participating in an exercise of the most frightful self-confrontation. In some perverse way, the guides were our teachers. Without their intervention, Betty and I would probably still be locked in the same desperate nothingness that our marriage used to be."

When Sandford and Betty first attended the sessions at Aviva's home each was unhappy with the other. At home, they subsisted in an emotionally arid climate and they felt unwilling and unable to discuss their problems. "The guides had a basic understanding of this," said Sandford, "and they worked at exacerbating our situation. In manipulating me, they pointed the finger at Betty because they needed a scapegoat. And, because I had abdicated my own sense of self, I allowed them to get away with it.

"The strange thing is that, although I had endless conversations with Tuktu, I never felt any resonance or familiarity with him. When Aviva and I were having differences of opinion, Tuktu always sided with her against me. In retrospect, it doesn't make sense that I was needed to channel healing energies in the first place. The guides said that healing was effected via the fourth level of Aviva's mind and, when I asked why they could not channel energies directly, Russell never gave me a straight answer. I think the guides always tried to give us the impression that they knew more than they did. They would tell us one thing that was accurate and then we would assume that everything they said was right."

Sandford's verdict in the aftermath of his entanglement is that Aviva's unconscious mind is somehow in league with mischievous and mendacious discarnates who seized the opportunity provided by her illness and the hypnotic state to make themselves known.

"My big mistake," he said, "was giving up responsibility for myself and letting these voices—whatever they represent—dictate the direction of my life. I firmly believe now that contact with such forces is not desirable, not natural, and not in our best interests.

"Who, or what, are these beings?" Sandford asked rhetorically. "It's very difficult to say. I do know they were right inside Aviva from the way her facial expression would change. They would even laugh through her. I tend to feel that they are lower astral entities who play on human frailty and feed on our energy and our emotions. They often dazzled with their remarkable knowledge and acute perceptions but they had nothing but contempt for us. I still believe they helped to keep Aviva alive. They needed her alive. Our communication allowed some light to shine into the darkness of where they are and wherever that is must be God-awful in the extreme."

* * *

Sandford's abrupt departure and my own subsequent desertion seemed to have little effect on the remainder of the group, which continued to meet on Friday nights. One or two people dropped out in the wake of our disillusionment but the group membership had always fluctuated. Back in May, 1986, Russell had even anticipated some form of rebellion:

> As a group, you will evolve, you will gain members, you will lose members. Each one who leaves, whether he or she leaves in a positive frame of a mind or in a negative frame, will have learned one thing: to access the self. If they do not like what they hear and are unable to process the information that they are given and even become quite strident in their remarks, they are still activating their thinking processes. They are still looking inside themselves to ascertain what their needs are and are learning to open up those areas which need to be opened up.

It was as if Russell knew that he would not be able to fool all of us all of the time and he was moving to defend the sessions against any tendency towards disintegration. I marveled at the guile that had inspired those words. His statement would have been interpreted entirely differently by the "staunch allies" who were still in thrall to the weekly performances of wisdom and unconditional love.

Because I moved out of the city just before becoming disillusioned with the guides, the impact of my departure from the group was somewhat muffled. Even so, the members who remained were unable to accept that I had gone for good. They knew how much I had loved Filipa and felt that so sublime a bond could not be broken. "He'll be back," Roger Belancourt was heard to remark. Roger was right ... but for the wrong reasons. On 5 February 1988 I showed up at Aviva's house for the last time. I had one aim in mind: to expose Russell in his duplicity by confronting him with the conflicting definitions he had given of Dr. Pinkerton. Six months had elapsed since my last visit and, although some familiar faces were there, many members of the group were strangers to me.

I seated myself on the floor among the true believers and watched as Roger hypnotized Aviva and talked her down to the level where the guides were waiting for the customary "Good evening, Russell." The sheep farmer sounded as hale and hearty as ever and the evening's interchange proceeded with the utmost conviviality until I took advantage of a lull to set forth my challenge. As soon as I stated my case, the atmosphere in the room chilled perceptibly and Russell's voice developed a hard edge of irascibility. He dealt with my challenge firmly and dismissively:

> Dr. Pinkerton is an alter-consciousness that is taking on the past-life personality. An alter-consciousness from a past life is still an alter-consciousness. This Dr. Pinkerton was, in fact, an acquaintance of the past-life figure that is now calling itself Dr. Pinkerton.

The peremptory reply had the semblance of clarity. But when I looked hard at the meaning of the words, there was no meaning. Obfuscation reigned. By the time I tried—and failed—to make sense of what he had said, another question had been asked and Russell, his geniality restored, was declaiming from his invisible podium on some other topic to the obvious pleasure of his listeners. My question and its mesmerizing answer was already forgotten and I was left in the dust, reminded of Russell at his most incisive....*Manipulators tend either to embellish or lie outright when challenged. Even if caught with their hand taking the bread, they will somehow explain it away.*

In search of indisputable evidence of double-dealing, I scoured transcripts of the sessions for flaws in the magnificent informational edifice the guides had constructed over the past five years. The voices didn't slip up very often. The few contradictions and inconsistencies that I managed to locate stood out like junkyards in the tundra.

On 14 December 1984, Russell had surprised and impressed us when he announced: "Did you know it was Nostradamus' birthday today?" He proceeded to display great knowledge about the sixteenth-century French seer, quoting from his work and saying that he had been apprenticed to Nostradamus' guide. Yet Russell had protested ignorance of his own birthdate. There was also conflicting testimony about guide intervention, whether or not the guides eavesdropped on conversations and whether or not they were inhabiting Aviva's body during trance. Then, after making some rough calculations, I realized that Filipa's knowledge of English could never have been garnered from an existence in Scotland one hundred lifetimes earlier, as she had claimed. In those days, the earliest version of the language did not exist!

Yet deep belief, like deep love, is not immediately discarded, despite the clearest oppositional evidence. For all their double talk, Filipa and the guides could not be jettisoned as casually as an outdated newspaper and I continued to mourn my loss even as I was relieved to have regained some measure of reality and common sense. Compulsively, I was still on the trail of the guides' identities. In hope of extricating myself from the thicket of perplexity represented by the mysterious voices, I sought out an expert qualified to analyze Filipa's descriptions of Thrace as well as her efforts to speak Greek.

In Dr. George Thaniel, a native-born Greek and professor of modern Greek at the University of Toronto, I found just the person I was looking for. Dr. Thaniel, who spent his childhood in Athens, is a quietly-spoken, philosophic man given to pondering the imponderable. He was intrigued to learn of my conversations with the guides and my futile investigations in Greece and agreed at once to scrutinize two tapes bearing Filipa's messages. Two weeks later, I sat in his study listening to his deliberations.

Most interesting of all was his assertion that Aviva's voice when speaking as Filipa was, in parts, the voice of a Greek woman who hailed from the north-eastern region of the country. That, in itself, was important. If the voice bore traces of one who was Greek by birth and not merely a speaker of Greek, it was likely that a discarnate being, rather than the uncharted realm of Aviva's unconscious, was the source of the communication. The tapes' most revealing section concerned Filipa's pronunciation of the name Gavrilos in both a Slavic-sounding dialect and formal Greek. At first, in vernacular which Dr. Thaniel could not understand, she uttered the name with a hard G before adding, "And now, in Greek, Gavrilos," with the G pronounced softly.

"This was a very revealing statement," said Dr. Thaniel. "First, of all, it was delivered spontaneously and naturally and sounded just like a peasant woman but, most significantly, it directed me to a tiny period of Greek history. Phonetically, she was comparing the modern Greek sound with the old way of speaking. Obscure yet specific information such as this would be very difficult to stage."

Dr. Thaniel explained that this simple remark could relate only to the years 1912-20 when unofficial changes in Greek phonetics were institutionalized at the time of Thrace's incorporation with Greece following the Balkan Wars. Therefore, Filipa's reference to Alexandroupolis—which was named in 1919 after King Alexandros—would be justified had she been alive in that era.

Dr. Thaniel was confident that Filipa's Greek did not belong to the eighteenth century, as she had claimed. Her descriptions of guerilla fighting between the Turks and the Greeks corresponded with hostilities at the time of the Balkan Wars and her mention of the *drachma* was anachronistic. Turkish currency based on a coin called the *kuruch* was used in Thrace during the eighteenth century, the modern *drachma* being resurrected from classical Greece in 1833. Filipa accurately described the landscape of north-eastern Greece but she did make some cultural errors. The old Greek calendar—which was abandoned in 1923—is thirteen days different from ours and not five, as Filipa had suggested. She spoke of people sitting down in church whereas Greeks have always remained on their feet during services.

Dr. Thaniel was mystified by what he heard. At times, he could identify the voice of a Greek speaking through Aviva's voice box but, sometimes, the voice sounded more like someone who was learning Greek. Turning over the riddle in his mind, he was at a loss to understand why I would wish to push so strenuously for answers.

Arguing that my investigation of the guides was hubristic, Dr. Thaniel suggested that I read what the Greek philosopher Heraclitus had to say about hubris, which the *Collins English Dictionary* defines as "an excess of ambition ultimately causing the transgressor's ruin." Heraclitus, who was known as "The Dark One" because his words were often misunderstood by his contemporaries in the fifth century B.C.E., told how the sun will not overstep its bounds for fear of attracting cosmic retribution.

"Do you have relationships with flesh and blood?" Dr. Thaniel wanted to know. It was an unusual question.

"Yes," I replied.

"Have you not found that these relationships have suffered as a result of your relationship with Filipa?"

I confessed that, yes, in Rachel's case, this had been so.

"That," said Dr. Thaniel, "would be a hubristic repercussion. Why tamper with another existence into which we will go anyway in due course? Is it not like disturbing a tomb?"

"Not at all," I responded. "I believe we must seek to understand our connection with the unseen world. If we are to develop greater understanding of ourselves, we must keep knocking on the door of the unknown."

Mid-way through my remarks I noticed that the professor was daydreaming. His reverie dissolved as soon as I fell silent.

"Eventually," said Dr. Thaniel, falling back on his penchant for philosophy, "we may explain all these things."

I hoped he was right on that score. In the meantime, I could only concur with another maxim of Heraclitus: *The nature of things is in the habit of concealing itself.*

CHAPTER 18

Tales of the Serpent

What to believe? That was the question that hounded me without respite in the wake of my disillusionment. Surely, I reasoned, just because I had encountered a gang of scoundrels on the astral plane didn't mean that *all* unbodily communicators were lying and manipulative. Genuine currency is very much in evidence despite the existence of counterfeit banknotes. Why should the discarnate world be any different?

I had left for Europe confident that Dr. Pinkerton was a charlatan. But on my return, beset with doubts, I wondered whether I had judged him too harshly. I asked myself whether the affably disquieting surgeon had been the victim of a smear campaign by Filipa and her cronies. After all, who were they to label him a mere past-life personality when their assertions about themselves had so miserably failed the test of scrutiny? Besides, Dr. Pinkerton appeared to have known that they were up to no good, having warned that I would be disappointed in my search for evidence in England and Greece.

However, my strongest incentive to reevaluate Dr. Pinkerton's credibility sprang from Claire Laforgia's insistence that she had located, in Belfast, the discarnate's great-grandson, a gynecologist bearing the family name. Claire told me that she was in the process of arranging an appointment with the Belfast doctor so that we could both travel to Northern Ireland where she would enter trance and present the gynecologist with his departed ancestor. I was reminded at once of mediumistic healer George Chapman and the remarkable verification—by surviving relatives—of his "spirit doctor" William Lang. Could it be that I was only a trans-Atlantic flight away from witnessing a startled Belfast specialist shake hands with his long-lost relative from beyond the grave?

Nonetheless, I could not discount the disturbing impression that Dr. Pinkerton had left with me and it was somewhat against my better instincts that I was lured back to the darkened consultation room where the surgeon without scalpel held court. Claire sat in repose with her hands folded in her lap and, breathing deeply, was an entirely different being within the space of ninety seconds. I knew that the old man had taken over when her body shifted slightly and leaned over to the left side. There was an accompaniment of throat-clearing and the smacking of lips and, when he had adjusted his seating position for maximum comfort, the unmistakably shaky tenor struggled to convey the elderly practitioner's greetings:

"Well, well, well. Did you have a pleasant journey, Son?"

Dr. Pinkerton spoke so sweetly that it was hard to tell whether his politeness was genuinely considerate or gloatingly sarcastic. Somewhat suspiciously, I replied in the negative, explaining why my travels had been anything but pleasant and telling how my investigations had exposed Filipa and Russell as arch-deceivers. While that masquerade was over, I said, there was still lots of explaining to be done. To begin with, I wanted to know why he had promised in vain that his "instrument" would channel messages directly from Filipa.

"You want me to be honest with you, Son?"

"Perfectly."

"I don't know how you're going to take this, but do you know the difference between earthbound spirits and real guides?"

My temples throbbed. I knew what was coming next.

"Yes," I replied apprehensively. "I know there is a great difference."

"Well, I do not want anyone to channel my instrument that is not of the light, that is not a true guide, Son. Does that answer your question?"

Just when I thought the emotional pummeling was over, Dr. Pinkerton's words left me feeling as though I had been punched in the stomach. He went on to say that Aviva's illness, lack of proper training as a medium and disinclination to protect herself, either mentally or verbally, while in trance had left her vulnerable to lost souls or earthbound spirits.

"So was this why you kept deferring when I asked you questions about Filipa? You didn't want to tell me that she was an earthbound spirit? You wanted me to find out for myself?"

"Indeed. Did I not say, 'Son, be careful when you go away?' I was quite sincere. I shall repeat myself: Who am I to change your will? I do not control anyone's will, Son. I am a friend who can advise you. Now the question is: Who is Albert? Is he the same as the others?"

While I was in Europe, Claire had attended the Friday night gatherings in Aviva's living room in hope of finding out more about Albert, whom Filipa had named as her guide. Russell had urged Claire to ask Dr. Pinkerton to step aside so that she could channel Albert. But once her suspicions were aroused by conflicting information Russell provided about Albert's past lives, she had decided not to follow his advice.

"So these earthbound spirits," I persisted, "are the dead who have lived rather unsavory lives and are hanging around and…."

"YES!" declared Dr. Pinkerton loudly. "These lost souls…." [he uttered the phrase with an attenuated cry of pain] "…these lower entities, they come in with great knowledge, they come in with love. They want you to believe in them. They are quite clever. They say that they do not control your will. Oh, no, no, no. They have a very lovely, sweet way to control you completely, do you understand me?"

"But what is to tell me that you . . ."

"That I am not of the same? I shall tell you why, Son. For many years I have been bouncing in and out of my instrument controlling organs, blood pressure, heartbeat and so on and so forth. Nothing bad has ever happened to her: she has never been possessed. I do not allow any lower entities around my instrument. But Aviva, she must stop at once. She's a very good medium, you know, and she could channel very well but she must retreat into herself for a while and have the proper training. If not, give her twelve to twenty-four months and you shall hear some very difficult news . . . Someone that comes through her shall remain there and we shall have to do an exorcism on this young lady."

The proposition was not an attractive one. Dr. Pinkerton knew that his words had incited anxiety and he pressed home the advantage.

"I am not lying to you, Joseph. I have no reason to lie to you, do you understand me? I've never lied to you."

Dr. Pinkerton concluded the session with a promise that, when we next met, he would withdraw and allow my true guide to speak through his instrument. He maintained that it was my true guide, not Filipa, who had earlier contacted Claire in her meditation. At our next meeting, however, the discarnate surgeon was as tantalizing and as tricky as ever.

"Your guide is right here, Joseph. She's saying: 'My Darling One. Do you truly want to speak to me or are you just ready to challenge me?'"

"Well," I began, far from convinced. "I think that she can understand what I've been through…."

"'Then I shall make you wait,' she's saying. 'You need more time to heal.'"

Dr. Pinkerton reminded me that he had sounded a faint warning about Russell and Filipa before my journey to Europe and stressed that he had purposely refrained from interfering with my free will.

"I did warn you, didn't I?" He smacked his lips loudly. "You went off just the same, didn't you?"

"Because I had to find out."

"I did not fight you, did I? I did not tell you to stay."

"Nor did Russell, Filipa and the others."

"They didn't need to. They felt that you trusted them one hundred per cent. The so-called master—Russell—is a serpent. He sweet-talks everyone, Dear. But the good always wins."

"So what are they gaining by this deception?" I asked.

"Controlling, My Dear," replied Dr. P. "Controlling, controlling. On the Earth plane, a lot of human beings like to control others. What makes you think it is different on the other side, Son?"

In spite of my doubts, Dr. Pinkerton was winning me over. My true guide, he said, had been engaged in a perpetual battle with Filipa to shield me from her seductive influence. Filipa had managed to be so credible and so effective because she had shadowed my true guide and impersonated her reincarnation history.

"But the buzzing in my ears," I asked him. "What is that?"

"That's her."

"That's my *real* guide?"

"Mm-mmm. She's been protecting you all the time….She does love you very much, Dear."

As always, I had a lot of thinking to do. For all his wheedling and evasiveness, Dr. Pinkerton appeared to exercise sound and careful judgement and had shown admirable restraint when the guides were dismissing him as a past-life personality. If Dr. Pinkerton could be established as the great-grandfather of the gynecologist in Belfast, if I was able to substantiate the claims concerning his life in Italy and if he could produce telling evidence of my true guide, Dr. P. would emerge as the genuine article against which the rogue spirits could be measured. As I prepared to check into Dr. Pinkerton's past-life claims, he never ceased to warn me about the devilish cunning of the lower entities.

"They are brilliant, Joseph, they are brilliant. You have no idea....These souls cannot cross over into the light. But they do have a lot of knowledge."

"How are they able to read one's thoughts?"

"They're around you. I've told you before, they're around you always. There's a constant fight here. We don't want to get too close to them, you know. We'll get caught."

"How?"

"They're quite powerful, these souls. We are protecting my instrument. We are protecting you. We are protecting a lot of souls. We're trying to make sure they stay away....You see, what these souls need...they need to be rescued, you know."

On 6 February 1988, I had my final audience with Dr. Pinkerton. Turning my investigative eye at last on the information he had provided, I discovered that the relatives he had named in Brussels and Vienna were nowhere to be found. Most revealing of all was the absence of his third claimed great-grandchild, who was said to be a London gynecologist called George Albert Pinkerton. The British Medical Directory for 1987 contained no mention of a doctor under that name.

Harboring incipient anger and distrust, I confronted Dr. Pinkerton in the gloom of his consulting room. To start with, he behaved as though he hadn't heard my declaration that the records bore no listing for a Dr. George Albert Pinkerton.

"What do you want to know about George?" he demanded unsteadily.

"Where can I find him? Why isn't he in the medical directory?"

"Just a moment. Yes, Nathaniel, yes, that is our friend Joseph. It's good to see his light, isn't it? Also, your guide is here, Joseph."

The carrot was no longer enticing the donkey. Dr. Pinkerton was employing his trusty tactics of distraction but I was not about to be swayed by yet another mention of my guide. I was thoroughly fed up with my compliance, with my tolerance, with my willingness to grant the benefit of the doubt to the utterances of one unfathomable voice after another. For years, I had encountered nothing but deceit and manipulation wrapped in the spirits' flattery, high-mindedness and exhortations of love and affection.

Watching Dr. Pinkerton performing his verbal dance, I condemned myself for acceding for so long to a being who, professing love and friendship, had done nothing but cajole and mislead with falsehood after falsehood. Something inside wanted to explode, but I smothered the impulse, knowing that any expression of anger would only be used against me. Responding with as much calm as I could muster, I refused to be diverted from the matter at hand.

"The British Medical Directory lists all medical practitioners in the British Isles. There's no George Albert Pinkerton listed as a doctor."

"That's nonsense," retorted Dr.. Pinkerton. "They're insisting here that you will find George….I don't see any problems."

We had to agree to differ.

"Joseph," Dr. P. went on, "do you realize what is going on in your inner self, in your inner conscious? Do you know how much anger there is there, disappointment….? Let go. Take one day at a time and get as much as you can out of whom you trust."

Those last few words left my throat constricted with a bitter chuckle. At long last, Dr. Pinkerton had been exposed in all his untrustworthiness. But I had to be absolutely certain that he was, indeed, as false as those entities he had taken such pleasure in reviling as earthbound spirits. First, I made contact with Dr. John Henry McKnight Pinkerton, the gynecologist in Belfast whom Claire Laforgia had supposed to be her controlling discarnate's great-grandson.

This flesh and blood Dr. Pinkerton was a renowned specialist and professor, the author of various papers on obstetrics and gynecology, and a Rockefeller Research fellow. In his reply to my letter, he denied any familial connection with Dr. Samuel Pinkerton.

> Dear Mr. Fisher,
> I was intrigued by your letter about my namesake. I am unable to confirm Claire Laforgia's hope; none of my grandparents or great-grandparents were physicians and all were born and died in Ulster. I may add that I know of no gynecologist with the name Pinkerton practicing in these islands during the past

eighty years—certainly none is listed in the Registry of the College of Gynecologists. So if any such descendant of this alleged "entity" exists, it would seem that he carries another name.

Yours sincerely,
J.H.M. Pinkerton

Even more damning was the response to an inquiry made of the archivist at the University of Bologna where Dr. Pinkerton claimed to have graduated in general surgery in 1830 at the age of twenty-nine. Translated from Italian, the letter was brief and to the point.

Dear Mr. Fisher,
With reference to your request for information concerning Dr. S. Pinkerton, please be advised that a check of our archives division of the University of Bologna has found that there is no record of this gentleman receiving a doctorate on the dates supplied.

The Director
Dr. Isabella Zanni Rosiello

As for all the other entities I had interviewed, only one—Dr. Frank George Jamieson, the "bone-setter" front Boston—lent himself to the possibility of verification. Richard J. Wolfe, curator of rare books and manuscripts at the Boston Medical Library, searched in vain for a record of the nineteenth-century practitioner. And if Dr. Jamieson's claims were rendered somewhat shaky by the results of Mr. Wolfe's inquiries, they were demolished by a letter from Ruth Marshall, a reference librarian at Boston Public Library. Not only was Dr. Jamieson absent from the records, there was also no trace of the medical college he supposedly attended and the graveyard where he was supposedly buried. Wellington Street, the address he had given, was not listed in the Boston directories until the alleged year of his death in 1872.

I was intrigued that both Pinkerton and Jamieson, whoever they were, had chosen to be known as "doctors." It seemed to be a favorite ploy among discarnate communicators. Doctors abound among the legions of entities channeled from coast to coast and they recur constantly in the history of Spiritualism. One can only assume that the prefix is adopted because of its power to generate instant deference and respect.

In his book *The Wanderings of a Spiritualist,* Sir Arthur Conan Doyle tells of attending a séance in Australia held by medium Charles Bailey whose "spirit controls" were both self-styled doctors. Sir Arthur wrote glowingly of the communicators' dignity and wisdom. Likewise, the great American psychologist William James was mightily impressed with a French "doctor" named Phinuit who spoke gruffly through the voice box of renowned medium Leonora Piper. I doubt whether anyone went in search of the past lives of Charles Bailey's "doctors," but a search was conducted for Dr. Phinuit and he was found to be absent from France's medical records.

The same problem dogged the well-known psychical researcher Sir William Crookes (1832–1919) who spent several years of his life attending séances in the hope of being able to prove the identities of a succession of discarnate communicators. As he wrote to Madame Boydanof of St Petersburg on 1 August 1874, his quest ended in disappointment.

> Madame,
> I have most earnestly desired to get the one proof you seek— the proof that the dead can return and communicate. I have never once had satisfactory proof that this is the case. I have had hundreds of communications *professing* to come from deceased friends, but whenever I try to get proof that they are really the individuals they profess to be, they break down. Not one has been able to answer the necessary questions to prove identity; and the great problem of the future is to me as impenetrable a mystery as it ever was. All I am satisfied of is that there exist invisible intelligent beings who *profess* to be spirits of deceased people.

Sir William Crookes would have dearly loved to obtain the heartwarming confirmation that he was looking for. So would many other psychical researchers, myself included. What could be more comforting than knowing beyond all doubt that one is in direct contact with a "guide" or departed relative who is dedicated to one's highest good? Unfortunately, mediumship is inclined to attract dark and tricky intelligences rather than act as a focal point for the genuine and the well-intentioned. It was always thus. As long ago as 1869, Andrew Jackson Davis wrote in *Spirit Mysteries:* "It is no difficult thing for certain spirits to impersonate others, to talk and dress up their thoughts like others, which they will do if such resemblance adds anything important to their communications."

Much more recently, in delivering the F.W.H. Myers Memorial Lecture in 1968 to Britain's Society for Psychical Research, Cyril Burt noted that even the most plausible examples of communication "seem nearly always to reveal on closer scrutiny flaws in the factual details and unexpected loopholes in the arguments based upon them."

Ruminating on Dr. Pinkerton's fall from grace, I chewed moodily on a meal of rice and mixed vegetables in Toronto's Chinatown. Finally, I pushed my plate away, called for the bill and bit into a Chinese fortune cookie. Inside was a sliver of paper bearing thirteen words typed in smudged purple ink: *Never be divided from the truth by what you would like to believe.* The message could hardly have been more appropriate.

Dr. Pinkerton was just another impostor who had made a great show of love, concern and the highest values, only to fail the basic test of integrity. He was able to assess Russell, Filipa and the others so adroitly because he was playing the same manipulative game. It takes one to know one. "The serpent," he had called Russell—an interesting choice of insult which could be applied to every discarnate of my acquaintance. Later, I was to read in Carl Jung's *The Seven Sermons to the Dead,* an obscure treatise on Gnostic symbolism, that the serpent was identified as an evil associate of earthbound spirits. The Sixth Sermon says:

> The serpent is an earthly soul, half-demonic, a spirit, and related to the spirits of the dead. Like the spirits of the dead, the serpent also enters terrestrial objects. The serpent also induces fear of itself in the hearts of men, and enkindles desire in the same. The serpent...is associated with the dead who are earthbound, who have not found the way by which to cross over to the state of solitude. The serpent...is a tyrant

and a tormenting spirit, always tempting people to keep the worst kind of company.

My publisher friend Alexander Blair-Ewart had anticipated that I would eventually become disabused of mediumistic communication. He likened the discarnate realms to a holy city which visiting strangers expected to be entirely inhabited by those who are spiritually developed. "More often than not," he noted, "one encounters only the riff-raff hanging around the temple gates." Alexander had seen enough mediums in his forty years to be thoroughly skeptical of all channeled voices and maintained that a genuine guide or teacher would never commandeer a physical body in order to make personal contact. "Truly spiritually aware entities," he said, "have better things to do than hang around incarnate beings who are not impeccable in their spiritual development."

Research both ancient and modern raises huge questions about the multitudinous channeled voices of the present day. If entities who claim to have lived in relatively recent times are shown to be suspect, how credible is the grandiose genealogy of so-called guides, teachers, ascended masters, off-planet beings, Oriental philosophers, contemporaries of Jesus, Atlantean overlords and other outlandish guardians whose far-flung assertions defy investigation?

All too frequently, these strange and unknowable voices brandish claims to past-life existences like complimentary passes to Nirvana and dispense instant reincarnation histories to the faithful in the same way that pablum is spoon-fed to uncomplaining infants. Their knowledge is impressive, their insight remarkable, their charismatic hold on their followers undeniable. Moreover, the voices' ostensible link to a higher and greater state of being seems to place them above suspicion in the minds of those who prize their counsel. Yet surely it is important—essential, even—to establish, if possible, the nature of the beast that is shuffling through the pipeline created by the trance state. Who are these entities *really?*

The answer to that question is as unwelcome as it is unavoidable. Months of soul-searching and examination of the evidence left me in little doubt that earthbound spirits or "hungry ghosts" have wormed their way into that juicy apple of spiritual regeneration known as the The New Age.

CHAPTER 19

The Siren Call of Hungry Ghosts

Mediumship is a mystery. For centuries, students of the mind have been confounded as to what exactly transpires in the trance state. While theories abound, no-one can define the process which opens the door of the personal unconscious to garrulous intelligences laying claim to nonmaterial existence and, in many cases, tutelary rights and privileges concerning certain earthly individuals. Is this babbling invented by the medium's unconscious mind? Are the voices speaking on behalf of multiple personalities? Are they past-life personalities re-activated? Is there reason to suspect either conscious or unconscious fraud? Or are we really hearing from discarnate beings, duplicitous though they may be, drawn by the medium's extraordinary state of receptivity?

These questions loomed large as I set to work comparing my own frustrating experience with historical observations, scriptural references, the casebooks of earlier investigators and contemporary medical evidence. No standard answers could be expected if only because each medium operated differently. All I could hope for were common characteristics which might function as an aid to understanding.

Whatever the voices represented, and however betrayed I felt by the spirits, I believed that conscious fraud on the part of the mediums was not a factor. Having observed the trance state on innumerable occasions, having witnessed marked personality changes reflected by a host of different accents and intonations, and having received a considerable amount of accurate information that could only have been acquired paranormally, there was no doubt in my mind that the mediumship itself, particularly in the cases of Aviva and Claire, was genuine. Other investigators from William James to Sir William Barrett have been similarly persuaded. As

Sir William commented in his 1920 classic *On The Threshold of the Unseen:* "Surely it would be as unjust to charge a deeply-entranced medium with conscious fraud as to accuse a somnambulist walking on a housetop with consciously jeopardizing his life."

Multiple personalities can also be dismissed from contention because multiple personalities always claim the same life span as the "host" individual. Past-life personalities, too, can be disregarded because, if genuine, relatively recent life histories would lend themselves to verification in historical records. And this was not the case.

Unconscious fraud is not so easily repudiated, however. The mind, as Aldous Huxley observed, is like the Earth of 150 years ago with its darkest Africas and Amazonian basins concealing unknown capabilities and potentials. Is the mind, then, somehow able to construct a fictional family of personalities, each with its own reincarnation life history? Possibly. Dr. Adam Crabtree, author of *Multiple Man* and one of the world's foremost authorities on multiple personality and possession, pointed out that thoughts in the unconscious tend to group together. These groups easily become personified.

But would the mind misrepresent itself as guides with distinct identities and then defend itself so steadfastly and so craftily against detection? No-one can say with certainty. "I don't believe," Crabtree told me, "that the process of channeling is purely self-delusion or purely the individual's unconscious or purely what the entities, so-called, would have us believe. I tend to go along with the notion that discarnate entities are, in many cases, responsible but that they are not who they say they are, although they are able to gain information in a paranormal fashion." Carl Jung also agonized over the meaning of mediumship and, while stressing the importance of being skeptical in each individual case, came to the conclusion that "the spirit hypothesis yields better results in practice than any other."

When Mrs. E. M. Sidgwick carried out a lengthy investigation of Mrs. Leonora Piper's mediumship, she suggested unconscious fraud as a probable explanation, but she also noted: "Veridical communications are received, some of which there is good reason to believe come from the dead, and therefore imply a genuine communicator in the background." Filipa's snatches of "natural" Greek likewise implied a disembodied source even as Aviva's unconscious will seemingly infiltrated the course and content of some conversations. Perhaps all mediums, to a greater or lesser extent, give voice in trance to unexpressed fears and unfulfilled desires in the same way that dreamers act out their unconscious feelings by producing a succession of images.

English medium Colin Evans has remarked that mediumship comprises a fusion of the deceased communicator's mind and the subconscious mind of the medium. The better the medium, the less his or her personality will intrude.

Whatever the source of the mysterious voices, there can be no denying the uncanny accuracy of many of their statements, particularly in regard to historical and geographical detail. This facility could be attributed to what Dr. Ian Stevenson, professor of psychiatry at the University of Virginia, has called "super telepathy." His theory suggests that any individual, living or dead, has the latent ability to tap into the complete memories of others, whether they be incarnate or discarnate. Unfortunately, there are no practical examples of this hypothesis. Telepathy appears, instead, to operate in a fragmented fashion. "Remote viewing" experiments conducted in the 1970s by the Stanford Research Institute, the Toronto Psychical Society and other professional bodies confirmed the reality of telepathy, but also demonstrated its erratic nature.

Then there is collective memory. Not Carl Jung's collective unconscious, which is ancestral and mythological, but the heavenly warehouse of memory known as the Akashic Records containing the impressions of everything that has ever happened. Disembodied entities might well be in a position to reach effortlessly into these vast immaterial archives which the great American clairvoyant Edgar Cayce visited regularly during self-hypnotic trance. In a lecture given in 1931, Cayce described a typical out of-body journey which gave him access to the Akashic Records. "I entered this temple and found in it a very large room, very much like a library," he said. "Here were the books of people's lives, for each person's activities were a matter of actual record, it seemed. And I merely had to pull down the record of the individual for whom I was seeking information."

Nevertheless, the most likely reason for the guides' hits and misses is that they *had* lived before in the locations they described so well. Because of their intention to deceive, however, their memory would be purposely selective and they would impart only enough accurate information to convince us of their earthly presence. The untruths and omissions testified to their parasitic behavior and penchant for making mischief.

Yet still the question nags: *why* would they lie about their identities? If bent on deception, would they not appear all the more believable if they were to provide their real names? Perhaps the solution to this riddle lies in their well-concealed dread of non-physical existence. If they gave their real names they would be forced to confront their deaths. And such a confrontation, which is clearly avoided at all costs, would activate their most hideous nightmare—that they no longer exist physically.

No matter how I mulled over the range of possible explanations, I always returned to the premise that the voices and their distinct personalities were generated by mischievous, and possibly malevolent, discarnates. Their eagerness to communicate, their concern for the medium's health and strength, their preoccupation with life after death and reincarnation and the occasional admission that they missed the pleasures of incarnate life, all suggested humans who no longer had physical bodies yet longed to live and breathe once more.

Just as the famed entity Seth occasionally asked for a glass of wine or beer and claimed to enjoy the material realm through Jane Roberts' senses, there were indications that Dr. Pinkerton and Russell hungered for vicarious sexual thrills. Russell and Filipa refused to discuss their deaths and declaimed, "We're not spirits!" as if unhappy with the *postmortem* condition. Dr. Pinkerton, claiming to know so much about earthbound spirits, uttered the phrase "lost soul" with a prolonged cry of anguish. I was intrigued by these clues.

But most of all I pondered the significance of the lying and manipulation channeled in the exalted name of guides and spiritual teachers and camouflaged as love, wisdom and solicitousness. And I concluded that if these various entities were to gratify themselves by tasting physical life, they had no option but to wrap their true intent in the guise of virtuousness. Only if they were seen as emissaries of the highest would their counsel be regularly requested. Only if they concealed their identities would they be unencumbered by the past. For ten years, Dr. Joel Whitton studied the trance utterances of several mediums while conducting research as a member of the Toronto Society for Psychical Research. In that time he learned that many of the voices he engaged in conversation belonged to mischievous discarnate entities "who would pose as whatever the inquirer, either consciously or unconsciously, wanted them to be." He also discovered that these entities were extraordinarily possessive of the body through which they were communicating. After listening, on tape, to the confrontation with Russell which followed my return from Europe, Dr. Whitton psychoanalyzed Russell's state of mind as revealed by his statements. Most revealing of all, he said, was Russell's accusation that I was negating the entities' earthly lives and karma.

"Russell is afraid of not existing," said Dr. Whitton. "You've stepped on his fear. His existence must be tenuous or he wouldn't comment on it. A true guide who had a conscious existence in the between-life state would not be threatened by your revelations. We always defend ourselves against that which we fear. In my opinion, he's attached himself to the medium because it's his way of continuing his existence vicariously, of trying to assure himself that he's alive. In his need to exist, he's playing the role of guide. He's a parasite. So are the others—very troubled, frightened, neurotic entities. Perhaps the medium has drawn these discarnates to herself because *her* fear is of dying, of not existing. Like attracts like. You have stumbled onto a nest of neuroses in both this world and the next.

"The red flag of neurosis is to do something that reveals your fear. Sigmund Freud called it 'the compulsion to repeat.' Unconsciously but deliberately, Russell and the others fed you false data so that they would be confronted with their worst fear—the fear that they do not exist. That's what they want to hear; that's what they are most afraid of. The mobilization of Russell's defenses proves the hypothesis."

The Benevolent Devil in P. D. Ouspensky's story of the same name admits to being terrified of the void of non-existence. "I have told you our biggest secret," he confesses. "It is on account of this fear, this terror, that we attach ourselves to you: you help us to ignore the dreadful nothingness and forget about it." I was reminded of the painting on Aviva's wall and its evocation of affliction. Titled "The Seekers," the painting struck me, belatedly, as an accurate portrayal of the plight of earthbound spirits: tormented individuals, condemned to darkness, who stretch beseechingly towards the light of incarnate humanity.

Every reference that I uncovered concerning earthbound spirits seemed to fit the channeling phenomenon at large. And the more I learned, the more it appeared that mediums were taking huge risks in allowing themselves to become the unwitting accomplices of questionable discarnate attentions. Ancient spiritual teachings from a wide range of cultures tell of hosts of disembodied beings inhabiting a dimension which lies closest to the Earth. This is the lower astral realm, a gloomy cesspool of the dead peopled by the spirits of those who have lived base, ignorant, or selfish lives. Afflicted with all manner of craving for terrestrial pleasure, their decadent existence thrives on attachment to needy and unsuspecting individuals on Earth. And so they masquerade as guides or teachers, developing emotional attachments to earthly humans and recycling the erudition available to all who inhabit the non-material universe. Their thinking processes are as rapid as they are machiavellian; their vampiric need of human energies is boundless.

These earthbound spirits or, in Tibetan Buddhist phraseology, *pretas* or "hungry ghosts," are individuals whose minds, at the point of physical death, have been incapable of disentangling from desire. Thus enslaved, the personality becomes trapped on the lower planes even as it retains, for a while, its memory and individuality. Hence the term "lost soul," a residual entity that is no more than an astral corpse-in-waiting. It has condemned itself to perish; it has chosen a "second death." In *The Astral Body*, Lt. Col. Arthur E. Powell asserts that entities who gather around mediums or sensitives are "people who have led an evil life and are filled with yearnings for the earth life they have left, and for the animal delights they can no longer directly taste." He goes on:

> Such "spooks" are conscienceless, devoid of good impulses, tending towards disintegration, and consequently can work for evil only, whether we regard them as prolonging their vitality by vampirizing at séances or polluting the medium and sitters with astral connections of an altogether undesirable kind....The more unselfish and helpful a person is, the less likely is he to be found after death lingering in full consciousness on the lower levels of the astral plane, from which the earth is most readily accessible.

In his out-of-body journeyings, Robert Monroe tells of encountering a zone next to the Earth plane populated by the "dead" who couldn't or wouldn't realize they were no longer physical beings. "It wasn't nice," writes Monroe in *Far Journeys*. The beings he perceived "kept trying to be physical, to do and be what they had been, to continue physical one way or another. Bewildered, some spent all of their activity in attempting to communicate with friends and loved ones still in bodies or with anyone else who might come along...."

This thickly-peopled "dead zone" just beyond the frontiers of physical existence tallies precisely with the realm of the hungry ghosts described in the teachings of Tibetan Buddhists. The hungry ghosts, characterized by intense greed, are depicted as beings with tiny mouths, thin necks and gigantic bellies. They are tortured by their insatiable hunger even more than the pain of not being able to find and consume what they crave. Their wants and desires are seen as a desperate attempt to feed their poverty of spirit as well as to obliterate their most basic fear, the fear that they may not exist. After death, say the Buddhists, the earthly individual's powers of resistance will be tried and tested by the hungry ghosts' siren call. *The Tibetan Book of the Dead,* an eighth-century guidebook mapping out the psychic territory to be negotiated once the body has perished, advises on the temptation to come:

> ...together with the wisdom light, the soft yellow light of the hungry ghosts will also shine. Do not take pleasure in it; give up desire and yearning....If you are attracted to it, you will fall into the realm of the hungry ghosts and experience unbearable misery from hunger and thirst. It is an obstacle, blocking the path of liberation....

Emanuel Swedenborg, who claimed to be able to pierce clairvoyantly the veil of the spiritual worlds, warned at great length about the brilliant and delusive nature of many communicating entities. Such evil, seducing spirits were said to be deceitful men and women who desired, in death, to hold the living in thrall to their duplicity. In *Arcana Caelestia*—published a century before the founding of modern Spiritualism—he explained how they cuddle up to their victims.

When spirits begin to speak with man they conjoin themselves with his thoughts and affections....They put on all things of his memory, thus all things which the man has learned and imbibed from infancy the spirits suppose these things to be their own.

Swedenborg maintained that the worst spirits of all were those "who have been in evils from love of self and at the same time inwardly in themselves have acted from deceit." In *Heaven and Hell* he tells how these entities like to flutter about mortals like phantoms, secretly infusing them with evil by penetrating the emotions.

They perceive and smell out the affections as dogs do wild beasts in the forest. Where they perceive good affections, they instantly turn them into evil ones, leading and bending them in a wonderful manner by means of the other's delights, and this so secretly and with such malignant skill that the other knows nothing of it....In the world these were the men who deceitfully captivated the minds of others, leading and persuading them by the delights of their affections or lusts....

Swedenborg's statements were echoed, in whole or in part, by the behavior of Filipa, Russell, Tuktu, Dr. Pinkerton and others. On 5 March 1987, the guides who spoke through Aviva were asked how we could be assured that they were not inhabitants of the lower astral plane. Tuktu responded by saying that no-one occupying the lower astral realm would be able to communicate directly by voice. Yet Dr. Carl Wickland, Dr. Edith Fiore and other medical specialists in de-possession therapy have spent much time conversing with entities occupying their patients' bodies in efforts to persuade them to leave. The possessors are always earthbound spirits.

"I view the possessing entities as the true patients," wrote Dr. Edith Fiore in *The Unquiet Dead*. "They are suffering greatly without even realizing it. Virtual prisoners, they are trapped on the earth plane feeling exactly as they did moments before their deaths, which may have occurred decades before."

Back in 1924, Dr. Carl Wickland told in *Thirty Years Among The Dead* how discarnate intelligences were attracted to the magnetic light emanating from mortals. Consciously or unconsciously, certain entities attached themselves wherever possible to these auras, finding an avenue of expression through influencing, obsessing or possessing their victims. Such encroachment might be facilitated by a natural and predisposed susceptibility, a depleted nervous system or illness. Less resistance was offered when the vital forces were lowered, allowing obtruding spirits to influence the "host" with their own thoughts and emotions, weakening willpower and contributing to mental confusion and distress.

Dr. Wickland, who discovered that some possessing entities claimed the status of guides or spiritual guardians, worked in a unique way. He would coax the spirits from the bodies of his severely disturbed patients and into the entranced form of his wife, Anna, a medium. He would then engage them in a two-way conversation, convincing them of their earthbound condition. If his commanding voice failed to dislodge a possessing spirit, Dr. Wickland sometimes applied encouragement in the form of terrifying electric shocks. He declared:

> These earthbound spirits are the supposed "devils" of all ages; devils of human origin, by-products of human selfishness, false teachings and ignorance, thrust blindly into a spirit existence and held there in a bondage of ignorance. The influence of these discarnate entities is the cause of many of the inexplicable and obscure events of earth life and of a large part of the world's misery. Purity of life and motive, or high intellectuality, do not necessarily offer protection....Many earthbound spirits are conscious of influencing mortals but enjoy their power, seeming to be without scruples.

Between 1977 and 1979, a hungry ghost masquerading as the late yoga master Sri Swami Sivananda (1887–1963) very nearly destroyed the worldwide yoga movement run by his protégé Swami Vishnu Devananda. The trouble started at the organization's headquarters north of Montreal, Canada when a senior staff member—a woman suffering from chronic abdominal pain—began to channel a spirit claiming to be the Master Sivananda. Swami Vishnu was quickly persuaded of the voice's veracity and his conviction led, in turn, to conviction among his followers. Soon, a large group was meeting nightly to listen to the "Master" expound wisdom and clairvoyance and occasionally demonstrate remarkable healing powers.

To Swami Vishnu Devananda, the channel's phrasing, intonation and effortless use of Sanskrit echoed the revered master's style of speaking and writing that he remembered so well from time spent in Rishikesh, India. Moreover, he was addressed by the pet name—Vishnu Swami—selected by his teacher many years earlier. The spirit offered guidance and inspiration and appeared to invest the very atmosphere with highly-charged positive energy. With protracted deviousness, however, the invisible presence deluded its audience into believing that they were the chosen Children of Light. Dire global predictions were made and, ultimately, the group was urged to stockpile food and weapons in readiness for the advancing breakdown in social order.

Swami Vishnu knew that such elitism contradicted Sri Swami Sivananda's abiding love and compassion for all beings. And he was already beginning to suspect that the spirit was encouraging laziness among his followers while subtly turning them against him. Consequently, he consulted the Master's teachings and discovered several passages in his book *What Becomes of the Soul After Death* affirming that great sages of the past cannot be invoked by a medium and that mediumship merely invites earthbound spirits. For example:

> The spirits have no knowledge of the highest truth. They cannot help others in attaining self-realization. Some are foolish, deceitful and ignorant. These earthbound spirits control the mediums and pretend to know everything regarding the planes beyond death. They speak falsehood. They put on the appearance of some other spirit and deceive the audience. The poor innocent mediums are not aware of the tricks played by their dishonest spirit guides.

Realizing that he had been duped by an impersonating spirit, Swami Vishnu called a halt to the channeling sessions. Too late, he saw the malevolence which pervaded the messages, one of which had advised that he undertake oral surgery without anesthesia. Too late, he perceived that the sessions were leaving him "completely drained like a discharged battery." The Swami's change of heart provoked anger and confusion among his followers, and some fifty people—many of them senior staff—deserted the organization in the belief that the wishes of the "Master" were being denied. Several Sri Sivananda centers around the world were closed down. As Swami Vishnu declared in an article in *Yoga Today:* "If anyone has stayed, it is by the grace of the true Sivananda."

In August, 1989, Swami Vishnu Devananda—a man who has dedicated his life to spiritual development and world peace—recounted the ordeal and told me ruefully: "Yes, I was fooled. But we have all learned from the experience. Earthbound spirits possess great knowledge and insight and, once you give them your hand, they will slowly pull you into their sphere of domination. Our scientists do not yet understand this dangerous phenomenon."

Edgar Cayce was well aware of the disruptive agitations of earthbound spirits. Although Cayce lulled himself into trance and spoke frequently of reincarnation while unconscious, he was not a medium in the strict sense of the word because his voice was always his own. No guides or controls came forward to identify themselves and take over his physical body. Instead, Cayce was able to attune his unconscious mind to communicate with the minds of people either living or dead. One day, while the "sleeping prophet" was stretched out in self-hypnotic trance, he warned explicitly about non-material mischief-makers:

> There are those influences from without the veil that seek, seek, that they may find an expression, that they may still be a portion of this evolution in the earth, not considering their present estate. And these bring turmoil and strife.

The Ouija board attracts earthbound spirits more readily than any other inanimate device and those who choose to "play" this trans-dimensional distraction run the risk of being influenced by the most devious tricksters imaginable. In *Ouija: The Most Dangerous Game,* Stoker Hunt presents a succession of cases in which people sacrificed their will and judgement to invisible guides—with disastrous consequences. "Because of the intimate nature of the information revealed," writes Hunt, "the Ouija board is incredibly seductive. The more suggestible a "player," the more dangerous the Ouija game." Seth, whose eloquence gave him ambassadorial status in the New Age movement, was first contacted via an Ouija board.

Occultist Alice Bailey maintained that common trance mediumship which allowed for communication with "old Atlantean degenerates and earthbound souls, the average Indian chief and guide" was a perversion of the natural relationship between the material and non-material worlds. "There is nothing to be learned from them and much to be avoided," she wrote of mediumship's innumerable voices in *A Treatise on White Magic*.

Madame Helena Blavatsky, the founder of the Theosophical movement, warned of the dangers of drifting into "unconscious black magic or the most helpless mediumship." In *The Key To Theosophy* she wrote that anyone who attempted to cultivate hypnotism or any form of mediumistic communication without awareness of the philosophic rationale of those powers was like a rudderless boat launched on a stormy ocean. "Happy are those who escape...," she added, "as they have neither test nor criterion by which they can distinguish between the true and the false."

The teachings of the Rosicrucians, a mystical order which can be traced to ancient Egypt, condemn Spiritualism and mediumship. The American edition of the Rosicrucian Manual states that many so-called mediums know little or nothing of the laws and principles which they are attempting to demonstrate, sometimes bringing serious situations and sorrows into the lives of those who are consulting them. The Rosicrucians insist that soul personalities who have left the physical plane do not return before the moment of their reincarnation and do not incorporate into a medium in order to communicate with the living. Not that communication with the departed is impossible. It is just that contact operates on a vibratory level without need of mediums, Ouija boards or any other paraphernalia.

Jesus Christ and the Biblical prophets had nothing good to say about communication with the dead, Jesus casting out "unclean spirits" and "devils" on many occasions. In the Bible, those who consult with spirits are placed in the same category as murderers, liars and fornicators.

Deuteronomy 18: 9-12 commands: "There shall not be found among you anyone that...useth divination...or a consulter of familiar spirits or a necromancer. For all that do these things are an abomination to the Lord." The Book of Revelation warns that those who unrepentantly practice spiritism invite the "second death" or everlasting destruction: to converse with earthbound spirits is to share their fate. Spirits and demons—followers of Lucifer who joined in rebellion against God—are often cited interchangeably as cunning and deceitful beings intent on corrupting the unwary. In the words of 2 Corinthians 14: "Satan himself masquerades as an angel of light. It is therefore a simple thing for his agents to masquerade as agents of good."

The Roman Catholic Church attributes mediumistic voices to fallen angels posing as the souls of the dead. In 1917, the Vatican's Holy Office decreed that priests should stay away from all spiritist demonstrations and conferences, no matter how well-intentioned because "one wishes to have no participation with evil spirits." Twelve years later, Cardinal Alexis Lépicier wrote a theological exposition in which he maintained that only corrupt and dishonest entities responded to communicative overtures. Because "these occult agents" spoke of the immortality of the soul, they induced the incautious and the credulous to accept other false statements. "Catholic theology holds," Cardinal Lépicier concluded, "that whatever the pretensions of modern spiritism may be, it is the continuation of Satan's revolt against God, and must end in the irreparable ruin of souls."

It was in the Middle Ages that a distinction was made between the supreme manifestation of evil known as Satan or the Devil and the host of lesser malevolent entities called demons. The word "Devil" is derived from the Latin *diabolus* and the Greek *diabolos,* meaning to slander, while Satan was born of the Hebrew *satan,* meaning an enemy. The word "demon" is based on the Greek *daimonion,* which signifies an evil spirit as opposed to *daimon,* a god or benevolent spirit.

Demons reverberate like a curse throughout the history of Christianity. The Jewish historian Flavius Josephus described them as "the spirits of wicked men" and Plutarch, the Greek essayist and biographer, made reference to "certain tyrannical demons" requiring for their enjoyment some soul still incarnate. But in modern times the notion of demonic influence has been laughed to scorn.

Towards the end of the last century, Dr. John L. Nevius studied strange psychical phenomena in the Chinese province of Shantung where the ability of evil spirits to usurp minds and wills had long been recognized. In his book *Demon Possession* (1896) Dr. Nevius recounted the behavior of individuals overwhelmed by controlling influences. He might as well have been describing a latter-day channeling session.

> When normal consciousness is restored after one of these attacks, the subject is entirely ignorant of everything which has passed during that state. The most striking characteristic...is that the subject evidences another personality, and the normal personality for the time being is partially or wholly dormant. The new personality presents traits of character utterly different from those which really belong to the subject in his normal state, and this change of character is, with rare exceptions, in the direction of moral obliquity and impurity. Many persons while "demon-possessed" give evidence of knowledge which cannot be accounted for in ordinary ways....They sometimes converse in foreign languages of which in their normal states they are entirely ignorant.

Whether voluntary or involuntary, possession always entails the invasion of one's will and thought by another, usually unknown, entity. Dr. Edith Fiore acknowledges that the condition has minor benefits such as companionship and exposure to whatever special abilities the possessing spirit might own. But she cautions that the relationship is *never* healthy and stultifies spiritual growth.

After completing an in-depth study of Mrs. Leonora Piper's mediumship, William James was so disturbed by the ramifications of the trance state that he was moved in 1909 to lash out at the intellectual establishment for its refusal to accept that demons or evil spirits might actually exist. He wrote, "The refusal of modern 'enlightenment' to treat 'possession' as a hypothesis to be spoken of as even possible, in spite of the massive human tradition based on concrete human experience in its favor, has always seemed to me a curious example of the power of fashion in things 'scientific.' That the demon theory...will have its innings again is to my mind absolutely certain. One has to be 'scientific' indeed to be blind and ignorant enough to suspect no such possibility."

Blindness and ignorance is, however, much in evidence in the New Age movement that champions the channeling experience. Having been seduced by the spirits myself in spite of my avowed investigative intent, I know how persuasive and convincing communicating entities can be. Their charm, clairvoyance and knowledge can work wonders in massaging ones frail hope that enlightenment might be within reach after all. Spiritual aspiration is often attended by tenderness and vulnerability, and earthbound spirits well know how to burrow into the most soft and pliable parts of the self in the cause of satisfying their own ends. Their mission is made so much easier by gullible New Agers, ever in search of the pure and the expansive, who readily embrace any influence which appears to be spiritually nourishing. Few care to probe beneath the platitudes and the plausibility to gain hard-won insights into what is really being said and done.

Channelers' disconcerting insouciance is sometimes matched by researchers who merely play at the task of investigation. Professor Jon Klimo tells in *Channeling* how sociologist Earl Babbie has supposedly devised a method of discerning good entities from bad entities: he simply asks them questions. In Babbie's words:

> We're starting to see some consensus emerging….It has to do with empowerment. If the entity is trying to get you to follow it or is trying to get you to give up your power to it, then you should really watch out….Many of the entities say they are intending to put themselves out of business.

Many entities *say* many things and Babbie should not be so artless as to suppose that such a procedure could ever hope to discriminate effectively. When John, the fourth evangelist, urged, "Test the spirits…" he must surely have had something more exacting in mind than ingenuous interrogation. Emanuel Swedenborg, of course, was fully cognizant of the devious practices of discarnates who allied themselves with the highest good. His sustained exposure to all manner of subversion left him eternally suspicious of all communications. "When spirits begin to speak with man," he wrote, "he must beware lest he believe in anything; for they say almost anything; things are fabricated of them, and they lie...."

Lying—and lying about lying—has always come naturally to earthbound spirits. As long ago as the third century, Iamblichus, the leading neo-Platonist philosopher of his time, unmasked an alleged Apollo speaking through a medium who was only the ghost of a gladiator. Minucius Felix, a Roman advocate and apologist, must have encountered impostors of his own. "There are," he wrote, "some insincere and vagrant spirits, degraded from their heavenly vigor...who cease not, now that they are ruined themselves, to ruin others." Centuries later, Swami Bhakta Vishita warned in his work *Genuine Mediumship* of a mischievous class of entities who impersonated other spirits. Wherever identity was claimed, he said, "positive and strict identification of the spirits is a duty on the part of investigators."

***

My thoughts turned back to George Chapman, the spiritual healer. He, too, insisted upon the need to verify the status of communicating entities, having established beyond all doubt that Dr. William Lang—the healing entity he has channeled for more than forty years—once lived as a highly-respected ophthalmic surgeon. Dr. Lang's surviving colleagues, patients and closest relatives had sworn that the entity speaking through George Chapman was, in truth, the genial medical practitioner who died in 1937. Why, then, was Dr. Lang so rare? If mediums at large were attracting earthbound spirits who were fond of fabrication, why was Dr. Lang so different? *Was* he different? Or was he simply more astute and sophisticated than the rest? Realizing that only George Chapman and Dr. Lang could answer my questions, I set out once more for the United Kingdom in September 1988.

Advance attempts to reach Chapman from Canada by letter and telephone had failed because he was working in the south of France. Nevertheless, his son, Michael, had told me that he was scheduled to return home to the Welsh village of Trer-Ddol, near Aberystwyth, by the middle of the month. Once I arrived in England, repeated messages left on Chapman's answering machine brought no response, even after Michael had confirmed that his father was once more in residence. So I climbed into my rented car and traveled more than three hundred miles to the west coast of Wales, a journey culminating in a steep climb up a narrow drive leading to Chapman's home, *Pant Glas* (Green Dip) perched high on a hillside.

When I arrived, *Pant Glas'* tiny forecourt was crammed with cars and a chartered bus bearing the sick and the disabled for appointments with Dr. Lang. A harried receptionist explained that Chapman was very busy and unable to see me. I scribbled a note of introduction and left.

The next day I drove back to the house on the hill before the start of the working day. It was a gloriously sunny morning and, as I stepped out of the car into the empty forecourt, a short, stocky man with a neatly-trimmed white beard appeared from behind the doctor's office set apart from the main building. He was smartly dressed in a blue blazer, dark slacks and a tie. Having seen photographs of sixty-seven-year-old George Chapman, I immediately recognized the man who greeted me. He apologized profusely for having been so difficult to track down. Then he invited me into his house, leading the way to a study furnished with relics of Dr. Lang; the surgeon's chair, his Bible, his retirement tankard and his appointment book for 1937 were all proudly indicated. Even the window curtains had been especially designed for Dr. Lang by the celebrated William Morris. Next, Chapman reached into a drawer for an envelope bearing a broken seal and showed me the enclosed letter signed by Dr. Lang's daughter, the late Marie Lyndon Lang, attesting to the genuineness of his mediumship.

Briefly, I told the story of my disillusionment with the claims of channeled entities and expressed the hope that Dr. Lang, the verifiable Dr. Lang, might possibly be able to throw some light on the darkness of my understanding.

"You're pretty well like me, you see," said Chapman in his pronounced Liverpool accent. "I would never satisfy myself until I had complete evidence....Maurice Barbanell, whose guide was Silver Birch, was a good friend of mine but I said to him: 'You've no evidence to prove it *is* Silver Birch.' To be honest, the only evidence I've had of life after death is from Dr. Lang."

I asked him why he believed he was the only person, to our knowledge, to verify so conclusively a possessing discarnate.

"I don't know," was Chapman's answer. "It was all so easy for me. I went into trance and Dr. Lang spoke through me, saying who he was, where he practiced, where he lived…all the information. My friend wrote away and it didn't seem difficult. But I don't mix with other healers or mediums. I never get involved with or worry about what the others are doing. There are so many different entities coming through and it's difficult to know what is truth or not."

Chapman spoke of his healing partnership with Dr. Lang as being "like a marriage." Apparently, Dr. Lang initiated the communication so that he could continue the work he loved, while at the same time exhibiting firm evidence for life after death. Chapman was chosen as intermediary because he had been a member of the same spiritual family as Dr. Lang through many incarnations. Dr. Lang has said that he will reincarnate on Earth following Chapman's death.

As Chapman enters trance, he can see Dr. Lang walking towards him. "It's like being smothered," he said. "I know no more. He has possession of my body but I remember nothing. It's like going into a deep sleep. But it's not the same as being hypnotized. During the war [Chapman served in the Royal Air Force] when we were tired we used to perform co-operative hypnotism on one another so that we could get some sleep. In that hypnotic state, the heartbeat and pulse rate are normal; but in the state of deep trance the heartbeat and pulse rate drop to a rate just above death. You feel fine when you come out of a hypnotic state. But I come out of my trance and feel nausea. I'm drained, yes…."

Checking his watch, Chapman realized that Dr. Lang was already late for his first patient of the day. Nevertheless, he offered to let me talk to the surgeon before he commenced his long list of appointments. Many of those who appear at *Pant Glas* have traveled long distances for a ten-minute appointment, which cost ten pounds, yet Chapman rarely meets his patients *consciously*. When they enter his darkened office, he is already installed in trance as Dr. Lang.

We left the house and walked over to the little office. Once more, the forecourt was packed with vehicles and overflowing with patients, some in wheelchairs, some on crutches. I waited in the anteroom with the receptionist as Chapman stepped into his small operating theatre to transform himself for the purposes of conducting an afternoon's healing. When I entered two minutes later, Chapman was practically unrecognizable. His blazer and tie had been discarded, his eyes were tightly closed and his forthright voice was transformed into the gentle, quavering tones of old age. He was smiling broadly when I shook his hand and I noticed how weak was his grip compared with Chapman's firm grasp.

"Why didn't you stay in the log cabin?" Dr. Lang wanted to know. Apparently, there was a cabin on the nearby hillside where guests often stayed.

I explained that I had been trying vainly to reach George Chapman by telephone for days and, in desperation, had driven unannounced to his door.

"Well, George gets such an amount of mail and—errr—he never gets a lot of time. He means well. He puts—errr—scribbles down on the paper but he never really—errr—gets round to doing things which I suppose he should….If you come again, you should drop George a line well in advance and say that I said you should. There's a very nice log cabin up there….."

I thanked Dr. Lang for the invitation and proceeded to explain my difficulties in trying—and failing—to verify information provided by various entities. He listened carefully, leaning forward with his fixed grin and sightless eyes. I had anticipated that he might have given me a lecture on the brilliance and trickery of earthbound spirits who use mediums' receptivity for their own ends. But he did no such thing. No matter how I worded my question, even suggesting that devious intelligences were taking advantage of the trance state, he continually laid the blame for my problems on the mediums concerned.

"Maybe mixed-up messages coming into the medium's brain," suggested Dr. Lang in an accent which, though more refined than Chapman's, still bore traces of Liverpudlian dialect. "It can be—errr—that the medium—errr—is not in so complete a trance and it's always a little worrying when one hears of mediums with so many people coming—errr—through them….I think it is the medium's brain or mind—call it what you will—becoming confused."

I told Dr. Lang that while much of the geographical and historical information supplied by the entities was amazingly accurate, the claimed identities did not stand up to scrutiny.

"Well, you get a lot of impostors," he replied. "Maybe the mediums are not developed enough to have built—errr—a good circle of protection?"

"But why are you so rare in that you are an entity who can be documented?" I demanded.

"Well, I think entities can be traced if you can find first of all a medium who is making genuine contact….I know as much about—errr—my life as I did when I was on Earth. You don't forget. One—errr—has memory…."

"But it seems that a lot of information given by discarnate entities is plainly wrong."

"You see, it could be, as I say, that—errr—the medium's not so perfect as one would like the medium to be."

"Or is it," I persisted, "that some entities are closer to the earthbound plane than others?"

"Well, I-I-I…when a person passes over they are very close to the Earth for a while. Therefore, if they make contact with a medium they can give all the evidence quite clearly. But they don't remain—errr—close to the Earth for very long. They start to move away, as it were."

"But you have remained close—for a purpose, presumably…."

"Well, yes, I'm linked with George….Spirits are about you all the time. It's just becoming sensitive enough to make contact—errr—with the spirit and, as I say, George and I have a closeness through our lives of being of one family, if you wish, and having worked through other lives in this way…I still blame a lot on mediumship….You find today that mediumship is not being practiced enough and there are not enough trance mediums that, I would say, are so fully developed. People seem to want to put—errr—a collar and tie on and become a type of medical doctor, which they're not…I think if you say the healing's coming from spirit, you have to *prove* the healing's coming from spirit."

"It's just that I feel the entities I have talked to are manipulative. Does that make sense to you?"

"It makes sense, yes. This can happen."

"Do you see those sort of people from your vantage point?"

"Yes. Because in this world you have playboys—errr—just the same and people wanting to believe they are important, giving so much evidence. I know I get many [incarnate] people telling me of the great guides they have, and they all seem to want someone very important. They talk of their great guides but when you—errr—ask them: 'Did you trace your guide?' they say: 'Oh, no, no, but he told me he was some famous surgeon. He's using a different name because, you see, he doesn't want his family to become involved.' Well, surely, when you've passed into this world you want your family to know where you are. That's what I wanted right away. My daughter and my grandchildren all came to see me."

"Do you see yourself as George's guide?"

"Well, I don't like the word 'guide.' I feel that I am George's close friend and I am here to help him and, if you wish, to guide him. When you come into the world you have a guide but it's not usually a Red Indian. It's usually a member of your family who loves you and wants to help you on the right road. Errr…if later on you develop a gift of mediumship, then— errr—no doubt someone will get connected with you to help you…."

Dr. Lang's healing mission is unprecedented. Over the years, thousands of people have benefited from his wondrous and specialized manipulation of the etheric or "shadow" body. Furthermore, the documentation of his personal history is a feat which knows no equal in the annals of psychical research. For all that, I felt much the same in the company of the charming and deferential Dr. Lang as I did while conversing with the spirits whose claims remain unsubstantiated. I couldn't put my finger on it, but something was wrong. While seeming to cooperate fully, Dr. Lang was fudging. He told me nothing new, nothing incisive. And when I raised the question of charlatan spirits who crave physical sensation, the discarnate surgeon avoided the topic completely.

Because my questions were not being answered directly, I wondered about Dr. Lang's ulterior motive in availing himself of George Chapman's mediation. Surely it was unnatural for any spirit entity, unless earthbound, to hang around the material world for more than forty years. Good works notwithstanding, was his true intent the satisfaction of misplaced desire for earthly experience? Dr. Edith Fiore noted in *The Unquiet Dead* that a misguided sense of unfinished business often compelled spirits to remain in the physical world. Was Dr. Lang, for all his altruism and meritorious reputation, just another hungry ghost?

Dr. Lang may not have been dishonest so far as his earthly credentials were concerned but I was by no means convinced that he was telling the whole story. Comparing him with other, blatantly suspect entities, I was haunted by one of Lt. Col. Arthur Powell's observations in *The Astral Body*. He wrote that it was impossible to distinguish truth from falsehood in communications from the next world "since the resources of the astral plane can be used to delude persons on the physical plane to such an extent that no reliance can be placed even on what seems the most convincing proof."

I was also mindful of the experience of a young woman called Johanna Michaelsen who, for fourteen months during the 1970s, assisted a Mexico City spirit healer called Hermanito Cuauhtemoc in more than 200 psychic surgery operations. Hermanito worked through an elderly Mexican woman, Pachita, whom he possessed intermittently for more than fifty years until her death in 1979.

Speaking in a deep, gruff voice, Hermanito claimed to be Pachita's guide who had once incarnated as an ancient Aztec warrior. He worked wonders far beyond the reach of medical science, removing inoperable brain tumors, replacing vertebrae, conducting lung transplants, healing cataracts and performing other "miracle" cures. Like Dr. Lang, Hermanito hugely impressed any medical doctors who witnessed his operations and went so far as to recruit a Mexican surgeon to help with his healing mission. Crowds of sick and disabled people—wealthy and poverty-stricken alike—flocked to Pachita's home in hope of ending their suffering.

In *The Beautiful Side of Evil* Michaelsen tells how she marveled at the spirit surgeon's abilities, encouraged in her appreciation by Hermanito's frequent invocation of the names of God and Jesus Christ. Once, however, she was paralyzed by a look of intense hatred which passed fleetingly across Pachita's face while Hermanito was in control. Then Michaelsen observed that not all of Hermanito's patients recovered even when he said they would and she realized that, although most people felt no pain while under Hermanito's care, committed Christians tended to suffer hideously. She noticed, too, that Hermanito acted with cruelty towards Pachita, refusing to treat her when she was sick. At last, Michaelsen severed her ties with Pachita and left Mexico City. She became convinced that evil forces were the source of Hermanito's powers and went on to denounce all mediumistic works as an abomination.

CHAPTER 20

The Challenge of Consciousness— Spirituality *versus* Psychism

More than four years have passed since my first chat with Filipa and I feel like a disaffected lover who likes to tell himself he never really cared. Intellectually, I can dismiss her as just another earthbound spirit who tricked me into making an emotional commitment that temporarily shored up her own condemned existence. I can protest self-righteously that she lied to me, which she did. But I cannot help but remember Filipa the tender-hearted confidante, Filipa the unearthly lover, Filipa the judicious interpreter of reality.

Even in duplicity, she knew and understood me more precisely than anyone and that quality of knowing can never be erased from the mind or the heart. Perhaps it is for the best that the mystery of our liaison remains intact and that, within the masque ball of discarnate deception, the slow dance of *Gideon* and *Micro Laluda* defies analysis. Perhaps. In any case, my conclusions and our estrangement notwithstanding, I shall always wonder who Filipa really was, what her past and future must be, and why she misled me in the guise of an eighteenth-century peasant girl from Thrace.

Likewise, I shall always wonder about Russell, Ernest, Harry, Kinnggalaa, Hanni, Tuktu, Mi-Lao, Dr. Pinkerton, Dr. Jamieson, Dr. Lang and all the others. As I write this, Aviva's living room still comes alive each week with the manifold voices of the dead, new "guides" from around the world replacing familiar voices as incarnate members of the group come and go. Claire Laforgia carries Dr. Pinkerton's counsel far and wide across the Americas and the other channelers who have appeared in this book continue to find audiences eager for their ministrations.

So long as there is suffering, insecurity, and the need to know, there will be a demand for possessing discarnates. The wise, however, will choose to rely on their own intuition which, after all, may well be prompted by the unspoken attentions of beings in the next world who genuinely seek our highest good. Kinnggalaa, the voice of tribal Africa, inadvertently gave the best advice when he told his charge one hot August night in 1985: "Never be fooled by what you see on the surface. When you look out upon the lake and it appears clear and placid, you do not see the undertows that are ready to grab the unwary."

In the absence of communication with my "friends" in the next dimension, my proclivity for nervous tension, insomnia and besetting uneasiness—all of which I had come to accept as normality—continues to recede. Like Sandford Ellison, I have reason to appreciate the self-confrontation precipitated by the eventual disillusionment with the mysterious voices. Indeed, I am grateful to have pulled through without scuttling for refuge into either skepticism or fundamentalism. And I know that the experience has, at last, enlarged my understanding and confirmed my sense of self. Without bitterness or even regret, I choose to believe in the words of eighteenth-century British philosopher Edmund Burke: "He that wrestles with us strengthens our nerves and sharpens our skills. Our antagonist is our helper."

The question remains: Do true guides exist and, if so, would they manifest through the body of a human being? In Chapter Seven I presented an extensive body of evidence suggesting that we are being watched by discarnate presences who know us intimately and have our best interests at heart. The awareness of evolved spiritual beings, however, must be distinguished from possession which, despite longstanding censure, gleams in the closing years of the twentieth century with the luster of the damned. Too often, as the reader has seen, earthbound spirits are mistaken for more enlightened intelligences because they congregate closer to the Earth and are much more accessible to our senses. Capitalizing on this confusion, they ride on the coat-tails of the truth, posing as invisible guardians who have interacted with man since the earliest times.

With the benefit of hindsight, it is hard for me to understand that mediums or channelers would consciously choose a course of folly which, ordinarily, they would shrink from even contemplating. No sane individual would run the risk of associating with, let alone surrendering to, another person or group of people without first being reasonably assured of their character and intentions. Yet to undertake mediumistic development is to send an open invitation to the next world of one's willingness to be controlled by any passing discarnate. Even though higher, evolved intelligences are aware of the medium's receptivity, only earthbound spirits are actively seeking opportunities to express themselves physically. Consequently, the likelihood is that the medium will attract the very type of loathsome individual who, in everyday life, would be shunned or deliberately avoided.

Channelers, then, are clearly asking for trouble—both for themselves and for those who are attracted by their "gift" of mediumship. In subjecting themselves body and soul to the whim of undesirable influences, they are also relinquishing their priceless faculties of personal will and self-responsibility. The possessing entities, exploiting this voluntary capitulation, are then able to extend their sphere of influence by subtly encouraging those within earshot of the compliant victim to sacrifice their selfhood.

Dependency is stealthily promoted in the name of personal growth. And the more the discarnates spoonfeed and stroke the egos of their listeners, the more flaccid becomes the will of each seeker after truth.

Only a small leap of imagination is required to see that channeling undertaken by thousands of unconscious receptors across the North American continent amounts to large-scale sabotage of the New Age and its ideal of ascendant consciousness. As Alexander Blair-Ewart has observed: "Anything is suspect which disarms, or attempts to disarm, the individualized consciousness. A passive relationship with the spiritual world is old age, not New Age."

In my own case, having been enthralled by entities claiming to be guardians of "forward development," it is easy to see, in retrospect, that their objective was not personal growth, but psychic subversion. Only after my disillusionment did I wake up to the fact that influences which sap or obliterate the authentic selfhood of the individual can only *obstruct* personal growth. True spiritual development is achieved neither by dependency nor by lapsing into unconsciousness. True spiritual development rises to the challenge of consciousness by demanding self-discipline, effort of the will, and as much awareness as possible. When all is said and done, there is no shortcut to Nirvana. But in this narcissistic age of instant gratification and swift solutions, the great deception of channeling is that we may glide effortlessly to the Godhead. All we have to do is pay our money, take our seats and dream on as loving discarnates lead us to enlightenment. Why, the Big E is just around the corner and anyway—didn't you know?—we *are* God.

There are those who believe that the multitude of channeled entities are not acting alone, that they are unified in their determination to undermine society's moral, religious and cultural values. Brooks Alexander, senior researcher at the California-based Spiritual Counterfeits Project, compares the entities' "glittering vision of possibilities" to the serpent's temptation of Eve in the Garden of Eden. In an article published in *Christianity Today,* he declared:

> The unnoticed reality is that spiritism has been steadily working its way into the mainstream of American culture for the last twenty years. The disturbing reality is that channeling is just the tip of an iceberg, the visible part of a much larger pattern. The sobering reality is that the new spiritism has moved beyond the weird and the supernatural into the normal and the mundane. Quietly but convincingly, the entities have been serving notice that they intend to shape our future.

The irony is that many who regard themselves as foot soldiers in the vanguard of New Age thinking are unconsciously settling for stupefaction and spiritual inertia by yielding to the persuasiveness of channelers' messages. It is as if a giant wand of delusion has been waved over the questing masses so that eyes do not see and ears do not hear. Fortunately, the casting of the spell has not gone entirely unnoticed. In an article titled *Ramtha, Channeling and Deception,* Dennis Stillings cautions that channeling and other wonders of the consciousness revolution "might be candy-flavored flypaper actually luring us into a New Age of unconsciousness that will make the Dark Ages look like dawn." Even Jon Klimo, for all his noncommittal posturing, suggests that channeling "may be offering early warnings of an impending break into a mass psychotic episode, a latter day Dark Ages with little redeeming value."

Back in 1912, when Spiritualism was enjoying a surge of popularity, the anonymous author of a book called *The Great Psychological Crime* argued that humanity's ability to persist and advance from lower to higher planes of existence relied exclusively upon the conscious exercise of independent faculties, capacities and powers. This evolutionary ascension was in accordance with nature's constructive principle and, as such, was the way of life. Humanity's alternative was to personify nature's destructive principle by abdicating personal stewardship to any intelligences who might wish to assume that responsibility.

> Mediumship, from the standpoint of the medium, is…a purely negative proposition. It is a self-surrender and not a "gift"….The medium does not develop himself. He is developed. That is to say, all the developing work is done by his controls and not by the medium himself. He is developed in precisely the same sense that a patient is delivered under the influence of an anaesthetic. That is to say, he is "developed" into a condition of subjectivity….

Eight years later, Sir William Barrett expressed similar concerns in warning that the danger to any medium lay "not only in the loss of spiritual stamina but in the possible deprivation of that birthright we each are given to cherish, our individuality, our true selfhood…." The medium's renunciation of personal sovereignty is perhaps even more central to the channeling debate than the question of who or what is exploiting the trance state. As Goethe pointed out, whatever liberates our spirit without giving us self-control is disastrous.

Madame Blavatsky affirmed long ago that "your best, your most powerful mediums, have all suffered in health of body and mind." Other authorities have stated that mediumship, while sometimes culminating in insanity, leads frequently to the atrophy of brain tissue, the degeneracy of mental powers and increasing egotism and emotionalism. Such testimony tallies, indirectly, with the contaminating presence of hungry ghosts. If mediumship is indeed synonymous with negativity and disintegration, only dissolute astral beings would participate in such a process. To quote again from *The Great Psychological Crime:*

> It may be accepted as an axiom of spiritual life that no spiritual intelligence...who has learned the meaning and the results of the mediumistic process, and who is honest, will ever subject any individual of earth to the blighting influence of mediumistic control. Whoever does so thereby convicts himself of either gross ignorance, deliberate dishonesty or unconscionable immorality.

This argument applies to celebrated entities—Seth, Ramtha, Lazaris, Dr. Lang and the like—as well as to Filipa, Russell, Dr. Pinkerton and other lesser-known stars in the channeling firmament. One must pierce the bombast and the grandiloquence to ask how it is possible that discarnate communicators can be emissaries of love, peace and wisdom if, simultaneously, they are subjecting those they control to a questionable fate. A healthy, balanced and vigorous life lies, after all, not in possession by another individual but in the marshalling of a fully-integrated consciousness through *self-possession.*

Knowing exactly who he is and where he is going, the self-possessed person is self-reliant and, consequently, is unlikely to be exploited by external influences. On the other hand, those who seek dependency and direction, looking to others to fulfill their needs, are asking to be duped and manipulated. This is where aspirations for an ally in the next dimension are to be substituted for an invocation of the higher self. "There is in all of us," wrote Plotinus, "a higher man...almost a god, reproducing God." Who is this inner helpmate if not a true guide on whom we can call in full consciousness?

So long as we remain in our physical bodies, we can never know the truth about genuinely benevolent spiritual presences, no matter what the myriad channeled entities would have us believe. As the Greek philosopher Xenophanes affirmed 2,500 years ago: "There is no man that has seen, nor any that will ever know, the exact truth concerning the gods....All things are wrapped in *appearances*."

Nevertheless, spiritual teachers are in agreement that evolved non-physical entities influence humanity telepathically, without speech. "Higher beings are silent—they simply radiate knowing and love," said The Venerable Namgyal Rinpoche, founder of the Dharma Center of Canada. "As a general spiritual law, no enlightened being would speak through an ordinary human. The discarnate spirits who are making themselves known through channeling are united in their desperate need for love. Their audience is a generation that is also hungry for love."

Rudolf Steiner, the Austrian occult scientist and founder of Anthroposophy who was able to perceive clairvoyantly the non-physical realms, told how each one of us has a personal angel, "a being who, being one stage higher, can lead the individuality over from one incarnation to the other." But in his work An *Outline of Occult Science* he cautioned that these beings....

> are not of a kind to be perceived by outer senses; they cannot even be described as thin and insubstantial forms of air, such as might still give rise to anything like sense-perceptible effects. All we receive from them are the impressions of purely spiritual sound, spiritual light and spiritual warmth. They do not find expression in material embodiment. Only the supersensible consciousness can apprehend them.

We have an obligation to sift the wheat from the chaff, if only because our immortality is at stake. Immortality must be earned and we are inviting setbacks and confusion if we allow ourselves to be distracted from this task by psychism's world of glamour and illusion. It is easy, much too easy, to be seduced by hungry ghosts and fall into the snare of dependency, a snare that can prove deadly. As Carl Jung observed, we die to the extent that we fail to discriminate. Or, to quote Virgil: "We make our destinies by our choice of gods."

I must admit to having yearned to confront the discarnates of my acquaintance one last time. Freed of my addiction and supported by the wisdom of the ages, I wanted to vent my feelings unrestrainedly, to unmask once and for all their conniving and deceitful ways. But even as I looked forward to a final showdown with the spirits, I knew they would be much too clever for me. No matter how ironclad my arguments and purposeful my intent, they would call on their native brilliance to sidestep the issue and somehow make me the culprit. Finally, I decided that the only worthwhile response was this book.

Despite my ordeal, the GUIDES WILL ASSIST YOU placard still adorns the wall of my study. I have never given up believing that there are wise and benevolent spiritual intelligences who are watching over us. I am simply less naive than before and more aware than ever that the search for truth and greater awareness is fraught with tests and temptations. As the odyssey continues, I can only reflect that the learning has been invaluable and....

Whoever is really looking after me out there, I thank you from the bottom of my heart.

Epilogue

Now it can be told.

Early in 1988, I was living in a little house facing Adolphus Reach on the northeastern side of Lake Ontario. During this time of soul-searching, while still grappling with the emotional upheaval of pulling away from the guides, I noticed an inflamed swelling over my navel. It was readily apparent that pus was gathering within and fuelling this growth, which was painful to touch. I tried to squeeze the suppurating appendage into submission, but without success.

A visit to my local doctor was of little help. Somewhat confounded, he could only recommend that I take antibiotics, wash away any discharge from the abscess and change dressings regularly. He prescribed a mild painkiller to ease my suffering, which would steadily intensify over the days that followed.

While in Toronto, I checked into the emergency ward of Toronto General Hospital where a doctor on duty was equally mystified by the inflammation. He recommended a different antibiotic and urged that I change dressings frequently. In time, he intimated, the abscess should heal.

But the abscess did not heal. In fact, it got progressively worse so that both the pain and my bewilderment about the infection would occupy my every waking hour. On the recommendation of some friends, I visited a veteran country doctor who was touted as a wilderness specialist, a man who had seen everything. As I lay in his office, this physician plunged a wooden-shafted swab into the inflammation, then tossed the barbarous accessory into a wastebin while I yelped with pain and surprise. "I've never seen anything like it," he muttered in a broad Scottish accent. After applying another dressing, he sent me on my way. Time heals, was the unspoken prognosis.

Nearly three weeks had passed since I had first noticed my umbilical infection. It was now late February, and the Canadian winter was in full spate. Under a leaden sky and on snow-covered roads, I headed across southern Ontario for home. Parking my red station wagon beside a barn on the main thoroughfare that skirts the brow of the escarpment overlooking Adolphus Reach, I walked 400 yards downhill to my white, stuccoed retreat. Indoors, alone, there was plenty of time to contemplate a reason for the malady that no doctor seemed to understand. Perhaps, I mused, I was under some kind of psychic attack. Were the various entities, who had ultimately failed to win me over, trying to ensure I would not reveal who they are and what they do? So went my distraught thinking as I manipulated my solar plexus and changed the dressing innumerable times.

Outside, the weather turned blustery. As pale sleet thickened into driving snow, my stomach pain intensified. That evening, I had no option but to take a strong painkiller every half hour just to keep the agony at bay. But even such heavy sedation failed to curb the mounting torment. It wasn't long before I realized that emergency action must be taken. Sometime after midnight, I decided to climb the steep slope behind my cabin and drive to the nearest medical refuge: Prince Edward County Hospital in the town of Picton.

The climb was difficult. Bent almost double, gripping my stomach, I struggled up the hill. At the top, I hobbled through snow drifts blanketing the highway and slumped into the driver's seat of my vehicle. In flying snow, on that desolate stretch of road, I drove for twenty minutes or more hunched over the steering wheel like a gut-shot cowboy in an unspeakably frigid spaghetti western. Reaching the hospital, I stepped back into the snowstorm and made for the main entrance. The doors were locked, but there was a night buzzer. I pressed it. Twice. An orderly appeared at the window and ushered me inside as, grimacing, I tried to explain my plight.

I was asked to lie down on a bed in the small emergency ward. Soon, a nurse was standing at the bedside peeling away the latest dressing from my navel. At the sight of the oozing inflammation she exclaimed under her breath "Oh my God!" Coming from a nurse, such a remark was hardly encouraging. I was told that the hospital surgeon would see me at his earliest convenience later that morning. In the meantime, an injection of Demarol dispatched me to dreamland.

Shortly after 9 a.m., Dr. Earle Taylor, a short, stocky man with a kindly air, appeared beside my bed. He carefully examined the stricken navel and, unlike the doctors who had preceded him, delivered a diagnosis. "You have omphalitis," he said. "This condition is rare in adults but occasionally affects newborns. After the severing of the umbilical cord, the navel is a potential portal of entry for organisms, and inflammation can occur."

I was then carried into a nearby room for an ultrasound scan. A small green screen showed a malevolent growth, like an inverted pyramid, lying beneath my belly button. Soon afterwards, I was wheeled into an operating room and given a general anaesthetic which, in the split-second before I passed out, smelled like the fumes of a gas station. Then Dr. Taylor—a veteran surgeon with 27 years' experience—went to work. He cut into the abscess, drained the toxin, and stitched up my navel.

Awaking later in my hospital bed, I felt groggy but relieved to learn that the operation had been successful. Within an hour, my semi-slumber was interrupted by a telephone call. Claire Laforgia was on the line.

"Joe, how are you?" she inquired.

"Fine," I replied. "But...but how did you know I was here?"

"My guide told me."

So Dr. Pinkerton had told her. Not a soul had been notified of my admission to the hospital.

My next thought was this: if Dr. Pinkerton had told Claire where I was, perhaps he had put me there. Perhaps he was the source of this strange affliction which had baffled three physicians and had puzzled even the practiced eye of Dr. Earle Taylor.

The site of the abscess was symbolic indeed; the navel, the very core of my being. In an abstract sense, the inflammation was undermining my central reality. To the ancient Greeks—and Filipa leapt to mind immediately—the omphalos was not only the human navel but could also be translated as "center" or "hub." Moreover, the omphalos was a sacred stone of conical shape in the temple of Apollo at Delphi, fabled to mark the center of the Earth. Omphalos. Omphalitis.

The source of the affliction was a mystery. Dr. Taylor later intimated that, in an adult, omphalitis would usually occur only if the navel were abraded, ulcerated, or left unwashed. None of these stipulations applied to me. Had I not driven to the hospital and undergone the operation, the abscess would eventually have burst. Then the accumulating pus might well have exploded internally, leading to peritonitis and death.

So perhaps I was facing a version of the psychic onslaughts already documented in the lives of other unfortunates who, after an initial embrace, had withdrawn from counseling spirits. Surely it is significant that this "attack" took place as I was preparing to write negatively about the influence of "the guides." Even—and perhaps especially—after my recovery, my resolve to write this book was constantly threatened by a deep-seated fear. Would the spirits find a way to prevent the story of my foray into the murky world of channeling from reaching the general public?

I can remember sitting at my computer and praying for deliverance so that the book could be completed. Even if my onetime friends ultimately found a way to take my life, I told myself, the book must be finished. Delivering a final manuscript to the publisher was all that really mattered. And all that mattered was finally achieved without further incident.

With the publication of the Canadian and U.K. editions of this book, originally entitled *Hungry Ghosts,* came sweet relief mingled with lingering distress. Even after the book appeared in Canada and the U.K. and Commonwealth, the emotional havoc caused by placing myself in such close and longstanding contact with earthbound spirits persisted. Because my belief system had been turned inside out, I was nervous, self-doubting, and a dyed-in-the-wool insomniac. My face and figure, people would tell me later, looked disturbingly gaunt and haunted. However, after meeting my wife-to-be, Emily Zarb, solace and peace of mind would gradually and blessedly replace fretful anxiety. I started to live without second-guessing myself. For the first time in years, I slept soundly. And for the next decade I avoided channeling and channelers.

After the book was published, I started to receive a long succession of letters; far more letters, in fact, than any other book of mine has generated. Most were penned by kindred souls who had suffered, in one way or another, from the practice of channeling. There were hosts of "thank you" letters from people who, while harboring doubts about channeling, had been encouraged to withdraw from spirit communication. Happily, the book seemed to boost confidence in genuine spirit helpers who, rather than pouncing on entranced humans to express themselves, work tirelessly behind the veil separating this world from the next.

Many of my correspondents had suffered excruciatingly from their contact with earthbound spirits. Usually, they had been won over by subtle manipulation masquerading as love and wisdom. A woman from Glastonbury, England told of being visited by the "guidance" of an unseen being whom, she believed, loved her very much.

She explained: "One night, I woke from sleep, terrified but fascinated as an 'energy' was rippling up and down my back and I heard a noise like a jet engine, blotting out any other sounds. My 'body' lifted from the bed and I rose up, fully conscious, to my bedroom ceiling, then slowly returned to my bed." This "energy" led her to meet a woman who said she had watched her for a long time. The experience was "so real it could have been physical. This woman was real; and I was alive—in another world."

The relationship developed in stages as the correspondent "went out" often. The entity, who became "like a spirit-mother," then offered to "train" her. By learning, she was told, she could help the spirit's own development. And that's when the trouble started.

She continued: "Something (from her) was pushing, darkening, irritating. I would stumble and fall sometimes. I felt so much love and support from her. Then I began to feel strangely ill. For no apparent reason, long waves of severe nausea would grip me. And a heavy 'thunderstorm' headache.

"'You are not ill,' [the spirit] told me. 'It's the training.' She showed me it was her doing it. She 'switched on' the sensations, then switched them off again, then on again. To show me. I didn't like it."

Despair was the pay-off for obedience to the wraith who had wooed and pursued her. "Deep down, I realized that this wasn't me," she wrote. "It wasn't my natural self. It was tremendous weariness. I struggled, trying not to lose life…I sank lower than I've ever been. I heard someone ask her if I'd ever considered suicide. I heard phrases in Latin and Spanish…"

Then she fought back with all her might. "Loss of dignity, humiliation, didn't matter. Nothing mattered but my survival and breaking, finally, all links with that woman. It took every ounce of strength I didn't know I possessed to get through. And it will take a long time to really heal."

A woman from Windsor, England related a series of trying experiences that occurred after she joined a ouija board circle. "I didn't realize for some time that I had drawn spirits to me and I had a few years of hell trying everything to get rid of them," she wrote. "But I was also too attached to one certain spirit which was running my life. I decided I had to be in control."

A wise decision. But, as in the time that followed my own contamination, questions remained. "I am not being touched or bothered so much these days," she concluded, "but I am left wondering: how can you tell the true spirits?"

A reader from Granum, Alberta was fascinated to learn about the "buzzing" that persisted in my ears, if only because he was afflicted by the same problem. He wrote me an unnervingly spooky letter which told of an entity that managed to make contact via his car radio, through telepathic communication, and in visions.

"The entity got stronger and stronger, and very demanding. I backed away, tried to shut it out of my space. From that point on my life became a nightmare, from waking up to a room full of smoke—my electric bed pad was smoldering with me on top of it—to being poked and jabbed, my heart being squeezed, and circulation in my legs being stopped!"

He went on: "It's 1995, and my ear still buzzes. It's been buzzing for about nine years now. I wish that was all... I am 67 years old—not a kid—and I really do need help!"

Then there was the tragic tale of a man from Ottawa whose wife of 22 years had left him and their three daughters in order to be free "to better serve God." In fact, according to the husband's letter, she had left home after undertaking an extensive search for her "true self," a search that led to meditations based on channeled messages.

The grieving husband wrote: "I am working to establish an environment that will encourage her to take a more objective look at the spiritual path that she has chosen [in the hope that] she will rethink her decision and avoid the exploitation that she is headed for."

Some readers challenged my conclusions. "As for earthbound spirits," wrote a man from Claremont, California, "I think you are too hard on them! You warn people about them as if they were demonic, yet they are simply people like you and me. They are manipulative because they are scared—an all-too-human tendency—and I see this as reason not to be angry with them but to be especially sympathetic and helpful."

He went on: "If we allow another spirit to speak or otherwise act through our body for spiritual purposes, it is called trance, or full-body, channeling and can be highly rewarding; the same process, if it involves earthbound spirits, is called possession and can be ruinous."

Here, of course, is where we disagree. I still maintain that no highly-evolved, spiritual being would ever speak through an incarnate human.

Of all the letters I received, the most powerful, the most instructive, and the most damning of the practice of spiritualism, came from an ex-spiritualist who lives on the south coast of England. I am reproducing most of her letter because her story illustrates, with eloquent clarity, just how devastating the act of communing with spirits can be:

"I read your book with a mixture of dismay that any last vestige of trust I may have had in spiritualism could no longer be entertained, tempered with a sense of relief that I am not alone in the conclusions I have reached. I felt that I must write to you and share at least in part my own story, if for no other reason than to let you know how desperately, I believe, the world needs books such as yours to paint the true picture of an evil that hides beneath a facade of love and spirituality.

"I called myself a spiritualist for ten years. I worked as a medium and a psychic consultant, and believed implicitly in what I did. I have had people cry with happiness at the so-called 'proof of survival' I offered them. They said what I have is a gift. And I believed them. Now I know it's a curse. I was born psychic so there was never really any hope for me. I was inevitably sucked into spiritualism at a young age, and I felt it was a relief to finally be with people who understood my abilities and accepted them. I was trained in a development circle to harness my talents into communication with the 'spirits' and to establish a relationship with my 'guides.' When I realized the extent of what I could achieve, it was like a fairyland of never-ending wonders. In reality, of course, it was a Pandora's Box of horrors.

"My guides manifested, as they do to all mediums and channelers, as beings of great wisdom with a desire to help mankind. I am sure you can fully appreciate the intense feelings of love and well-being you receive from these beings during direct, mind-to-mind contact. It is heady stuff that hooks you totally. Right from the beginning, my guides appeared to groom me for a 'great work' that I had supposedly been born to perform as a spiritual teacher. Wherever I went, I was assailed and brainwashed with this idea. Countless independent mediums gave me the same messages over and over. And it was true that I could stand in front of an audience and torrents of inspired philosophy would pour from my lips. My guides were adept seers, and their predictions of future events were flawless, prolific, and amazingly detailed. How could I not have faith in these wonderful beings who were never wrong?

"And then it started. Slowly, insidiously. The manipulation. Your friends, Sandford and Aviva, were lucky in that they escaped in time. I was not so fortunate. My life has been devastated by these guides. The full details of my life are too lengthy to be given here, but I feel it would be true to say that I have never met anyone who has suffered as much tragedy, hardship, and misfortune as I have. Around 95 per cent of this can be seen to be directly attributable to the guides and their influence on me. Through the use of skillful brainwashing, I was maneuvered into not one but two marriages (made not in heaven, as the saying goes, but literally in hell). Both my husbands were spiritualists and heavily influenced by their own guides. One was sadistic and violent, the other a twisted, compulsive liar who made my children and I destitute. These are only two of the spirit-related disasters in my life; there have been many more, including the full year I was stalked by a psychopath who was obsessed by the psychic abilities I possess and felt that he himself was 'spirit-influenced.'

"In passing, I would like to point out that your own experiences tend to corroborate my own observation that most of their manipulations revolve around personal relationships, especially sexual ones. This may be partly because, perhaps, these are our most vulnerable points, the things which mean most to us. But also they do appear to have a great interest in sex itself and are always apparently present at the most intimate of moments. It does seem as if the thing they require most from us is whatever they gain from earthly sex as 'observers!'

"After reading of all the ways I have been successfully manipulated by the guides, it may surprise you to learn that I actually consider myself a very strong person and not easily influenced. [This] should testify to their skillful talents in psychological warfare, which is, after all, what we appear to be dealing with. Incidentally, I have spoken to many spiritualists who have had their lives almost as badly manipulated as my own, yet they refuse to see what stares them in the face. None of them appear to have the strength I have had to acquire, to admit it to themselves. Believe me, I have had to have unimaginable strength just to survive the horrors set upon me by my involvement with the guides.

"I have a little sign like your 'Guides Will Assist You.' Mine reads, 'It's hard to fight an enemy who has outposts in your head.' And therein lies the essence of their skill: they know their victims inside out. They know our strengths, our weaknesses, and what makes us tick. That's why it's so easy for them. I read with interest your view that what we are dealing with are 'lost souls.' Personally, I feel this is too kind an interpretation. The typical image of a lost soul would be of a spirit trapped between worlds, perhaps unaware of its physical death, groping in an ignorance which prevents it [from] having the ability to progress. Compare this to the entities we have both experienced. They are masters of deception; they are articulate and eloquent with vast knowledge of philosophy at their disposal, whether fabricated or otherwise. They are able to cooperate and liaise sufficiently with others of their kind to devise strategies against us and maintain a continuity of information given to us. They have apparently limitless powers of precognition and access to any information they choose—past, present or future—enabling them, among other things, to impersonate whomsoever they wish with ease. This is not my idea of a poor lost soul stumbling in the darkness.

"The one thing I think we have both established beyond doubt is this: they are smart. They are *very* smart. Any lost soul this intelligent would surely have the ability and knowledge to progress to some higher state. If these souls are simply too evil to do so, and therefore have no knowledge of any supposedly higher realm, where do they obtain their vast understanding of philosophy? Not from living in a dark void trapped between worlds, that's for sure.

"I feel the answer to the riddle, if an answer is even possible, lies in a study of the history of our race. The plain fact is that mankind has been dogged by bizarre supernatural phenomena since the dawn of time. These phenomena change to fit changing belief systems and expectations. In other words, if you lived in the Middle Ages, you might be visited by the fairies. If you were an early Christian, you might expect to see angels (and many modern Christians still do!). And now, in the space age, thousands of people have experiences with supposed aliens from other planets. The vast mass of people who have had these experiences are not mad or deluded. They are victims as surely as you or I. Interestingly, the sexual component I have mentioned frequently appears in many of the documented experiences relating to the above. (Consider the ancient tales of the incubus and the succubus.) In fact, many key elements appear again and again in all areas of supernatural experience. I believe it is all the same thing, manifesting in different ways. If you are a spiritualist and believe in life after death, the phenomena simply provide you with that particular manifestation. The outward facade they present is all illusion.

"What I am saying—and I am not alone in the conclusions I have reached—has very serious and very sinister implications. Perhaps if we begin to accept that these beings have been present among mankind as far back as our records go, we have to acknowledge a horrifying fact. Our race has been directly shaped by these beings, and not in any beneficial way. The manipulation you and I have experienced is nothing compared to the manipulation inflicted on civilization on a mass scale. Nearly every religion in the world was initially based on psychic manifestations, visions on mountaintops, images of God appearing to prophets, voices in the mind—just as our modern day mediums hear voices, see visions. Indeed, I have heard of certainly more than one medium who claims their contact is Jesus or God himself.

"These beings, in their different guises, have directly formed our very religions. And anyone who has studied the history of organized religion must be aware that [religion] has been responsible for more death and destruction than just about anything else. And yet we all stagger blindly on, oblivious to this manipulation for thousands of years. Perhaps I sound paranoid or overly dramatic in my belief of the magnitude of the situation. I would love to be proved wrong, but doubt I ever can be.

"I hope that perhaps my opinions and experiences have been of some interest to you. I wanted, if nothing else, to let you know that you are not alone in your discoveries. I believe your book is an extremely significant work which should be compulsory reading for all who call themselves spiritualists. You have my admiration for daring to face the facts which others deny even to themselves. As for my own life...I am learning to pick up the shattered remnants and carry on."

These conclusions are more far-reaching than my own. I have never sought to place the guides in the context of the evolution of the human race. But that doesn't mean that the ravenous ones have had no role in shaping our destiny for millennia. Indeed, my correspondent's view of earthbound spirits as arch deceivers of humanity is not as far-fetched as it might sound on first hearing. This, surely, was what Edgar Cayce was talking about when he declared: "There are those influences from without the veil that seek, seek, that they may find an expression, that they may still be a portion of this evolution in the earth, not considering their present estate. And these bring turmoil and strife."

It took at least four years after my final chat with Dr. Pinkerton before I felt fully reconstituted in body and soul. Today, the rapture and disillusionment precipitated by my rushing in where angels probably would have feared to tread seems, in the rosy glow of hindsight, more like a bad dream than an extended nightmare. Only by rushing in and staying the course until many—but far from all—of my questions were answered, could I have learned the hard lessons that lie beneath channeling's beguilingly warm and fuzzy carapace. Now that the ordeal is over, there is nothing I would do differently. Like a secret agent, I had to expose myself to danger in order to retrieve important information. I am simply grateful to have survived my confrontation with the liars and deceivers of the spirit world. Only when the struggle was far advanced did I finally comprehend the meager state of my resources as well as the might and swiftness of the unseen enemy. Let this be a warning to all.

Acknowledgments

This book has been in the making for more than five years and many are those who have contributed, directly and indirectly, to its development. First and foremost, I am grateful for the co-operation of certain, selected mediums who gave of their time, effort and hospitality. My special thanks to Aviva Neumann and Claire Laforgia who spent countless hours in trance so that I could chat with their channeled entities and research their pronouncements. I am also grateful to several members of "the group," notably Sandford Ellison, Roger Belancourt, Rachel Ezra, Ruby Beardsley, Tony Zambelis, Helen Fields, Erik Muller, Valerie Edson and Jane Barkalow. My heartfelt appreciation extends especially to:

David Kendall, for his matchless friendship and rigorous revisionary eye.

Patrick Crean, for his editorial wisdom and guidance.

Dominick Abel, for helping to bridge the gap between outline and publication.

Dr. Joel L. Whitton, for loaning me his brilliant mind.

The Canada Council, for providing invaluable financial support for research.

John Pearce, Jill Lambert, Alexander Blair-Ewart, Kelly Watt, David Kopman, Frances Hanna, Steven Waring, Michele Hawkins, James O'Neill, Rita DeMontis, Mike Jackson, Jim "Ginger" Ware, Walton Houston, Kevin Scanlon, David Buchanan, Ann Emerson, Brian McLeod, and Alan Edmonds, who told me that I had a book when all seemed lost…Muchisimas gracias one and all.

Finally, I would like to acknowledge the inspiration of Henry Miller, Richard Brautigan, the music of Level 42 and the cosmic nudge of Pluto in Scorpio (1984 to 1995) which signifies the elimination of old life forms and the end of secrecy.

Select Bibliography

Allen, T. G., translator, *The Book of the Dead,* Chicago: University of Chicago Press, 1974.
Barrett, Sir William F., *On The Threshold of the Unseen,* London: Kegan Paul, Trench, Trubner and Co. Ltd, 1920.
Beard, Paul, *Living On.* New York: Continuum Publishing Corp, 1981.
Beardsworth, Timothy, *A Sense of Presence.* Oxford: The Religious Experience Research Unit, 1971.
Berger, Peter L., *A Rumour of Angels.* Harmondsworth, Middlesex: Penguin Books, 1971.
Bernard, Raymond, F. R. C., *Messages from the Celestial Sanctum.* San Jose, California, Supreme Grand Lodge of AMORC Inc., 1980.
Blavatsky, H. P., *The Key to Theosophy.* Pasadena, California: Theosophical University Press, 1946.
Blunsdon, Norman, *A Popular Dictionary of Spiritualism.* London: Arco Publications, 1961.
Brunton, Paul, *The Notebooks of Paul Brunton, Volume I: Perspectives.* Burdett, New York, Larson Publications bic., 1985.
Cavendish, Richard, editor, *Man, Myth and Magic.* New York: Marshall Cavendish Corporation, 1970.
Cayce, Hugh Lynn, *Venture Inward: The Incredible Story of Edgar Cayce.* New York: Paperback Library, 1964.
Chapman, George, with Roy Stemman, *Surgeon from Another World,* London: W.H. Allen, 1978.
Clifford, Terry, *Tibetan Buddhist Medicine and Psychiatry: The Diamond Healing.* York Beach, Maine: Samuel Weiser Inc., 1984.
Conan Doyle, Arthur, *The Wanderings of a Spiritualist.* New York: George H. Doran Co., 1921.
Crabtree, Adam, *Multiple Man: Explorations in Possession and Multiple*

Personality. Toronto: Collins, 1985.

Crabtree, Adam, *Animal Magnetism,* Early Hypnotism, and Psychical Research, 1766-1925. New York: Kraus International Publications, 1988.

Davis, Andrew Jackson, *Spirit Mysteries.* Boston: William White and Co., 1869.

Elbe, Louis, *Future Life in the Light of Ancient Wisdom and Modern Science.* Chicago: A. C. McClurg and Co., 1906.

Evans, Hilary, *Gods: Spirits: Cosmic Guardians.* Wellingborough, Northhamptonshire: Aquarian Press, 1987.

Findlay, J. Arthur, *On The Edge of the Etheric.* Philadelphia: David McKay Co., 1931.

Fiore, Edith, PhD, *The Unquiet Dead: A Psychologist Treats Spirit Possession.* New York: Doubleday and Co. Inc., 1987.

Fisher, Joe, *The Case for Reincarnation.* London: Grafton Books, 1986.

Frazer, Sir James George, *The Belief in Immortality, V61. 11.* London: Dawsons of Pall Mail, 1968.

Frazer, Felix J, *Parallel Paths to the Unseen Worlds.* Los Angeles: Builders of the Adytum Ltd.

Fremantle, Francesca, and Trungpa, Chogyam, commentators, *The Tibetan Book of the Dead.* Boulder, Colorado: Shambala, 1975.

Gallup, George, Jr. with William Proctor, *Adventures In Immortality.* London, Corgi Books, 1984.

Gauld, Alan, *Mediumship and Survival.* London. Paladin Books, 1983.

Gooch, Stan, *Creatures From Inner Space.* London: Rider, 1984.

Graham, Billy, *Angels: God's Secret Agents,* London: Hodder and Stoughton, 1975.

Grof, Stanislav, MD, *Realms of the Human Unconscious.* New York: Viking Press, 1975.

Hardy, Sir Alister, *The Spiritual Nature of Man.* Oxford: Clarendon Press, 1979.

Hay, David, *Exploring Inner Space.* Harmondsworth, Middlesex: Penguin Books, 1982.

Highwater, Jamake, *The Primal Mind.* New York: New American Library, 1981.

Hoeller, Stephan A., *The Gnostic Jung and The Seven Sermons To The*

Dead. Wheaton, Illinois: Theosophical Publishing House, 1982.

Huntley, Florence, editor, *The Great Psychological Crime: The Destructive Principle of Nature in Individual Life*. Chicago: Indo-American Book Company, 1912.

Jaffe, Aniela, *Apparitions: An Archetypal Approach To Death Dreams and Ghosts*. Irving, Texas: Spring Publications Inc., 1979.

James, William, *The Varieties of Religious Experience*. New York: Crowell-Collier, 1961.

Jaynes, Julian, *The Origin of Consciousness in the Breakdown of the Bicameral Mind*. University of Toronto Press, 1976.

Klimo, Jon, *Channeling: Investigations On Receiving Information From Paranormal Sources*. Los Angeles, Jeremy P. Tarcher Inc., 1987.

Krickeberg, Walter; Trimborn, Hermann; Muller, Werner; and Zerries, Otto, *Pre-Columbian American Religions*. London: Weidenfeld and Nicholson, 1968.

Leadbeater, C. W., *Invisible Helpers*. Adyar, Madras, India: Theosophical Publishing House, 1980.

Lepicier, His Eminence Alexis Henry M., Cardinal, *The Unseen World: An Exposition of Catholic Theology in Reference to Modern Spiritism*. London: Sheed and Ward, 1929.

Lewis, C. S., *The Screwtape Letters*. London: Collins, 1987.

Lilly, John C., MD, *The Center of the Cyclone*. New York: Bantam Books, 1973.

Medhurst, R. G., collector, *Crookes and the Spirit World: The Writings of or by Sir William Crookes OM, FRS*. New York: Taplinger Publishing Company, 1972.

Moody, Raymond A., Jr., MD, *Life After Life*. New York: Bantam Books, 1981.

Moses, Revd W. Stainton, *Spirit Identity*. London: Psychic Book Club, 1954.

Murphet, Howard, *The Undiscovered Country*. London: Sawbridge Enterprises Ltd, 1984.

Nevius, Dr. John L., *Demon Possession and Allied Themes*. London: 1896.

Oesterreich, T. K., *Possession: Demoniacal and Other*. Secaucus, New Jersey: Lyle Stuart, Inc., 1966.

Ouspensky, P. D., *Talks With A Devil*. London: Arkana Paperbacks, 1988.

Powell, U, Col. Arthur E., *The Astral Body*. Wheaton, Illinois: Theosophical Publishing House, 1982.

Schapira, Laurie Layton, *The Cassandra Complex: Living with Disbelief*. Toronto: Inner City Books, 1988.

Sri Swami Sivananda, *What Becomes of the Soul After Death*. Himalayas, India: The Divine Life Society, 1985.

Steiner, Rudolf, *The Influence of Spiritual Beings Upon Man*. New York: Anthroposophic Press, 1961.

——*An Outline of Occult Science*. Spring Valley, New York, Anthroposophic Press, 1939.

Swami Bhakta Vishita, *Genuine Mediumship or The Invisible Powers*. New York: 1919.

Swedenborg, Emanuel, *Heaven, and Hell*. London: The Swedenborg Society, 1966.

Tibetan Lama Geshey Ngawang Dhargyey, oral teachings of, *Tibetan Tradition of Mental Development*. Dharamasala, India: Library of Tibetan Works and Archives, 1976.

Trungpa, Chogyam, *The Myth of Freedom*. Berkeley, California: Shambala Publications Inc., 1976.

Underhill, Evelyn, *Practical Mysticism*. New York: E. P, Dutton and Co., 1943.

Ward, Theodora, *Men and Angels,* New York: The Viking Press, 1969.

Whitton, Joel, MD, PhD, and Fisher, Joe, *Life Between Life*. New York. Doubleday and Co. Inc, 1986.

Wickland, Carl A., MD, *Thirty Years Among The Dead*. London: Spiritualist Press, 1968.

Periodicals and Pamphlets

Alexander, Brooks, "Theology from the Twilight Zone: Spirit Channeling is the Newest Fad in Upscale New Age Spiritism." Christianity Today, 18 September 1987.

Anderson, Rodger, "Channeling," Parapsychology Review, September/October, 1988.

Blair-Ewart, Alexander, "Life, Death and the New Age," Dimensions, November, P487,

———"Channeling: The Beginning of a New Culture,"Dimensions, February, 1988.

———"New Age Retrospective '88," Dimensions, January, 1989.

Burt, Cyril, "Psychology and Psychical Research." The Seventeenth Frederic W. H. Myers Memorial Lecture, 1968. Society for Psychical Research, London.

Davis, Susan, "Science Looks at Channeling," San Francisco Examiner, 19 November 1988.

Devananda, Swami Vishnu, "The Sivananda Spirit Messages (parts one and two)," Yoga Today, March/April, 1980.

Huzinec, Mary, "The New Soup-to-Nuts Cookbook: A Channeler Says She's Getting Recipes from the Late James Heard," People Weekly, Match, 1988.

James, William, "Report on Mrs. Piper's Hodgson Control," Proceedings of the English Society for Psychical Research 23: 1-121.

Lowry, Katharine, "Channelers," Omni, October, 1987.

McLaughlin, Corinne, "Evaluating Psychic Guidance and Channeling," Venture Inward, January/February, 1988.

Knight, J. Z., "First Word," Omni, March, 1988.

Pope John Paul 11, "Angels: Free Beings, Unseen and Seen," The Pope Speaks. Vol. 31, No. 4, 1986.

Rojcewicz, Peter M., PhD, "Strange Bedfellows: The Folklore of Other-Sex," Critique No. 29,1989.

Stillings, Dennis, "Ramtha, Channeling and Deception," Critique No, 2.5, 1987.

Stump Keith W.," Communication with the Dead: Is It Possible?" The Plain Truth, September, 1986.

"Unseen Spirits: Do They Help us or Do They Harm Us?" Pennsylvania: Watchtower Bible and Tract Society, 1978.

Van Dusen, Wilson, PhD, "The Presence of Spirits in Madness: A Confirmation of Swedenborg in Recent Empirical Findings," New Philosophy, 70, 1961.

Vaughan, Alan, "Channeling," New Realities, January/February, 1987.

www.ingramcontent.com/pod-product-compliance
Lightning Source LLC
Chambersburg PA
CBHW021039200426
43507CB00001B/5